TRAMWAYS OF
METROPOLITAN MIDDLESEX
AND NORTH LONDON

by George Atkins

LRTA
Since 1937

Published by the Light Rail Transit Association
138 Radnor Avenue,
Welling,
DA16 2BY

www.ltra.org

Copyright © Light Rail Transit Association 2013

Designed by Steve Middleditch

Printed by Latimer Trend and Company Limited
Estover Road, Plymouth PL6 7PY

ISBN 978-0-948106-41-5

Front Cover
Type UCC Car (Feltham) No. 370 at Finchley Depot
About 1931. *Illustration Ashley Best*

Back Cover
Type H Car No. 314 at Wood Green Depot.
July 1924. *Illustration Ashley Best*

TRAMWAYS OF METROPOLITAN MIDDLESEX AND NORTH LONDON

by George Atkins

A history of

The North London Suburban Tramway Company Limited

The North London Tramways Company

The North Metropolitan Tramways Company in Middlesex

The Metropolitan Electric Tramways in North Middlesex

connecting London County Council Tramways

the tramways of London Transport in North Middlesex

and subsequent recollections of MET tramcars

Contents

Chapters

Type UCC Car (Feltham) No. 370 at Finchley depot about 1931.

Illustration Ashley Best

4

5

6

MAPS AND DIAGRAMS

ILLUSTRATIONS

NOMENCLATURE

Original sources quoted in the text use terms of distance, currency and local government administration which may confuse the modern reader. Some have been clarified in the relevant parts of the text but as a general guide:

Distance
1 mile = 1.609 kilometres
1 mile consists of 1,760 yards, each yard of 3 feet (ft) and each foot of 12 inches (in). Additionally 22 yards are known as 1 chain and there are 10 chains in 1 furlong and 8 furlongs in 1 mile.

Currency
Prior to the introduction of decimal currency in 1972, one pound (£1) was divided into 20 shillings and each shilling into 12 pence with transactions written as, for example, £7 10s 6d.
Some transactions were recorded in guineas; 1 guinea having the value of £1 1s 0d

Local Government
The rapid expansion of London in the nineteenth century resulted in the local government structures of the surrounding areas, which had been designed for rural communities, being unable to cope with the resultant social, health and welfare issues. The frictions between the responsible bodies as they evolved and their boundaries changed are part of the history of the development of tramways in the area and are mentioned at relevant points in the text. It should be noted that from medieval times until 1965, when it was abolished, local government of what are now the northern and western parts of the Greater London area was vested in the County of Middlesex. The abbreviation MCC is used in the text, as it was at the time, to refer to the Middlesex County Council and not the Marylebone Cricket Club.

SOURCES AND ACKNOWLEDGEMENTS

I was born and grew up near Finsbury Park and frequently travelled on the MET and LCC cars in the north Middlesex area of this history as my family had relatives who lived near Turnpike Lane and also in Tottenham and Edmonton.

When we visited them at weekends, the last possible public service vehicle we could catch to return to Finsbury Park was a number 49 tram running into Stamford Hill Depot - where we had to change onto a bus along Amhurst Park to Finsbury Park. Travelling on the ex-LCC cars late at night to Stamford Hill was interesting; very little traffic was about and it was quiet, the track was in good condition, very few stops were made to set down or pick up passengers, so the tram had an open road and took advantage of it.

I have included my clear memories of the MET trams in the later parts of the text of this history.

I undertook much of the original research relating to the histories of the tramways of north Middlesex in the period 1949 – 1950. Credit must be given to the helpfulness of the staff at the local councils of Edmonton, Tottenham, Wood Green and Hornsey at that time, and later those of the respective London boroughs, for producing all the horse and steam tramway photographs from their collections (and allowing me to reproduce them), and particularly the archivist for Tottenham Library at Bruce Castle and Edmonton Reference Library. I also searched through the pages of the Tottenham Weekly Herald from 1880 to 1892 which are held at Bruce Castle Museum and Library.

Thanks must also be given to my great friends, the late V. E. Burrows for his own information on horse and electric tramways in the area and the late J. B. Norris, who lived at Childs Hill on the north west section of the MET, for information about that company and the experimental and standard Feltham cars which he saw come into service and travelled on. V. E. Burrows left the extensive Gratwicke / Burrows Tramway Collection of photographs, and those of G. N. Southerden, in the care of Mr Green, the then archivist of West Ham Corporation Libraries – now known as the London Borough of Newham Libraries, whom I also met and from whom I received permission to reproduce these photographs. I am very grateful to my sister-in-law, Beryl Jackson, for permission to use a number of photographs from the collection of my late brother-in-law, Alan Jackson.

I must also thank London Transport for the photographs and depot maps I obtained when they were located in a building adjoining the Edgware Road Metropolitan and Circle Lines Underground station.

By accident, I came across the original minute books of the North Metropolitan Tramways. I happened to be at the former British Railways Western Region Archive Office at Royal Oak during the time of the British Transport Commission, when I saw a number of large hampers on the floor. Looking through one of them, I found the original minute books of the North Metropolitan Tramways and the Metropolitan Electric Tramways. Inquiries revealed they had been sent over from London Transport at 55 Broadway and were waiting to be catalogued. I then obtained permission from the archivist to go through the minute books of both companies and make notes from them.

I would like to thank Ashley Best for his two excellent colour paintings of MET trams, executed from my black and white photographs, which are used on the front and back covers of this book.

Information was also obtained from:

Board of Trade
    Returns of Street and Road Tramways
    Returns of Tramways and Light Railways
    (Street and Road)
    Railway Inspectorate - Index to Reports

Companies Registration Office

Edmonton Local Board
    Minute Books (1880 – 1894)
    Works Committee Volumes 1 and 2
    (1882 – 1886)

London Transport Archives
    North London Suburban Tramway
      correspondence and papers
    North London Suburban Tramway Acts
    North London Tramway Acts
    North Metropolitan Tramways Minute Books
    North Metropolitan Tramways Acts

Middlesex County Council Acts

Newspapers and periodicals:
    Enfield Gazette and Observer (1881)
     'Townsman's Notes'
    Electrical Review
    The Engineer
    Engineering
    Modern Transport
    North Middlesex Chronicle
    Railway News and Joint Stock Journal
    Railway Times
    Tottenham and Edmonton Weekly Herald
     (Wood Green Edition)
    Tottenham Weekly Herald (1880 – 1892)
    Wood Green Herald

Not least, I have to thank my wife Mavis for typing the manuscript and reading the drafts, my son Paul for proof-reading the manuscript and making useful comments, and my grandson Samuel Shaw for enhancing and enlarging the photographs and documents reproduced herein.

George Atkins

St Margarets at Cliffe, Kent

July 2013

Type H Car No. 314 at Wood Green depot. July 1924.
Illustration Ashley Best

Introduction

This is a history of the tramways in north Middlesex and the connecting lines in north London. It covers the area northwards from Finsbury Park and Manor House to Wood Green, Palmers Green and Enfield and to Tottenham, Edmonton, Ponders End and Waltham Cross. In addition, it includes the routes from Seven Sisters Corner to Stamford Hill and from Wood Green to New Southgate and North Finchley.

It is an area I know well since I was born and grew up near Finsbury Park and frequently travelled on the Metropolitan Electric Tramway (MET) and London County Council (LCC) cars in the north Middlesex area of this history as I had relatives who lived near Turnpike Lane and also in Tottenham and Edmonton.

Before beginning the history of these tramways, it is important to understand the background to both the local area and the legal framework required to promote tramways in the UK during the last quarter of the nineteenth century.

The locality

In the late 1870s, the population of London was expanding rapidly into the surrounding areas of Middlesex. While Middlesex was administered by a county council, the inner London area was controlled by the Metropolitan Board of Works – the London County Council had yet to be created. Under each of these bodies was a number of local boards. The local boards in Middlesex were reconstituted as urban district councils by the Local Government Act of 1894.

The population growth in the area can be illustrated from the censuses:

	1871	1881	1891
Edmonton	13,860	23,463	36,350
Enfield		19,119	31,799
Hornsey			
(incl. Highgate)		37,061	61,404
Tottenham			
(incl. Wood Green)	22,860	46,441	97,166

Developments in the area had already been encouraged by the passenger and freight services provided by the Great Eastern Railway. Industry was concentrated along the Lea Valley – including the Royal Small Arms factory, which employed a considerable number of people, and the Ponders End jute factory, which closed in May 1882 throwing 450 people out of work.

Even so, by 1886 Ponders End was still only a hamlet and the surrounding Durants Estate was still to be sold for housing developments. However, it was attracting considerable crowds of pleasure-seekers at weekends intent on enjoying the countryside.

Tramway Legislation

Street tramways originated in the United States of America by providing local services along the railway tracks which had often been laid along the main streets of towns. The first street tramway in Britain, with the cars pulled by horses, was opened in Birkenhead in 1860 and promoted by the eccentric American George Train. His various ventures suffered from both the difficulty in obtaining parliamentary powers for tramways and the special L-shaped rails he patented for his tramways which stood proud of the road surfaces in which they were laid.

Train built a number of trial tramway lines in the UK, by agreement with the local authorities, including three short, disconnected lines in the London area in 1861. However, by mid 1862 permission for each of these had been rescinded and they were removed.

Nevertheless, the potential for urban public transport had been demonstrated and the Board of Trade promoted the Tramways Bill in 1870 to simplify and regularise the procedure for promoting and constructing street tramways. Despite the Board of Trade's good intentions, as the bill passed through Parliament powerful opposition to the concept of tramways resulted in the procedures specified in the Act, as passed, becoming complicated and expensive, with a requirement to obtain a Provisional Order for each line from Parliament even where agreement had been reached with the authorities responsible for the streets to be used.

Additionally, frontagers (generally those who owned or occupied properties facing onto a road in which a tramway was to be laid) obtained a right of veto where that line was to run within 9 feet 6 inches of the kerb for a length of at least 30 feet and one third of their number opposed. However, the promoters of a tramway were able to overrule the veto of local interests if their line was to run through several districts and it was supported by the authorities for at least two-thirds of its length.

The Act also specified that the maximum speed of horse-drawn tramcars was to be 9 mph and the minimum speed was to be 6 mph, except around curves with a radius of 60 feet or less. Drivers were required to maintain a distance of at least 100 yards between cars on the same track, except on single lines, at junctions, at a terminus or at intermediate stops. At stops, drivers had to leave a gap of at least 10 yards between their car and that stopped on a parallel track.

Another piece of legislation of significant relevance to this history is the Light Railways Act of 1896. While it was clearly intended that this Act was to simplify the promotion of light railways to serve rural districts and boost rural economies at a time of agricultural depression, the preamble of the Act did not define a 'light railway'. Since the procedure to promote a light railway was much simpler than that for a tramway, requiring only for an application to be considered by three commissioners of the Board of Trade rather than for a separate Act to pass through parliament, and avoiding the right of veto held by local authorities under the Act of 1870 (although they could petition the commissioners) and requiring only a quarter of the general district rates to be paid, the imprecise wording of the Act of 1896 was soon used for the development of urban tramways – including those in Middlesex.

This is the background against which the metropolitan tramways of North Middlesex were conceived.

Chapter
One

The North London Suburban Tramway Company Limited

(1879 – 1882)

Inauguration

The North London Suburban Tramway Company Limited was incorporated in December 1878 *"to construct, equip, maintain and work by horses or other motive power Tramways in the Counties of Middlesex, Hertford and Essex"*. The nominal capital of the company was £100,000 divided into 20,000 shares of £5 each with power to increase.

The principal promoters were the O'Hagan brothers, who were behind a number of tramway schemes at the time. Thomas O'Hagan was the freeholder of the property which later became Edmonton Depot. He was the brother of Henry Osborn O'Hagan, a financially successful business man but said to be of doubtful character. He was also a partner of the contractor Charles Phillips and Company and was later involved with the City of London Contract Corporation.

An Order was obtained from the Board of Trade early in 1879 for the construction of a single track tramway from Stamford Hill, in the county of Middlesex, to Cheshunt, in the county of Hertford, via Tottenham, Edmonton, Ponders End and Waltham Cross, a distance of 10¼ miles. The Order included passing places, permitted joint traffic arrangements with the North Metropolitan Tramways Company (subject to that company's approval), and stipulated a track gauge of 4 feet 8½ inches (standard gauge), tolls for the carriage of parcels and maximum fares for workmen.

"The Promoters ... are hereby required to run at least two carriages every morning in the week (Sundays, Christmas Day and Good Friday always excepted) at such hours, not being later than 7 in the morning or earlier than 6 in the evening respectively, as the Promoters think most convenient for artisans, mechanics and daily labourers, at tolls their charges not exceeding ½d per mile. (The Promoters nevertheless not being required to take any fare less than 1d)".

Construction

On 10 October 1879 a contract was entered into by the Company with Mr Albion Chadbourn of Brixton for construction of the line, but only the section between Stamford Hill and Edmonton, Hertford Road (Tramway Avenue). It included paragraphs requiring Mr Chadbourn to provide all the equipment for operating the line by horse traction.

"Twelve one horse cars capable of holding twenty persons or such other number and type of cars of an aggregate equivalent value as may be required by the Company". *"The cars to be of a type and quality similar to those used on the Metropolitan Tramways, to be of the best material and made and constructed of such pattern and style as shall be approved by the Directors and their Engineer according to his specifications and drawings"*.
"Twenty four sets and seventy five horse collars, one forage van, one break for breaking in horses, one cart, ... one water cart, two riding saddles and bridles, twelve whips and twenty waterproofs for horses". *"Complete working equipment of stable implements"*, *"smiths' and farriers' tools and implements"*
"Seventy five horses of the average value of £40 each subject to their being passed as sound and suitable by the Company's Veterinary Surgeon. Each horse to have its complete clothing".

Other materials to be supplied included:
"One fitters bench". *"One complete set of Fitters and Carpenters tools ... Implements and utensils and usual requisites for cleaning and keeping cars in working order"*.
"One track trolley, one cleaning trolley for cleaning rails". *"One screw jack, complete working equipment for one platelayers gang of four men, including paviours with all necessary road guards and lanterns"*.
"Twelve uniforms for drivers and conductors,

complete with belts and waterproofs and capes". "Twelve ticket and fare boxes subject to approval of the Directors". "Twelve mouth whistles, twelve leather money bags".

Soon afterwards, on 29 October 1879, a further agreement was entered into between the Company and Mr Chadbourn in which the previously agreed initial and subsequent monthly cash payments for the construction on the line would be made partly as shares in the Company.

"The Company, as soon as in a position to do so, forthwith pay to the Contractors in lieu of the sum of £3,000 in cash, the sum of £2,000 in cash and allot 200 fully paid shares numbered from 1 to 200 to the said Contractor and

"The Company reserve to themselves the option of paying to the Contractor and the Contractor agrees to accept the balance of the contract price, namely £35,500 in lieu of the said monthly cash payments provided for in the agreement, 5,500 shares which shall be issued fully paid up at par value and £8,000 in cash or such lesser number of fully paid up shares and larger payment in cash as the Company may from time to time deem advisable. The allotment of the shares and the payment in cash to be made pro-rata seven days after the certified statement of the value of the work done and equipment and materials used delivered less the proportion authorized to be retained under the Agreement".

Mr Chadbourn tried to make arrangements to reassign his part of the original contract to Messrs Charles Phillips and Company, of 20 Bucklersbury, E.C. 4, but, as the contract gave him no powers to do so, the Company was able to insist on certain conditions before giving their agreement. The principal of these was that Charles Phillips and Company, having financial connections to the principal promoters and later also with the City of

London Contract Corporation, should pay interest to the shareholders from 1 January 1880 as security. Eventually, Messrs Charles Phillips and Company was the contractor for constructing the line between Stamford Hill and Edmonton, using Mr C. A. Wilkes as a subcontractor, while Mr Wilkes was the contractor for the later extension from Edmonton to Ponders End.

Under the terms of the contract, the line should have been constructed and opened by May 1880 but in fact work only commenced from Stamford Hill on 3 May 1880. The contractors opened up the centre of the road for a width of 8 feet and a depth of 15 inches to lay the tracks, throwing the excavated material to the sides of the trench. The method to be used for the construction of the tramway was for the rails to be secured to wooden creosoted sleepers bedded in 6 inches of concrete and for the road surface to be reinstated flush with the top of the rails. However, although the sleepers for the track were delivered, the rails had not been - so the work was then left. The situation was aggravated by the contractors opening up the road from Stamford Hill through to Bruce Grove, which was a much greater distance than allowed under the provisions of the Order. As a result, road accidents were a frequent occurrence, vehicles were overthrown, footpaths driven over, cut up and spoiled and gullies blocked by road materials.

In June 1880, the Tottenham Local Board applied at Edmonton Magistrates Court for a summons against the tramway company for failing to carry out the work in a satisfactory manner, for which the Company was fined £10. In mitigation, the Company stated that a contract for the supply of rails necessary for the construction of the tramway had been entered into with a firm in Germany but these had not arrived. To avoid further delay, alternative arrangements were made for the rails to be delivered from Liverpool but these had gone to the wrong railway station.

In August 1880, the Tottenham Local Board applied for a further summons because still very

3

little had been done to complete the works and the Company was fined £2 per day. The summons was adjourned for one week to ascertain whether work on the section of the road which had been opened up could be completed. As it was not, the Company was fined a total of £61 10s 0d.

The Edmonton Local Board also considered issuing a summons against the Company for delay in the construction of the tramway, but the contractors requested the Bench to stand it over for a fortnight as progress was being made with the work.

By November 1880 work on the tramway was proceeding apace and the depot and stables were being constructed at Tramway Avenue, Edmonton. (See Chapter 6). Nevertheless, the Surveyor to the Tottenham Local Board felt compelled to write to the Board of Trade on 18 November

"Work not done to my satisfaction. Let me know when inspection taking place"

and again on 31 January

"Beg to direct your attention to dangerous condition in which Company allowed their Works to remain. The paving throughout their line has sunk from two to four and five inches below the level of the rails".

Additional lines proposed

Although the initial construction works were well behind schedule, the Company applied for another Provisional Order in November 1880, which was granted in 1881. This authorised powers for the construction of a tramway from Waltham Cross in Hertfordshire to Waltham Abbey in Essex to be constructed to a gauge of 3 feet or such other gauge as approved. Also included were tramways to be constructed to standard gauge along Seven Sisters Road from Tottenham High Street (now High Road), connecting with the tramway already

under construction, to Finsbury Park and along Green Lanes from the Manor House Tavern to Wood Green.

The Edmonton Local Board, already in dispute with the Company about a number of issues regarding the construction of the initial line, consulted its solicitors. The clerk to the Board later reported that he had received a letter from the Board of Trade, dated 5 February 1881, in reply to a letter written by the Company withdrawing its application for further powers under their Provisional Order of 1881. It is thought that the Company withdrew its application because of the stringent regulations which had been attached to it by the Tottenham Local Board.

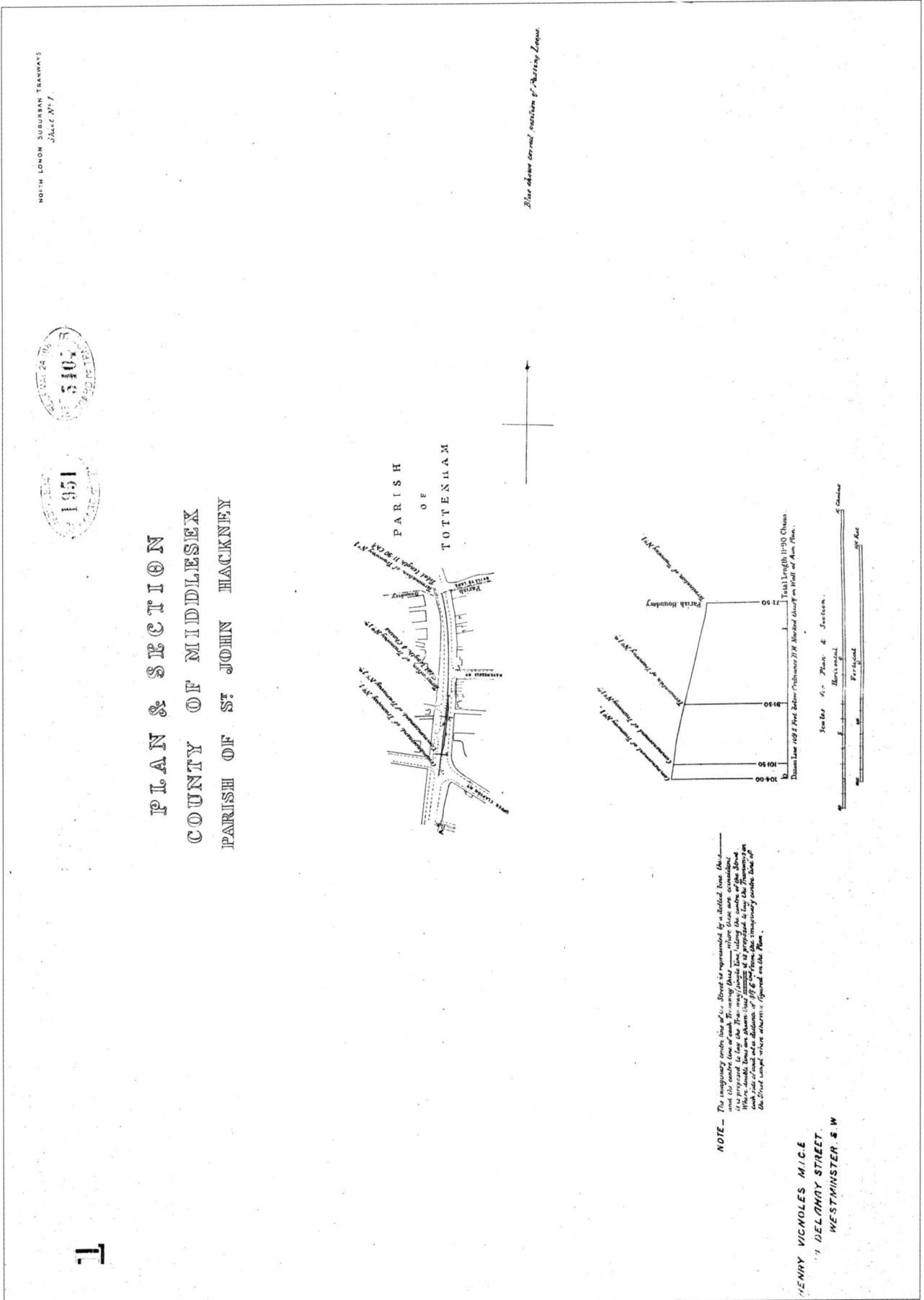

Figure 1a. The plan and section of the NLST laid in the parish of St John Hackney, as filed with the Board of Trade (1881).

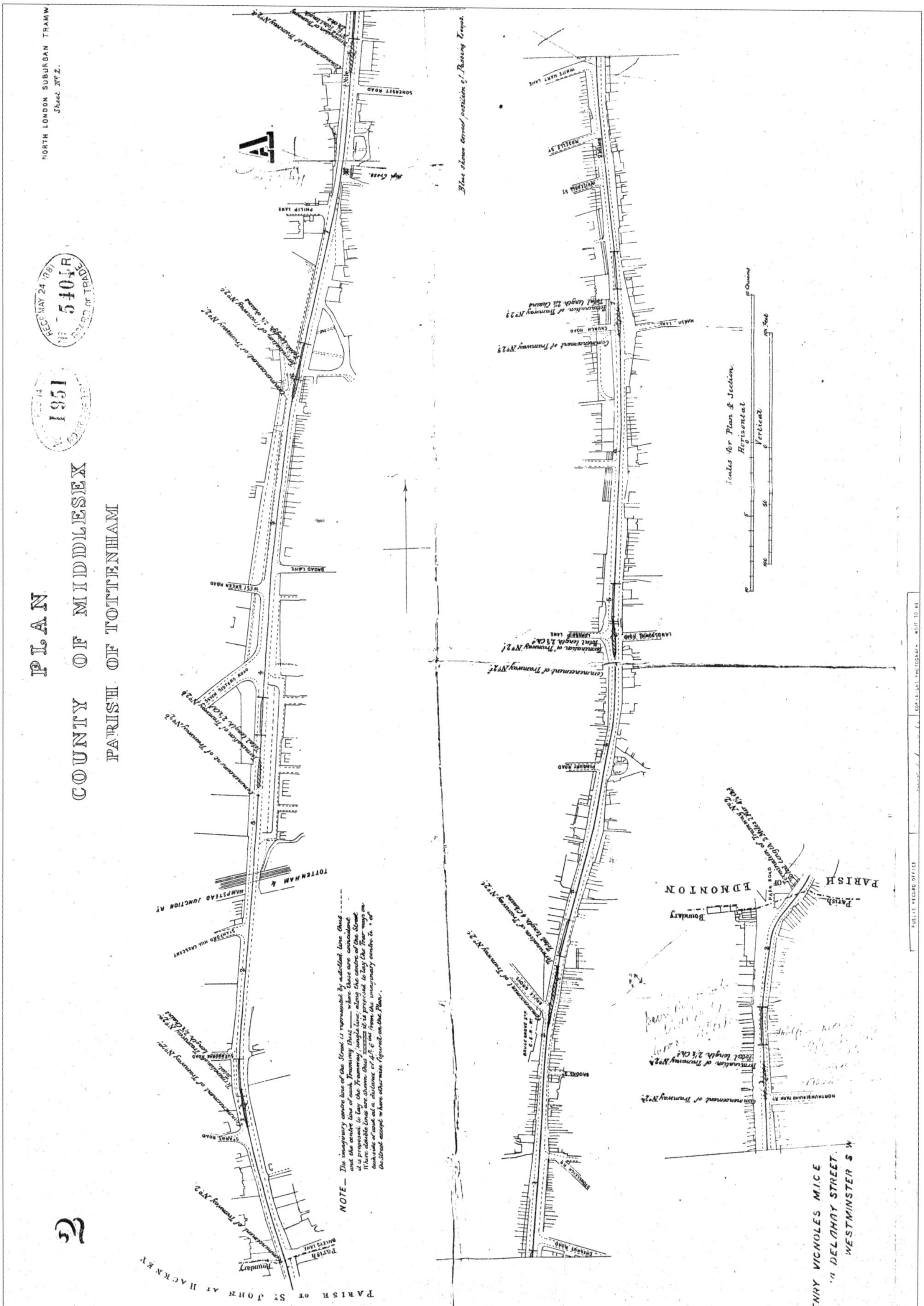

Figure 1b. The plan of the NLST laid in the parish of Tottenham, as filed with the Board of Trade (1881).

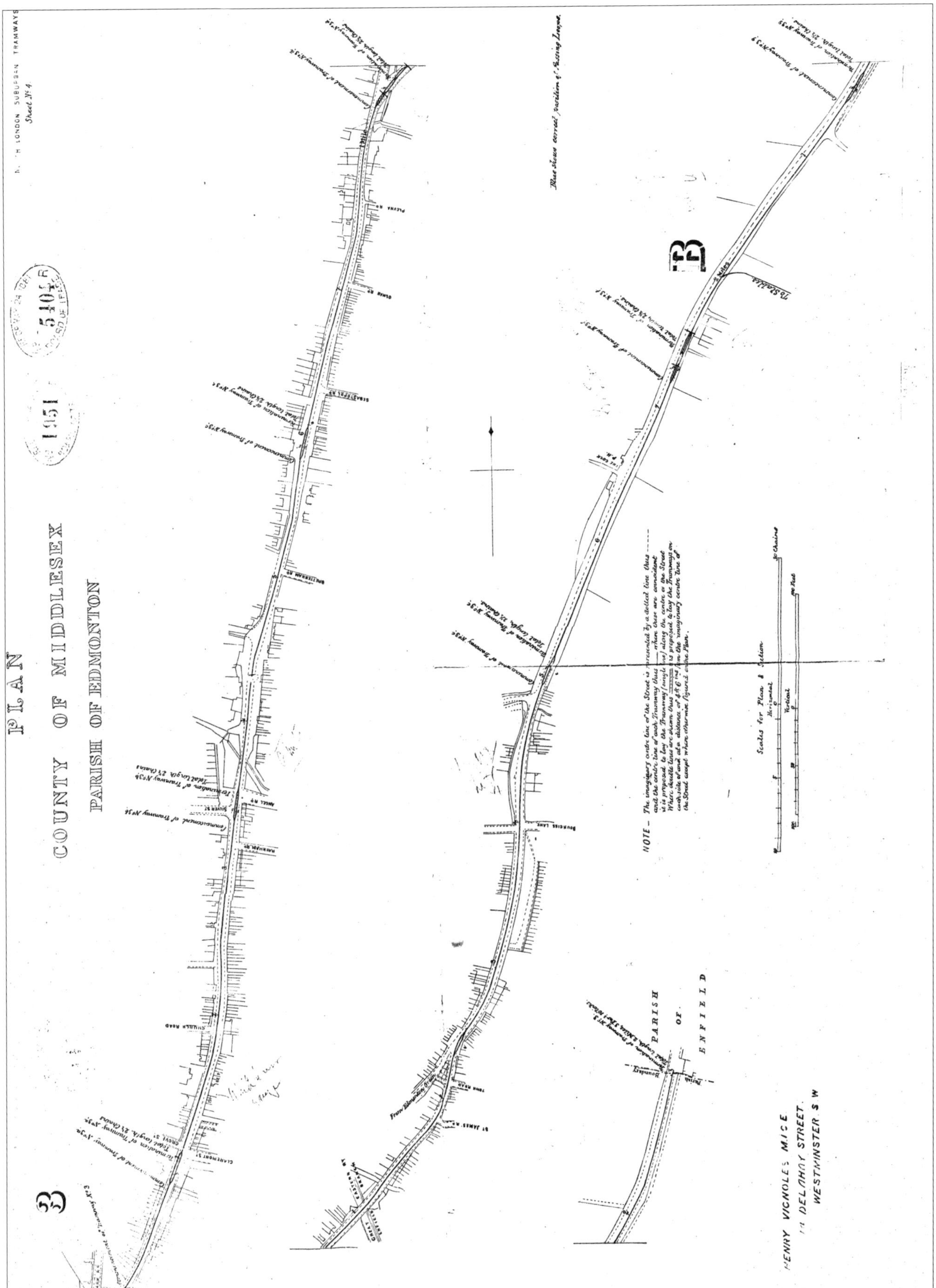

Figure 1c. The plan of the NLST laid in the parish of Edmonton, as filed with the Board of Trade (1881).

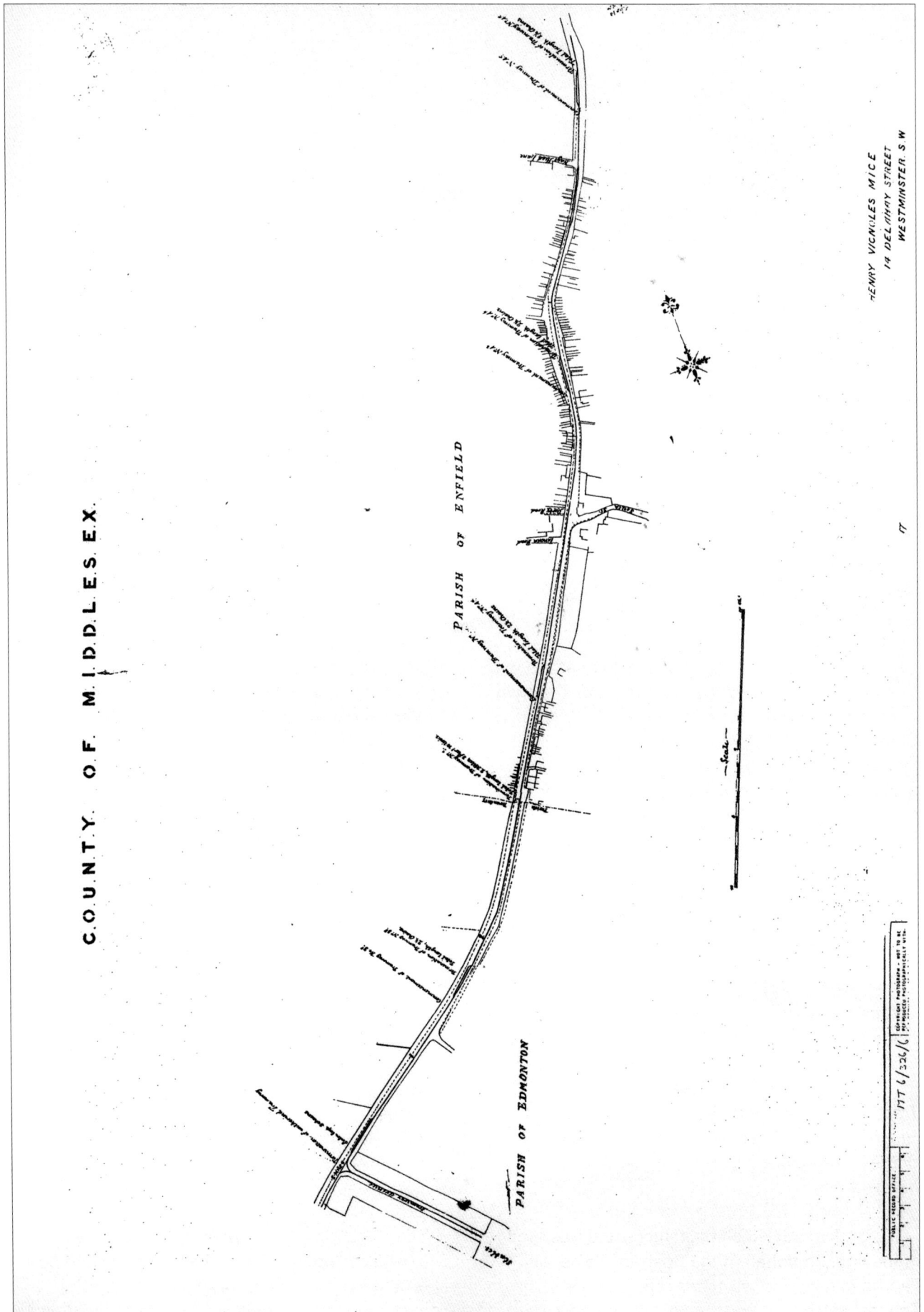

Figure 1d. The plan of the NLST laid in the parish of Enfield, as filed with the Board of Trade (1881).

Inspections

By 14 February 1881, the Company considered that the section of line between Tramway Avenue in Edmonton and White Hart Lane in Tottenham was ready for operation. It wrote to the Board of Trade:

"Sir,

I beg to inform you that the portion of the above tramway from Tramway Avenue, Edmonton to White Hart Lane will be ready for inspection on the 16th instant and shall be glad therefore if you will instruct one of your officers to inspect the same.

Herewith I beg to hand you a copy of the Act and Provisional Order authorizing the Tramway, together with tracings [reproduced as Figure 1], of the section to be inspected showing the passing places, and to inform you that the Road Authorities are Mr. T.W. Grindle, Surveyor to the Edmonton Local Board and Mr. W.A.H. de Pope, Surveyor to Tottenham Local Board.

Your Obedient Servant
(signed) Thomas Jervis
Secretary"

A note attached to this letter in the Board of Trade file reads

"Let Major Hutchinson inspect this portion of the Tramways. Inform the Company. Major General Hutchinson's attention is called to the complaints of the Tottenham Local Board in the papers and herewith".

Major General Hutchinson inspected this section of the line, on behalf of the Board of Trade, on 21 February 1881 and wrote his report the next day. The inspection commenced at White Hart Lane, Tottenham, and proceeded northwards to Hertford Road (Tramway Avenue) Edmonton, a distance of 2 miles 19 chains.

"The level and gauge of the rails appears to be very fair throughout, but I myself do state that the condition of the paving is very unsatisfactory (particularly on the outside of the rails), the curbs, which towards the edge of the paving in the Parish of Edmonton has almost entirely disappeared, having sunk into the macadam and the setts, whether stone or wood, are for the most part either too high or too low, presenting, only in exceptional cases, a proper surface in Tottenham where there has been a dispute between the Tramway and the local Board as to the maintenance of the level of the road, there are to me some spots (or crossings) where the tramway is about 5 inches above the level of the road, with an abrupt decent from one level to the other, thus".

The Inspector also had concerns that there were sections of line where the method of construction was not that approved by the Board of Trade, the position of one of the passing loops had been relocated from the approved plans, the consent of the frontagers at that location had not been obtained, angle plates had not been fitted to the points for each of the passing loops and the entrance to the tramcars was unsatisfactory and required alteration.

"I must therefore now report that the above mentioned portion of the tramway cannot be certified as fit for traffic, owing, principally, to the unsatisfactory condition of the paving; the deviation from the approved also, I submit, requires explanation."

In order to open the line, the Company had no alternative but to comply with the inspector's recommendations. However, it wrote to the Board of Trade on 1 and 3 March to explain that the

9

deviations from the approved methods of construction and authorized location of the passing loop were at the request of the Tottenham Local Board.

On 4 April the Company requested the Board of Trade to re-inspect the 2 miles of the tramway wholly within Edmonton; the report of the inspection, again undertaken by Major General Hutchinson, is dated 9 April 1881.

"This portion of the tramway is now in a tolerably satisfactory condition having been much improved since I first went over it, the outside edges of the paving has been entirely re-laid and are now [?] so as to make a proper junction with the macadamised surface of the road".

"The Chairman and Surveyor of the Local Board of Edmonton were present at the inspection and expressed themselves as being generally satisfied with the state of the Tramway, there had been a dispute as to the making good of the sides of the road at The Crescent and at the foot of the railway bridge, and it was arranged in my presence that the Tramway Company should at once do this to the satisfaction of the Surveyor".

"An angle plate had been fixed at one of the points as a sample of what is intended to be done at all of them as soon as the rest of the plates shall be supplied".

"Subject to the sides of the road at The Crescent and at the foot of the railway bridge being made good and the angle plates fixed as soon as possible, I can now recommend the Board of Trade to certify that the above sited portion of the North London Suburban Tramways are fit for public traffic".

Written confirmation was received in a letter from the Board of Trade dated 12 April

"The Certificate is enclosed on the understand-

ing that the road is made up at two points to the satisfaction of the Surveyor to the Edmonton Local Board, and angle plates are fitted".

The service within Edmonton, between Tramway Avenue and Snell's Park, commenced later the same day.

On 16 May Major General Hutchinson re-inspected the line in Tottenham between the Edmonton boundary and White Hart Lane and also the section from there to High Cross, a total distance of 1 mile 50 chains. The party walked over the line from Bruce Grove to the Edmonton boundary and rode back as far as Bruce Grove in one of the Company's cars. They then walked over the section of the line between Bruce Grove and the High Cross and the inspector announced he was satisfied with the work.

The service of tramcars was extended from Edmonton to Tottenham with immediate effect. A Board of Trade minute dated 17 May confirms that the Company had not been held in the highest regard.

"The Promoters appear now to be laying their Tramways in a proper manner. Major General Hutchinson recommends the issue of the certificate but suggests that the true position of the passing places, which have been altered with the consent of the Road Authority and of the frontages, where necessary, should be shown on the plans".

The final section of the line from High Cross Tottenham to Stamford Hill, a distance of 1 mile 5 chains, was inspected by Major General Hutchinson on the afternoon of 4 June.

"The construction is similar to that of the last portion inspected and the tramways being in good order I can recommend the Board of Trade not to object to certify that they are fit for public traffic".

"The inspection was also attended by the Surveyor of the Tottenham Local Board, who expressed himself satisfied with the mode in which the work had been carried out. The Hackney Board of Works were not represented at the inspection".

The same afternoon cars commenced running through to Stamford Hill, where they met those of the North Metropolitan Tramways line.

To Ponders End

In July 1881 the Company had to consider that the remainder of the authorised line from Edmonton through to Cheshunt would not be completed within the permitted timescale. It served the Enfield Local Board with notice of an intended application to the Board of Trade for an extension of time from 11 August 1882 to 11 August 1883 for the completion of works authorised by the North London Suburban Tramways Order 1879 and the subsequent Tramways Confirmation Act 1879.

Meanwhile, a separate contract was concluded with Mr C. A. Wilkes for the construction of the section of line from Tramway Avenue in Edmonton along Hertford Road and High Street to Ponders End, a distance of 1 mile 3 chains. The terminus in Ponders End was 200 yards north of Nag's Head Lane (now Nag's Head Road). The completed line was inspected by Major General Hutchinson on 3 January 1882.

"The lines on the whole are fairly well laid but in Edmonton some of the setts require raising and in Enfield, at the overlapping lines and passing loop 4c they require lowering. Angle plates have also to be supplied at the north end of the over-lapping lines and one of those in the curve at Tramway Avenue is not properly fixed".

"Subject to these defects being made good, and the [?] of the Surveyors of Edmonton and Enfield, the Board of Trade need not [?] refuse to certify that the above cited parts of Tramway Nos.3 and 4 are fit for public traffic".

The tramcars

The 12 original tramcars of February 1881 were single deck vehicles, licensed to carry 20 passengers, supplied by Greenwood's Carriage Company of the Pendleton Works in Manchester. They were of a single ended, lightweight design which could be pulled by one horse, known as Eades Reversible Patent type, developed by John Eades, the manager of Greenwoods since 1867. At the rear of the car was something little better than a cupboard, intended as a smoking compartment but not used as such. When new, these cars were fitted with crimson cushions, put on polished and perforated longitudinal wooden seats, but they were removed by October 1881 after they had been damaged by passengers habitually placing their feet upon them. The horses had bells fitted to their head harness to warn the public of the approaching tram.

At the end of each journey, the whole bodywork of the tramcar was turned on a pivot in its truck. While the horse was walked round the car by the driver for the return journey, the locking pin, holding the body in position on the under frame, was released and the tramcar body was reversed by hand before being locked in position again.

The company very soon tried to convert some of the single deck cars to double deck. However, the underframes were so light as to be hardly capable of supporting the single deck bodies and passengers, let alone the double deck bodies which each weighed 1¾ tons. Consequently the fleet of cars was augmented by purchasing some double deckers in 1882 - taking the fleet to 20 cars.

Operations

From the beginning, all the drivers, conductors, stable hands and workshop staff were employed on a daily, not weekly, basis.

Overloading the trams was not uncommon from the start of operating the services. Joseph Elliot, the manager of the Company, was issued with a summons in July 1881 for allowing a workman's car, licensed to carry 20 passengers, to have 32 on board; shortly afterwards a conductor was fined for having 27 passengers on a car licensed for 20.

Over the Whitsun holiday of 1882, a police officer stopped a double deck car and found 25 passengers inside (downstairs) and 33 outside (upstairs), a total of 58 and 16 more than the car was licensed to carry. The conductor was summoned to appear at court for allowing the overloading to occur.

On 13 September 1881 the Bye Laws of the North London Suburban Tramway Company were approved by the Board of Trade and came into force the next day. (See opposite).

In October 1881 the Tottenham Local Board agreed to an application by the Company for permission to construct an additional passing place between the terminus at Stamford Hill and the passing place north of South Tottenham Railway Station on the grounds that great delay was caused in the running of the trams by the passing places being so far apart.

In August 1882 a tramcar broke down on a single section of track near Lordship Lane and remained there for a considerable time. Drivers of other cars, travelling in both directions, avoided any delays by jerking their vehicles off the track and driving them along the road surface around the broken down car before regaining the track. A large crowd gathered to watch the spectacle, amongst whom were two policemen controlling the traffic. One of the other tram drivers arriving at the scene refused to follow the example of the others, out of consideration for his horses, and suggested to the crowd that there

were enough men around to lift the broken car off the track and carry it bodily to the side of the road, which was then done.

On Saturday, 5 May 1883, a carman was returning from London with a large van drawn by three horses; he was about half way down the northern slope of Stamford Hill when he heard a strange noise behind the van. He looked round and saw a tramcar out of control being drawn rapidly downhill towards him by two horses, there being no driver in charge of them. It was a strange sight as the tramcar was a double decker of the Eades Patent type and the body of it was swinging round on its pivot and projecting over the sides of its truck. The carman endeavoured to get his van out of the way of the approaching tram but was unable to do so in time. The front part of the tram struck the rear part of the van with such force as to almost overturn it, throwing the carman and the boy, who had been riding with him, onto the road. The accident appears to have been caused by the sudden bolting of one of the tramway horses whilst the tramcar, to which it was still attached, was being reversed at the end of the journey at Stamford Hill.

On 15 June 1883 the Company commenced a parcels van delivery service but in the first fortnight of operation only 24 shillings in revenue was taken.

Fares

Initially, the route was split into several stages costing 1d (one penny) each and fares were paid by the passengers dropping a separate 1d coin into a box carried by the conductor each time a fare stage boundary was crossed.

By January 1882, the method of fare collection was revised and passengers were at liberty to pay the total fare at the end of the journey. By agreement with the Company, a local firm in Tottenham undertook to pay for 200,000 tickets to be printed by Mr Whiting, a printer and stationer in City Road, London, on the understanding that his advertise-

BYE-LAWS AND REGULATIONS

MADE BY THE

NORTH LONDON SUBURBAN TRAMWAY COMPANY,

LIMITED.

Under the powers conferred on the Company by the Tramways Act, 1870.

1. The Bye-laws and Regulations hereinafter set forth shall extend and apply to all carriages of the Company and to all places with respect to which the Company have power to make Bye-laws or Regulations.

2. Every passenger shall enter or depart from a carriage by the hindermost or conductor's platform, and not otherwise.

3. No passenger shall smoke inside any carriage.

4. No passenger or other person shall, while travelling in or upon any carriage, play or perform upon any musical instrument.

5. A person in a state of intoxication shall not be allowed to enter or mount upon any carriage, and if found in or upon any carriage shall be immediately removed by or under the direction of the conductor.

6. No person shall swear or use obscene or offensive language whilst in or upon any carriage, or commit any nuisance in or upon or against any carriage, or wilfully interfere with the comfort of any passenger.

7. No person shall wilfully cut, tear, soil, or damage the cushions or the linings, or remove or deface any number plate, printed or other notice, in or on the carriage, or break or scratch any window of or otherwise wilfully damage any carriage. Any person acting in contravention of this Regulation shall be liable to the penalty prescribed by these Bye-laws and Regulations, in addition to the liability to pay the amount of any damage done.

8. A person whose dress or clothing might, in the opinion of the conductor of a carriage, soil or injure the linings or cushions of the carriage, or the dress or clothing of any passenger, or a person who, in the opinion of the conductor, might for any other reason be offensive to passengers, shall not be entitled to enter or remain in the interior of any carriage, and may be prevented from entering the interior of any carriage, and shall not enter the interior of any carriage after having been requested not to do so by the conductor, and, if found in the interior of any carriage, shall, on request of the conductor, leave the interior of the carriage upon the fare, if previously paid, being returned.

9. Each passenger shall, upon demand, pay to the conductor or other duly authorised officer of the Company the fare legally demandable for the journey.

10. Each passenger shall show his Ticket (if any) when required so to do to the conductor or any duly authorised servant of the Company, and shall also when required so to do either deliver up his Ticket or pay the fare legally demandable for the distance travelled over by such passenger.

11. A passenger not being an artisan, mechanic, or daily labourer, within the true intent and meaning of the Acts of Parliament relating to the Company, shall not use or attempt to use any Ticket intended only for such artisans, mechanics, or daily labourers.

12. Personal or other luggage (including the tools of artisans, mechanics, and daily labourers) shall, unless otherwise permitted by the conductor, be placed on the front or driver's platform, and not in the interior or on the roof of any carriage.

13. No passenger or other person not being a servant of the Company shall be permitted to travel on the steps or platforms of any carriage, or stand either on the roof or in the interior, or sit on the outside rail on the roof of any carriage, and shall cease to do so immediately on request by the conductor.

14. No person, except a passenger or intending passenger, shall enter or mount any carriage, and no person shall hold or hang on by or to any part of any carriage, or travel therein otherwise than on a seat provided for passengers.

15. When any carriage contains the full number of passengers which it is licensed to contain, no additional person shall enter, mount, or remain in or on any such carriage when warned by the conductor not to do so.

16. When a carriage contains the full licensed number of passengers, a notice to that effect shall be placed in conspicuous letters and in a conspicuous position on the carriage.

17. The conductor shall not permit any passenger beyond the licensed number to enter or mount or remain in or upon any part of a carriage.

18. No person shall enter, mount, or leave, or attempt to enter, mount, or leave, any carriage whilst in motion.

19. No dog or other animal shall be allowed in or on any carriage, except by permission of the conductor, nor in any case in which the conveyance of such dog or other animal might be offensive or an annoyance to passengers. No person shall take a dog or other animal into any carriage after having been requested not to do so by the conductor. Any dog or other animal taken into or on any carriage in breach of this Regulation shall be removed by the person in charge of such dog or other animal from the carriage immediately upon request by the conductor, and in default of compliance with such request may be removed by or under the direction of the conductor.

20. No person shall travel in or on any carriage of the Company with loaded fire-arms.

21. No passenger shall wilfully obstruct or impede any officer or servant of the Company in the execution of his duty upon or in connexion with any carriage or tramway of the Company.

22. The conductor of each carriage shall enforce or prevent the breach of these Bye-laws and Regulations to the best of his ability.

23. Any person offending against or committing a breach of any of these Bye-laws or Regulations shall be liable to a penalty not exceeding Forty Shillings.

24. The expression "conductor" shall include any officer or servant in the employment of the Company and having charge of a carriage.

25. There shall be placed and kept placed in a conspicuous position inside of each carriage in use a printed copy of these Bye-laws and Regulations.

26. These Bye-laws shall come into force on the 14th day of September, 1881.

Secretary of the Company.

I hereby certify that a true copy of the foregoing Bye-laws and Regulations has, in accordance with the provisions of s. 46 of the Tramways Act, 1870, been laid before the Board of Trade not less than two calendar months before such Bye-laws and Regulations came into operation, and that such Bye-laws and Regulations have not been disallowed by the Board of Trade within the said two calendar months.

An Assistant Secretary to the Board of Trade.

13 4 September 1881

Figure 2. NLST bye laws and regulations (1881).

ment appeared on the back. The tickets were to be delivered to the offices of the Company for issue to the conductors.

In October 1882 the 1d fare and the stages were abolished and a flat fare of 2d was charged, the maximum fare had previously been 4d. One result of this was it cost 2d to travel by tram from Bruce Grove to Stamford Hill and only 1d by the parallel Great Eastern Railway. This situation lasted until February 1883 when the consequential loss of revenue caused the Company to revert to the 1d fares and stages.

Further additional lines proposed

Still searching for more profitable traffic opportunities, the Company applied for another Provisional Order in November 1881 to construct and operate some of the lines in the Order it had withdrawn the previous year. These tramways were to be constructed to standard gauge along Seven Sisters Road from Tottenham High Street (where it connected with the existing line) to Finsbury Park (where it met the line of the North Metropolitan Tramways Company), and also along Green Lanes from the Manor House Tavern to Wood Green. However, construction of these lines was again not commenced because of a lack of capital.

Financial results

The year 1882 was not a financial success; this was partly attributed to the unfavourable weather, which prevailed during the greater part of the year, and also to the closure of the Ponders End Jute factory in May, throwing 450 people out of work.

In retrospect, the Company considered that it had been a mistake to build the line at all since the population of the district was not sufficient to sustain such an undertaking. It had also been an error to allocate shares and commence operations when only about 15,000 of the 20,000 shares, about £75,000, had been subscribed.

The Company had come to regard the whole line from Stamford Hill to Ponders End as essentially a pleasure route, with insignificant business traffic despite following the main road. On fine Saturdays and Sundays more money was taken than on all the other days of the week together. The route was considered to be too far from the City of London to act as a feeder to the North Metropolitan Tramways route operating to there from Stamford Hill.

The North London Suburban Tramway Company approached the North Metropolitan Tramways Company with a view to the latter taking over and working the line, but it was not interested.

A new start

Not only was the revenue below expectations but the lack of working capital was causing operational difficulties. An extraordinary general meeting of the Company took place at the Guildhall Tavern, Gresham Street, in the City of London on Monday, 30 January 1882, when a resolution was put forward for approval.

"that the Bill now being promoted by this Company in Parliament, and now submitted to the meeting, entitled a Bill for dissolving the North London Suburban Tramway Company Limited and reincorporating them under the name of The North London Tramway Company, and to confer upon them powers to construct and maintain additional Tramways and for other purposes".

The resolution was passed on 22 February and forwarded to the Companies Registration Office on 25 February.

In April 1882 notice of the Bill was given for that parliamentary session. In addition to reconstituting

STAMFORD HILL TOTTENHAM AND EDMONTON

NORTH LONDON SUBURBAN TRAMWAY CO.

Above: 1. One of the original single deck Eades patent cars.

Left: 2. One of the Eades patent double deck horse cars, with knifeboard seating, in Tottenham High Road.

the Company, it gave the new company powers to refinance the operation, to abandon routes authorised but not constructed which were now perceived as having no commercial potential, to construct additional routes regarded as being more profitable and to use steam and other mechanical motive power on the existing and intended tramways (see Chapter 2).

The Bill was enacted; consequently, the North London Suburban Tramway Company Limited was dissolved on 20 August 1882 and reincorporated under the name of the North London Tramways Company Limited.

Chapter
Two

The North London Tramways Company

(1882 – 1891)

A fresh start

The North London Tramways Act of 1882 gave powers to the new company to refinance the operation, to abandon routes authorised but not constructed which were now perceived as having no commercial potential, to construct additional routes regarded as being more profitable and to use steam and other mechanical motive power on the existing and intended tramway.

The North London Suburban Tramway Company Limited was dissolved on 20 August 1882 and reincorporated under the name of the North London Tramways Company Limited. The first directors were listed as Christopher James, John Beattie, Henry Lee Corlett, Thomas O'Hagan and Arthur Randolph Robinson; most of whom had been directors of the North London Suburban Tramway Company. The capital of the Company was to be £115,000, consisting of £73,020 stock representing "the original capital" and £41,984 of "new capital" divided into 4,198 preference shares of £10 each.

The directors were empowered to abandon construction of the portion of the tramways previously authorised by the North London Suburban Tramways Order of 1879 from Ponders End High Street (near its junction with Nag's Head Lane) northwards to Waltham Cross and Cheshunt and, consequently, were able to secure release of the deposit made earlier in respect of that section.

The Company was permitted to construct a tramway from the existing line at Tottenham High Street (Seven Sisters Corner) along Seven Sisters Road via the Manor House Tavern to Finsbury Park, a distance of nearly 2 miles. Although a connection was authorised at Finsbury Park between the new line and the existing tramway of the North Metropolitan Tramways Company, it was not to be constructed without the consent of the latter company. Consequently, the new line terminated 15 yards short of the existing one.

A further new line was authorised from Manor House along Green Lanes to Wood Green (Sidney Road), a distance of about 2½ miles, and, to protect the Hackney Board of Works, the Company had to widen the Green Lanes bridge over the New River at its own expense. The newly authorised lines were to be completed within two years of the passing of the Act.

Responsibility for the roads along which the new lines would operate was fragmented and this would cause the Company operational difficulties in the future.

Hornsey Local Board:
The north side of Seven Sisters Road between Finsbury Park Gate and Manor House Gate and the west side of Green Lanes from Manor House Gate towards Harringay.

South Hornsey Local Board:
The south side of Seven Sisters Road from Finsbury Park Gate to Manor House Gate.

Stoke Newington Parish:
Seven Sisters Road from Amhurst Road to Manor House but then only the east side of Green Lanes from Manor House towards Harringay.

Tottenham Local Board: Seven Sisters Road from Seven Sisters Corner to Amhurst Road and Green Lanes from Harringay to Wood Green.

Bye Laws

The Edmonton Local Board, having submitted copies of the proposed Bye Laws in respect of the Tramway Company to the Board of Trade, was informed on 4 September 1883 that the Board of Trade could see no objection to them providing the Company had been consulted and two copies had been forwarded to them.

" *1. The Bye Laws shall come into force on the day of 1883.*
2. The rate of speed to be observed for tramway traffic shall in no case exceed 8mph.
3. No carriage using a tramway shall follow

another carriage using the same tramway at a less distance from such other carriage than 100 yards.

4. *Every driver or conductor shall stop the tramway carriage when required so to do by a passenger desirous of leaving the carriage, or by any person   desirous of travelling by the carriage and for whom there is room.*

5. *No driver or conductor shall, by loitering or stopping needlessly or otherwise, impede the ordinary traffic of the street in which the tramway is laid. If at any time a block occurs in the ordinary traffic in any street, any tramway carriage in such street shall, either stop running or move in such direction as may be necessary to relieve such block in the traffic. No tramway carriage shall stand within 50 yards of the following places for more than three minutes that is to say:* [left blank in original document]

6. *In default of compliance with any of the foregoing Bye Laws the Company or persons offending will be liable, upon conviction, to a penalty of not exceeding 40 shillings and in a case of a continuing offence to a further penalty of not exceeding 10 shillings for every day during which the offence may be continued."*

The Bye Laws could not come into operation until they had been laid before the Board of Trade for two calendar months after notice had been published in the 'London Gazette' and local newspapers.

Conversion to steam traction

In February 1883 Edmonton Local Board became aware the Company was promoting a Bill to enable them to use steam traction on the tramway and decided to petition against it unless a clause was inserted *"that no steam or mechanical power was to be used in the Edmonton District without the consent or approval being first obtained of the*

Board". The Company came to a satisfactory agreement with the Board at a meeting on 10 April 1883 at which the clerk to the Board and the parliamentary agents were instructed to obtain the insertion of such a clause, provided the costs incurred by the Board would be paid by the Company.

Petitions against the Bill had also been received from the New River Company, which later withdrew its objection, and from the Metropolitan Board of Works (predecessors of the London County Council). The latter objected generally to the use of steam traction on tramways in its district and the Company decided to offer to discontinue its service in Hackney (the area administered by the Metropolitan Board of Works) from the top of Stamford Hill northwards to the Middlesex boundary at Baileys Lane, a distance of about 250 yards.

In July 1883 it was announced that the Bill had passed the House of Commons, had been read a second time in the House of Lords and would shortly receive the Royal Assent. The passed Act authorised the use of steam traction for seven years.

The Company intended to construct the two new lines with heavier materials than the earlier line, so they could be operated by steam traction from their opening, and a contract for the construction was entered into with the City of London Contract Corporation. The new line from Seven Sisters Corner to Finsbury Park ran across the boundary between Middlesex and the area of the Metropolitan Board of Works at more than one location. The Board's objections meant that, although the whole line was in Seven Sisters Road, there was only a clear run of ¾ mile from Tottenham on which steam could be used since there were then three short sections where it could not. It was proposed to operate a service on the existing line from Ponders End to Seven Sisters Corner and through onto the new lines from Seven Sisters Corner to near the junction of Seven Sisters Road with Amhurst Park by steam traction before continuing to Finsbury Park by horse power. This would require the retention of 40 of the 125 horses and the provision of stabling for them on a convenient site.

At a meeting of the Edmonton Local Board on 2 October 1883 it was agreed jointly with the Company that the contractors upgrading the original line for steam traction should alter the location of the passing places, as agreed, and widen Edmonton Fore Street, adjoining the Broadway, between Knights Lane and Plevna Road. New Road was built as a bridge over the railway at Lower Edmonton Station to avoid the tramway crossing it on the level.

In June 1884 the Company promoted a further Bill seeking an extension of the time required for the construction of the works, powers to raise additional capital and to be able to use steam and other forms of mechanical traction within the Metropolitan Board of Works area. However, when the Bill came before a committee of the House of Commons, although the Board opposed it as they had on previous occasions, it was decided unanimously that the preamble of the Bill was proved and the use of steam traction on all the Company's lines was authorised for seven years.

The steam engines

In the same month that unrestricted powers to operate the tramways by steam traction were authorised, an order was placed with Messrs Merryweather & Sons of London (Greenwich) for 15 steam tramway engines.

The Company rebuilt the depot at Tramway Avenue with commodious workshops and running sheds for the new rolling stock. The stud of horses had to be considerably reduced in order to permit the conversion of the stables into a steam depot and the receipts decreased in consequence during this period.

Mr Aldworth was recruited as the Engineer for the new rolling stock under Superintendent Hill.

He was a man of considerable experience, coming from Batley, in Yorkshire, where he had had some years' training in the practical working of steam tramways.

Also, in preparation for the operation of steam engines, Edmonton Local Board agreed to a hydrant, with hose and meter box, being placed in New Road for watering them. The first engine was delivered towards the end of 1884 and satisfactory trials of it took place at the beginning of December.

The Merryweather "Economical" steam tramway engine had duplicated controls so that the driver always drove the engine standing at the forward end. A powerful centrifugal governor was driven directly from the main axle, without chains or belts. The governor operated on a throttle valve, which closed when the speed reached 8 mph. Should the speed not be checked, as for instance when descending a gradient, a small steam valve was opened giving steam to the brake cylinders and applying the brakes. This acted automatically and ceased to operate when the speed had been reduced below the given limit. An ordinary screw hand-brake was also provided at each end of the engine. The steam brake, besides being actuated automatically by the governor, could also be applied by the pressure of the driver's foot on a treadle. The weight of the engine was 9 tons.

The engine was fitted with a condenser of a type known as the "Merryweather Air Condenser" from which the manufacturers claimed neither the exhaust steam nor the vapour from the chimney was visible, even when ascending hills. Coke was used as a fuel to reduce the amount of smoke emitted and the ash pan, which could be operated from both ends of the engine, was specially arranged to prevent dropping cinders or showing fire but could easily be raked out when required.

At the end of January 1885 the Merryweather engine was run over the line from Edmonton to Stamford Hill and back during the evening. The distance traversed was 9¼ miles, which it covered in 80 minutes including stops. The route was fairly level but in parts there were gradients of 1 in 37 and even 1 in 26. By 6 February a second engine had been running. One of the engines was exhibited at the Inventions Exhibition held that year.

The tramcar trailers

Consideration was given to converting the single ended horse cars for use as steam tram trailers by strengthening the trucks. However, it was thought better to dispose of the lightweight cars and to purchase more substantial ones in their place.

Seventeen bogie cars, weighing 4 tons each, were ordered from the Falcon Engine and Car Works Company, Loughborough; each car seated 46 passengers, 20 on inward-facing longitudinal seats inside and 26 on back-to-back longitudinal seats along the centre upstairs. Low bridges along the route determined the upper deck should be open top. The trailer car brake blocks were operated through the medium of a chain connected to a steam brake cylinder on the engine.

Operations: 1885 – 1886

Major General Hutchinson inspected and tested steam operation, on behalf of the Board of Trade, on 29 March 1885 and expressed himself satisfied but the police stopped the running of the engines until the Company had obtained the necessary licenses. However, a partial service of steam traction was commenced over the Easter holiday, on 2 April, since an insufficient number of engines had been delivered. During this period, the steam tramway engines and trailers, and the horse cars worked alternate journeys on the same line. All 15 engines were not delivered until the end of the year.

On 12 May Edmonton Local Board debated an application by the Company to install further hydrants in the streets for watering the steam engines in the streets and its Surveyor was instructed to meet the Company and discuss the matter.

The horse cars were finally withdrawn on 31 May, by which time the revenue from the conductors on the steam tram trailers amounted to double that of those on the horse cars. The horses were retained for some time after finishing work in order to get them into a good condition for sale.

Arrangements were made for placing advertisements on the engines and for tickets to be supplied free of charge to the Company in return for the placing of advertisements on the back.

The line from Seven Sisters Corner, Tottenham, along Seven Sisters Road to Manor House was opened for traffic on 19 October and extended from there to Finsbury Park on 12 December. At Finsbury Park the line met the tracks of the North Metropolitan Tramways, but no direct connection was made. The service was now revised to operate through from Finsbury Park to Ponders End and the line from Seven Sisters Corner to Stamford Hill became a backwater which was only worked at infrequent intervals.

In connection with opening the new line in October 1885, a second depot was provided off Seven Sisters Road, by St. Ann's Road, to avoid running dead mileage back to Tramway Avenue, Edmonton. (See Chapter 6).

Almost from the start of steam tram services, complaints were received from passengers travelling on the upper, open top deck of the trailer cars that they were obliged to inhale the suffocating fumes emitted from the chimneys of the engines. One person riding on the last car at night from Finsbury Park complained that the passengers sitting on the top deck were subjected to a continuous emission of steam and sulphurous fumes until the engine arrived at Manor House, when it ceased abruptly - no doubt because he had called the conductor's attention to it. The company could not raise the height of the chimneys because the engines had to pass under a very low bridge at

21

St. Ann's Station in Seven Sisters Road and also, even if they were able to do so, this would increase the draughting and generate more steam than was desirable or permitted. Trials were undertaken by fitting a chute over the chimney, which was reversible according to the direction of travel, to deflect the fumes high over the heads of those riding on the open top cars.

At an Extraordinary General Meeting of the Company in November 1885, the Managing Director stated that the wages of the drivers were five shillings a day and those of the conductors were between three shillings and threepence and three shillings and sixpence.

The attention of the Company was called to the practice of the engine drivers keeping their engines standing on the passing loop near the Finsbury Park Tavern, to the inconvenience of the public, and also to the danger of shunting engines at this point.

In June 1886 complaints were being made regarding the service between New Road, Edmonton, and Ponders End; some of the engine drivers were in the habit of terminating journeys about 500 yards short of the actual terminus, just north of South Street, Ponders End, leaving the passengers to continue on foot.

Not all the passing loops were easy to see at night. It was usual practice for a steam tram travelling from The Crescent, Edmonton, in the direction of Tottenham to stop at the passing loop opposite The King's Head and for the conductor to go ahead to see that the single line was clear and, if all was well, to signal the engine driver by whistle.

Fares

By July 1884 white tickets were used for penny (1d) fares and blue ones for two-penny (2d) fares. It is known that 1d was charged for the stages between Stamford Hill or South Tottenham Station and Bruce Grove and between Bruce Grove and the Edmonton boundary (Snell's Park) while Stamford Hill through to Ponders End was 4d. A printed scale of fares was posted inside the cars for the benefit of passengers.

By March 1885 the 1d fare stages had been revised and lengthened. As an example, Tottenham White Hart Lane to Tottenham High Cross became Edmonton Snell's Park to Tottenham Chestnut Road.

For a period in 1886 double the normal fare was charged on Sundays.

In the autumn of 1887 notices were posted inside the cars to the effect that no cars would, in future, stop to pick up or set down passengers within a short distance of a passing loop. Any person wishing to enter a car before it reached a loop or remaining in one after it had passed a loop would be charged the appropriate extra fare, however short the distance.

In November 1889 the Company started issuing adult season tickets at reduced rates, compared to the single fares, and at half fare for school children.

Additional rolling stock

Reviewing the position after the opening of the line to Finsbury Park, and with a modest profit being made, the Company decided it required 10 additional engines and trailers. Consideration was given to operating two trailers attached to one engine but it was thought the police might object to this.

The first of the new steam engines was delivered in August 1886. This time they were built by Messrs Dick, Kerr & Company at its Britannia Works in Kilmarnock and were more powerful than the Merryweather engines. The new trailers delivered by the Metropolitan Carriage Company of Birmingham were open top bogie cars, each seating 60 passengers. The 'garden seats' on the top deck were arranged laterally and had open backs. The Company had considered lighting the cars by electricity but this option was not pursued.

One of the new engines and a trailer were taken for a trial run from Tramway Avenue to Manor House and back. The engine proved satisfactory even on the fairly steep gradient in Seven Sisters Road, between St. Ann's Road and Amhurst Park. On Saturday, 31 August, Major General Hutchinson, the Government Inspector, arrived to observe and test the new engines and trailers before they were allowed to enter public service. Following another test run with an engine and trailer, he declared he was satisfied with the results. The following Thursday an engine and two trailers, loaded with four tons of iron, were taken on test to Stamford Hill – up which the engine ran easily.

The line to Wood Green

The only remaining matter was the completion of the line to Wood Green. The delay in starting work on this line authorised by the 1882 Act required the Company to promote a new Bill for the 1886 session of Parliament. In addition to the authorisation required to obtain a further extension of time for completing the remaining portion of the Wood Green line, the opportunity was used to secure powers to construct an additional line, 4½ miles in length, from the terminus at Finsbury Park to Kings Cross Station and Islington, near The Angel, via Seven Sisters Road, York Road (now York Way) and Amwell Street, to raise the necessary capital for this additional line and to consolidate the preference shares into stock.

The Company called an Extraordinary General Meeting on a Sunday afternoon at the end of November 1885 at the Guildhall Tavern Gresham Street in the City of London for the shareholders to agree to such a Bill being promoted. A director, Mr Christopher James, presided and moved the adoption of a resolution authorising the directors to exercise the borrowing powers, given to the Company under section 25 of their Act of 1882, and

also to raise an additional £20,000 of capital by the creation of 6 per cent preference shares. He stated that the new line from Tottenham along Seven Sisters Road had been built and the prospects for the Wood Green line were very good as building developments were increasing on all sides.

Mr Wain, Managing Director of the Company, seconded the motion. He explained that no doubt the shareholders had noticed traffic receipts had fallen off, to a very considerable degree, earlier in the year. The simple explanation for this was that, in order to convert the stables into engine houses, they had had to get rid of some of their horses. This had resulted in a poorer service; up to the end of the previous March they had lost £300 in traffic receipts. At first they had only been able to put on a part service of steam engines to work together with the horse trams – but, even so, this had not only wiped off the deficit but received (sic) an increase in receipts of £500 more than the same period in the previous year. After the answering of questions, the resolution was carried and the meeting closed.

The Bill came formally before the Examiners of the House of Lords in June 1886, when compliance with the necessary Standing Orders was proved. However, at the fifth Ordinary Meeting of the Company, held in February 1887, the directors noted that that part of the Bill promoting the additional line had received an objection from the Metropolitan Board of Works. Consequently, Parliament, having declined to suspend the Standing Orders which would have enabled the Company to dispense with the consent of the Board, could not sanction that part of it. The remaining provisions of the Bill, being unopposed, had been duly enacted.

Even though Green Lanes was mostly a wide straggling country lane at the time, the Company wrote to the Tottenham Local Board asking it to arrange for the widening of it at certain places and to fix the levels of it at which the line to Wood Green was to be laid. It suggested that the works required should be undertaken at the same time as the construction of the line. The Board then approached the Company, asking it to divert the line from the locations indicated on the parliamentary plan to a position where, when the Board made up the road, it would occupy the centre of the road. The Company consented to do this, but there was no mention at the time that it would have to make any financial contribution.

Construction of the line commenced on 6 October 1886. The Board then made a claim for £6,000 against the Company for work it had to do in making up the road, raising it, widening it and other improvements. This claim resulted in construction work on the line being suspended on 20 December. Since the powers for the construction of the line would have lapsed again on 10 August 1887, it was necessary for the two parties to come to an agreement to permit the construction to be resumed. To this end, the Board reduced its claim to a quarter of the sum originally sought.

On Monday, 8 August 1887, Major General Hutchinson made his official inspection of the line from Finsbury Park to Wood Green (by the Nightingale public house on the corner of Truro Road). He was met by Company officials at Green Lanes Station (now known as Harringay Station) who were waiting with an engine and trailer as well as a horse car. First he proceeded to Finsbury Park, alternately riding and walking along the route. He then continued his inspection as far as The Nightingale public house in Wood Green High Road, where he expressed entire satisfaction with the construction of the line. However, in consequence of the delay by the Tottenham Local Board in widening the road, it was only passed fit as a horse tramway until such time as the road was widened. As the Company did not want to operate a new service of horse trams for only a few months, it decided to delay the opening of the line until the road widening was completed and it could use the steam trams.

The steam tram service, of through journeys from Finsbury Park to Wood Green, commenced on 24 December 1887. No alteration was made to the existing service between Finsbury Park and Ponders End.

Operations : 1887

The first annual dinner for the employees took place on the first Thursday of January 1887 at the Golden Lion, Edmonton. To facilitate this, it was arranged that all cars would cease to run at 8 p.m. As the cost of the dinner could not be afforded by the Company, it was paid for by "public subscription".

A conductor wrote a letter to the Weekly Herald, published on 21 January, regarding an earlier letter printed about North London Tramways.

"Sir

Having noticed in your last issue a letter signed "Ex Conductor", stating that our hours averaged 14 per day, I beg to give that statement an unqualified denial. We servicemen rotate at our work and thus all get the same proportion of long and short days. Now there are two, and in the summertime four, or more cars that do not work until after 1 p.m. and on which we all take a turn and we all have a rest day once a fortnight. For all these half days and also for our rest day we get a full day's pay. Taking the year through, our hours average 10 hours 50 minutes per day or about 4 hours per day less than any other company I have ever worked for. (etc)

Conductor Badge No. 2987"

By May, six of the new engines built by Messrs Dick, Kerr & Company had been delivered, as had the 10 new bogie trailers. The rolling stock now consisted of 21 engines and 27 trailers – 10 of which carried 60 passengers, 16 had a capacity of 46 passengers and one carried 54 passengers.

Difficulty was still being experienced coping with crowds at weekends, when all available staff were required for duty. The police were needed to prevent the public crowding onto the cars in such numbers as to almost wreck them. Returning from Ponders End on Saturday evenings, the crushing was so tremendous that many had to be turned away.

Not only had the weekend pleasure traffic built up but considerable residential developments were now taking place in the districts served by the Company. This particularly affected Edmonton, which at one time had been the financially poorest section of the line. The Company ran as frequent a service as the line would permit but, because of the single line and passing loops, the maximum headway was only every 15 minutes.

On 9 May, at about 10 p.m., an engine and trailer were standing on the single track in Edmonton, at the end of Tramway Avenue, when the driver of a horse and van overtook them. The engine suddenly let off steam as the horse came level with it, causing the animal to swerve round, pulling the van against the kerb and overturning it. The driver of the engine said it was his last journey of the day and he had to uncouple it at Tramway Avenue.

The first fatal accident on the tramway happened on Wednesday 18 May 1887, along Tottenham High Road by Scotland Green. It was raining at the time and a small girl ran across the road in front of the engine. It was only moving slowly, as the driver had shut off steam when he left the loop and then applied the brakes, let sand run onto the track to improve traction and put the engine in reverse when he saw what was happening. However, the rails were greasy and the engine slid forwards to hit the girl on the shoulder, knocking her to the ground and causing her death. The engine driver was held not to blame for the accident.

In September a tram conductor was charged with stealing one metal punch valued at £5 and embezzling £3 16s 1d in fares whilst a servant of the Company. It was stated in Court that on 2 July, at about 8.20 a.m., an inspector employed by the Company handed the accused 1,628 tickets, representing a value of £16 17s 3d. It was the custom for conductors to retain the takings for one journey throughout the day and to pay in two at the end of their turn of duty. The last journey scheduled for the accused that day finished at 11 p.m. When the tram arrived at New Road, Edmonton, with twenty to thirty passengers on board, the conductor was not on it. He had disappeared, with the punch and the fares taken for two journeys, leaving the car unprotected and with a number of passengers on board. Subsequently, 906 unsold tickets were found on the car and returned; by deduction it was estimated that tickets to the value of £3 16s 1d had been sold. The case was proven and the conductor convicted and sentenced to two months hard labour.

In November 1887 a hearing took place at Clerkenwell County Court of a case between Bertolle and the Company. The plaintiff gave evidence that on the previous 26 June, whilst he, accompanied by his daughter, was pushing a tricycle up Woodberry Hill, a steam engine overtook them and in so passing ejected steam and water, slightly scalding his legs. Inspector Freshwater appeared on behalf of the Company and offered 21 shillings compensation, without admitting liability. The plaintiff was awarded the 21 shillings but no costs.

Two more incidents took place during November. The first occurred when a one horse dray, travelling along Tottenham High Road by Scotland Green, was met by a steam tram en route to Finsbury Park. The horse became restive and, just as the trailer car was level with it, backed the dray into the car, completely smashing the whole side of the dray. No injuries occurred. The second accident took place outside Edmonton Police Station when a steam tram and trailer collided with a horse and wagon, causing the horse to fall and smash both shafts. The accident was caused by the horse backing the wagon into the tram just as the engine approached. Apart from breaking the shafts, no further damage was done.

Other extensions proposed

On 17 November 1887 a Bill was lodged with the Board of Trade for promoting in the 1888 session of Parliament. This sought powers to construct and operate three additional lines. The first was from Seven Sisters Corner, Tottenham, along West Green Road to Green Lanes. The second was from Green Lanes via Turnpike Lane and High Street, Hornsey, to Priory Road at a point 43 yards west of Middle Lane. The third was an extension of the original Ponders End line along Hertford Road to the Bell Inn.

This time the Tottenham Local Board raised objections. The principal point of contention was the Board required West Green Road to be widened for a short distance westward from Elmar Road, even though this could not be done without private property being acquired. The Company wrote to the Tottenham Local Board asking it to reconsider its decision since the Company believed construction of the line would be beneficial to the district and, if carried out, it would consider extending it along Turnpike Lane to Hornsey. Since the contentious issues had still not been resolved, the Board decided to maintain its objection.

In February 1888 a deputation of owners and ratepayers attended the offices of the Tottenham Local Board and presented a petition against the proposed tramway in West Green Road. In March the Company and the Board met to discuss the proposed lines along West Green Road and Turnpike Lane. The Board, having considered the signed petition from along West Green Road, decided it could not consent to that proposal. However, it gave its approval to the line along Turnpike Lane, provided that there were never more than two tramcars (including engines) along any part of Turnpike Lane within the district of the Board.

Islington Vestry was still interested in the Company's proposals, under the 1886 Bill, for a line from Finsbury Park to Kings Cross and The Angel and wrote to the Metropolitan Board of Works and petitioned Parliament in favour of it. It hoped that the South Hornsey Local Board would do likewise, so was disappointed when South Hornsey decided to oppose the proposals and sent a deputation to attend Islington Vestry and explain its reasons for doing so. While the directors of the Company thought they should make a final effort to get into the metropolis, the shareholders indicated they would prefer to remain a suburban company.

Operations : 1888 - 1890

South Hornsey Local Board considered that engines and trailers waiting at the Finsbury Park terminus caused inconvenience by standing opposite the park entrance. By agreement with the Company, this arrangement was altered so that they would stand clear of it.

In July 1888 an unusual accident occurred in Wood Green High Road one afternoon. Engine Numbers 3 and 16 were in the Gladstone Avenue passing loop together with trailers. Instead of one driver waiting until the other was clear, or owing to slippery rails, both continued to run resulting in a collision which caused Number 16 to leave the rails and each engine to sustain slight damage. Fortunately there were only six passengers in the two cars at the time and no one was injured.

On 2 August a large number of employees of the Company assembled at The Golden Lion, Edmonton, to present a testimonial to Mr Aldworth, the Locomotive Superintendent, who was leaving his post following his appointment as Manager of the Coventry Steam Tramway Company.

The service on the line between Seven Sisters Corner and Stamford Hill was withdrawn early in August because it was uneconomical to run. Even when a 1d fare, and then a ½d fare, had been tried in order to stimulate traffic, the takings only averaged 1d per mile. Nevertheless, it was recommenced from 18 August.

Complaints were being received about the state of the track, one of which, in September 1889, was from the Enfield Local Board about Ponders End and another from the Tottenham Local Board. The Company replied that it spent enough money on the original line, through Tottenham and Edmonton, to keep it in repair but it had been built for horse traction and was not as solid as it would have been if it had constructed for steam engines from the start. At the end of June 1890 the Edmonton Local Board instructed its Engineer to call the attention of the Company to the serious liability it was incurring by non-repair of the tramway. The Board would hold the Company responsible and liable for any accident or damage that occurred by reason of the defective tramway.

In view of the worsening financial situation of the Company, it was decided that there would be no 1d fares issued on Good Friday, Easter Sunday, or the bank holiday Monday of 1890.

On 29 July 1890 an engine and car were standing in the loop at New Road, Edmonton, waiting for the next engine and car to pass. Presently, the latter came down the hill from the railway bridge at a good speed, jumped the points and ran into the stationery engine. The driver said he applied his brake but it failed to act. The result was considerable damage to both engines and personal injury was caused to several passengers.

On Saturday, 27 September 1890, an engine and car left Finsbury Park terminus for Ponders End. On arriving at the junction outside the Manor House Tavern, where the Wood Green branch turned left, the engine, correctly, went straight ahead and so did the front bogie of the car, but the rear bogie jumped the point and was derailed. The driver of the engine did not immediately notice resulting in the car being dragged to one side and colliding with a large lamppost in the middle of the road. The lamp was knocked over and the protective railings along one side of the car's top deck were torn off.

Steam traction 'nuisance'

By April 1888 complaints were being made regarding the nuisance arising from the smoke and steam being emitted from tram engines at Wood Green. In May the Tottenham Local Board wrote to the Board of Trade on the subject and received a reply that the Company was liable to penalties for any breach of the regulations. The Board of Trade raised the subject with the Company which stated, in its reply, that it regretted that there should be any grounds for complaint since it had given its attention to the question of the emission of steam and fumes from the engines and would continue to do all possible to prevent inconvenience to the public by adhering to the regulations under which the trams were worked. As an additional safeguard, all the new engines constructed in the last twelve months had steam condensers fitted. The Board of Trade noted the reply and said it would take proceedings against the Company if any further complaints were made.

Until now, the district known as Wood Green formed part of the area administered by the Tottenham Local Board. However, a Bill of local importance, known as the Wood Green Division of District Bill or the "Separation Bill" was introduced into the 1888 session of Parliament on the initiative of Ralph Littler, a wealthy barrister with specialist knowledge of tramway legislation and a dislike of steam trams. The Tottenham Local Board, with the approval of its ratepayers, was determined to oppose the Bill but eventually agreed before it was enacted. Wood Green became administered by a separate Local Board, of which Ralph Littler became a member, from 29 September 1888.

Also arising from the Local Government Act 1888, the London County Council came into being on 1 January 1889 with a remit, amongst other things, to take over all the functions of the former Metropolitan Board of Works and with powers to acquire (but not operate) all existing tramways within the new county boundary.

The new Wood Green Local Board wrote to the Company calling its attention to further complaints, which had been made about the steam, smoke, noise and reckless driving of the engines. The Board stated that it was impossible for the engines to climb Jolly Butcher's Hill, Wood Green, without extra steam being used.

A two-year agreement had been made on 24 February 1887 between the Company and the Tottenham Local Board which gave powers to the Company to operate trams (of unspecified type) throughout the district, which then included Wood Green. Prior to this agreement expiring on 24 February 1889, the Company applied to the Wood Green Local Board for a renewal of that part of the agreement relating to the lines now in the new Wood Green district. However, the Wood Green Local Board declined to grant permission whilst steam was the motive power employed. To make matters worse, the South Hornsey Local Board followed suit. The Company wrote to the Board of Trade, asking it to appoint an Arbitrator to decide the terms of the contract between the Wood Green Local Board and the Company.

In January 1889 the Tottenham Local Board applied to the Edmonton Magistrates' Court for a summons against the Company for using steam power within its district without having entered into a statutory agreement. It transpired that there had been two agreements; the first, to operate steam traction, had been made when steam traction was introduced and this had already expired but the second was the agreement of 1887 to operate trams generally for two years. On the basis that the period of time permitted for the first

agreement had expired, the summons was granted. The Wood Green Local Board then decided that, since the original agreement with the Tottenham Local Board had expired by the time the Wood Green district had been separated from Tottenham the previous September, there could be no agreement in force between the Wood Green Local Board and the Company. The clerk to the Wood Green Local Board was instructed to attend court and watch the proceedings.

The summons was heard on 7 February, when the Company asked for the case to be adjourned on the grounds that the situation had already been put before the Board of Trade, which was going to appoint an Arbitrator as provided for in the Act of 1883. The Tottenham Local Board opposed the adjournment as it considered that any decision of the Board of Trade could not affect the decision of the magistrates on a question of a contract be-tween the Company and Tottenham Local Board. The Company responded that although the Act provided that the agreement should not remain in force for more than two years, the Tottenham Local Board had allowed eighteen months to pass since the alleged expiration of the existing agreement before taking any steps. In those circumstances, the magistrates decided to adjourn the case. The case was resumed at the end of February when, on behalf of the Tottenham Local Board, it was requested that the case might be further adjourned for a week, by which time the two parties might have come to agreement. Indeed, the new agree-ment between the Company and the Tottenham Local Board was signed shortly afterwards.

However, with no agreement in sight between the Company and the Wood Green Local Board, the trams suddenly stopped running in the Wood Green area after 24 February. Shortly afterwards, services were also suspended in the South Hornsey area. The trams only ran from Manor House to Ponders End and from Manor House to The Wellington public house in Green Lanes, thus lopping off the most important end of the system.

Board of Trade Arbitration

The Referee (Arbitrator) appointed by the Board of Trade held the inquiry to settle the differences that had arisen between Wood Green Local Board and the Company at Wood Green in May 1889 over several sittings.

A local newspaper of the time reported:

"A deputation from the Wood Green Local Board protested against the use of steam by the Company within the district of the Board, stating that the use of steam on the Company's lines was dangerous. The Wood Green Local Board had only come into existence the previous year; had they been in existence at the time the Company's Act was passed they would certainly have opposed granting of powers to use steam traction. They considered the Company had broken every regulation of the Board of Trade and no agreement with the Wood Green Local Board had been entered into."

"The South Hornsey Local Board also stated that the Company had no agreement with them but simply ran in defiance of all laws and regulations. Owing to the smoke and smell from the trams, they considered the rateable values in the district had been seriously depreciated."

"The Arbitrator stated that his terms of reference from the Board of Trade were to not to enquire whether the Company should use steam traction but only to the terms upon which it should be used. The Local Boards then asked that the Board of Trade should also refer this question to the Arbitrator. They stated that should the Board of Trade decline to refer the matter, the responsibility for this dangerous traffic could not rest with the local boards. The Board of Trade replied by suggesting that the local boards had legal remedies under the Tramways

Act 1870; unless they had exhausted these powers before approaching the Board of Trade, it could be accused of exceeding its own remit."

The Referee, in giving his findings, stated

"The Tramway Acts require that where steam is to be used upon a particular roadway, a contract agreement or arrangement shall exist between the road authority and the Company."

"These two bodies were unable or unwilling to agree upon terms and this Department has been appealed to, thereby raising a number of questions of the highest public importance; some of them within and some of them without the scope of such an agreement. The Wood Green Board avowedly disliked steam tramways in the district. They treated them as a nuisance and wanted to get rid of them. Their objection to enter into an agreement (it was hardly denied by their counsel) proceeded from a desire, first to delay and if possible defeat the operations of the Tramway Company; failing in this, to impose upon them new and extremely onerous conditions of paving, of road widening and of hostile supervision. Evidence tended to show that there had been accidents and depreciation of property and the tramways ought to be worked by horse. The Company, through their counsel, opposed these demands as unreasonable. They proceeded from a Local Board established only a couple of years ago, and no similar terms had been required by any of the adjoining districts, through which their trams ran."

"As to complaints, the Wood Green Board had advertised for them. None had been put forward until this enquiry. Evidence was called to what pecuniary loss and inconvenience the temporary stoppage of the Tramway had caused. It had been admitted on behalf of the Local Board that

the Company had satisfied the original require-ments of the Board of Trade but further experi-ence, they contended, had shown that additional safeguards were necessary."

The Referee decided that he could only deal with the undertaking as an authorised steam tramway but he had no doubts as to his jurisdiction and was prepared to make the contract of agreement which the parties themselves had failed to enter into. As to whether it would be better if the tramway was worked by horses or some other power than steam, *"that question must stand over until next year, when an opportunity will arise legitimately for considering it under the power of revision exercis-able by the Board of Trade every seven years."*

The Referee subsequently made his written award, under which the Company was enabled to exercise its powers of running steam in the district as hitherto. He gave instructions regarding the terminal points which the Company might use – but the precise details are now uncertain. This enabled the Company to resume services, along the sections where it had been suspended, in time for the Whitsun holiday.

Labour relations

A meeting was held at the Edmonton Liberal and Radical Club in New Road at midnight on 9 July 1889 to vent the frustration of Company employees at the length of the hours they had to work and the pay they received. About thirty men, employed on the steam trams between Finsbury Park and Ponders End, attended and the meeting lasted until 2 a.m.

The Rev. D. Russell took the chair and opened the meeting by remarking that it was never in-tended that men should work the long hours for the small pay, which all omnibus and tramway men were doing; it was only just and right that consideration should be given to them, as well as the shareholders of the company which employed them. He then called for the first resolution.

The many grievances and hardships of the life of the tramway men on this line were recalled:

● They had to work an average of fifteen hours a day, seven days each week with only one day off at wide intervals of three or four weeks. There was no payment for the day off.

● The pay was paltry; in the case of conductors it was less than 3d per hour. They were allowed no meal times and, if they lost any of the tickets stock, the full value of those tickets was deducted from their pay even though the tickets could not be used by the public.

● The drivers' pay was very little better; paid by the hour, they averaged from four shillings to five shillings and three pence per day (with one in-stance of five shillings and sixpence being known).

● The conductors were fined for sitting down, kept later than the usual time to settle their accounts of tickets and for this, men who had been over three years in the service, received three shillings and three pence per day.

● Drivers were fined for being late on the journey (one shilling) and for bending [the skirting] bars due to the jumping of cars they were fined two shillings and sixpence. The fines certainly went into the sick fund, but the men who were never fined still had the benefit of the fines imposed on drivers and conductors.

● Sunday was the hardest day of all, always over fifteen hours per day.

It was moved "That a branch of The Tramway Employees Union be formed in this district".

The Company commented that it was a matter

of common knowledge that neither the ordinary shareholders of the Company nor the preference shareholders had received a dividend from their investment. The Rev. Russell admitted this was so and said he had been misquoted.

Insolvency

Neither the North London Tramways Company nor its predecessor, the North London Suburban Tramway Company, was financially successful. The curtailment of services along some of the key sections of line from February to May 1889, as a result of legal actions and disputes with some of the local authorities, brought it to its knees.

An action, entitled Lowe v. North London Tramways Company 1889 L No. 857, was commenced in the High Court, Chancery Division, on 2 April by John Shaw Lowe on behalf of himself and other debenture holders in the Company. The plaintiff asked the High Court for the Company (as the defendant) to be declared insolvent and for a receiver and manager be appointed to sell the Company and deal with the re-assignment of the tramway undertaking and the freehold and lease-hold properties. He suggested that the Company could be sold as a going concern to the North Metropolitan Tramways Company. A history of the North Metropolitan Tramways Company and its services is given in Chapter 3.

The hearing of the action took place on 18 December 1889 and was granted; consequently an Order for winding up the Company was made on 21 January 1890. By a subsequent Order of the Court, dated 17 February, Arthur Edwin Preston, chartered accountant, was appointed Liquidator of the Company and a further Order of 25 March stated that the undertaking should be sold as a going concern.

On 10 April William James Carruthers Wain, the previous Chairman of the Company, was appointed manager and receiver of the undertaking on behalf of the debenture holders. He was a civil engineer, an authority on steam tramways and had an involvement with a number of other systems – including the Birmingham Central Tramways Company which had 70 steam engines.

On the petition of the Judgement Creditor, an Order was made in the High Court on 21 June 1890 for the compulsory winding up of the Company.

More 'persecution' of the tramway company

The Board of Trade inquiry did not satisfy those who had petitioned against the use of steam traction on the tramway. As a result of a memorandum signed by 700 residents of South Hornsey, and passed to their local board, four summonses were issued against the Company, which were heard at Dalston Magistrates Court on 20 December 1889.

1. For emitting steam from engines so as to cause a nuisance
2. Causing the engines to make a noise by blasting
3. Also causing steam to escape
4. For not concealing the fire of the engine from view.

Summons No.1 concerned engine No.2 attached to car No.1. The first witness for the Prosecution said he saw steam emitted from the front of the engine at the bottom, and a dense volume at the side. In his judgement that was enough to frighten horses. A second witness corroborated this. For the Defence, it was stated that the engine and car in question were at Finsbury Park Terminus, the conductor uncoupled the car from the engine and the driver had occasion to put his foot on the brake. This was only half a second and there was not enough steam escaping to frighten a horse. The steam in question came from the foot brake at the side.

Summons No.2 concerned engine No.25. The first witness alleged that a noise was created by the blast of the engine. This was being done by turning steam into the funnel to cause a draught. The machinery of the engine also shook a good deal and caused a great clatter. This was corroborated. For the Defence, the engine driver said he always drove engine No.25 when he was at work, and the Company stated that the engine was always kept in proper repair.

Summons No.3 The number of the engine was not known. The same two Prosecution witnesses gave evidence that they were passengers on a car and saw steam issuing from the condenser in large volumes and also from the funnel. There appeared to be leaks in the pipes and an immense volume of steam was emitted. When the steam was shut off, the steam did not escape but all the time it was on it did so. The Defence asked for an adjournment of this Summons because the number of the engine was not known and it was not in a position to call any rebutting evidence.

Summons No.4 was for not complying with the regulations. In this case the Prosecution witness stated that he saw the furnace door open, with the fire plainly showing, for a quarter of a mile. For the Company, this was pointed out that this was an offence by the engine driver, for which it was not liable.

The Magistrate dismissed the first summons; on the second he fined the Company forty shillings; the third he adjourned for 14 days and on the fourth he thought the summons ought to be taken out against the driver.

The adjourned summonses were heard on 3 January 1890.

For that against the driver in the employ of the Company, for allowing the light of his fire to be seen, the driver was convicted and fined. For

Summons No.3 the night foreman employed at the Seven Sisters Road depot was called. He gave evidence that he had charge of the depot where the engines were stationed after completing the day's work. It was his duty to do any necessary repairs. He had had no report whatever that the condensing pipes of the engine in question needed repair. He had seen the same engine that morning and found it working satisfactorily. The Magistrate imposed the full fine of forty shillings in this case.

Three new summonses against the Company were then heard; these being

1. For causing a noise
2. For the clatter of machinery
3. For the emission of steam

The witness for the Prosecution stated that he rode in one of the cars of the Company from Finsbury Park to Lordship Road and during the journey the blast was put on and a buzzing sound was heard all the way. This noise was calculated to frighten horses. The Company was found guilty and fined twenty shillings.
On the second Summons two witnesses deposed to riding on the same car and experiencing a noise from the clatter of loose rods and bolts which could be heard 300 yards away. The Company was fined forty shillings.
The third summons was for emitting steam from the engine, the details of which were similar to those already stated and in this case the Magistrate imposed a fine of twenty shillings.

Trying to improve the tramway

Representatives of the local board areas served by the North London Tramways Company, by now in the process of going into receivership, met at the Guildhall, Westminster, offices of Middlesex County Council on 31 January 1890 to consider steps which could be taken to secure improvements to the tramway, its rolling stock and mode of working. A sub-committee, appointed by the representatives of the local boards, met with the receiver of the Company, the solicitor to the debenture holders and the solicitors to the Company to discuss the complaints made against the Company. The receiver of the Company undertook to do all in his power to deal with the complaints arising out of defective roads, steam, sulphurous smells etc. but asked for time to be able to take action. The meeting was adjourned for five weeks on the understanding that the representatives of the Company would lay before the representatives of the local boards, within four weeks, details of repairs to roads, stock etc. which had been taken together with proposals for future action.

A further meeting took place on 24 February. The representatives of the local boards approved the contents of a letter asking the Board of Trade not to renew the Company's powers for the use of steam traction without first giving any interested local boards the opportunity to make any comments they might wish.

In June 1890, the Company in receivership obtained a High Court ruling in favour of it applying to the Board of Trade for the renewal of its powers to use steam traction for a further seven years. Knowing of the disapproval of these powers by some of the local boards in the area, the Board of Trade called a further inquiry and informed the local boards accordingly.

Board of Trade Inquiry : Operation of Steam Trams

The Inquiry was held by the Board of Trade Inspector, Major General Hutchinson, at the offices of the Tottenham Local Board at Coombes Croft House. It opened on 1 July 1890 with the Inspector stating that he would firstly take evidence and then make an inspection of the line and machinery. Middlesex County Council and all the local boards except Enfield were represented.

Evidence was given on behalf of the South Hornsey Local Board who reiterated the previous complaints, which had been raised at the Board of Trade arbitration inquiry in May 1889, and also mentioned the proceedings against the Company in the Police Court. A further complaint was depreciation of property along the route of the tramway. There were 906 yards of the Company's line in the South Hornsey district, one half of which, longitudinally, was in Hornsey District, and the other half in South Hornsey. The Board maintained the road on behalf of Middlesex County Council, who might withhold payment if the County Surveyor did not certify it as being in proper repair. It was suggested that horse trams replace the steam trams. Various independent witnesses were called in support.

The Inquiry was then adjourned until 5 July when evidence was given on behalf of the Wood Green Local Board concerning the state of the road and track in their area and also the condition of the rolling stock. In particular, it was reported how the engines had to blast frequently when going up Jolly Butcher's Hill (an average gradient of just over one in twenty four) while some had to stop at the bottom of the hill for some minutes to enable them to get up steam to climb the hill.

The Hackney Board of Works put in a report and evidence was given on its behalf. About half a mile of the tramway was in their area in Seven Sisters Road; it was in fairly good repair but there was room for improvement in the rolling stock.

Evidence was given on behalf of the Tottenham Local Board that the tramway line (under its jurisdiction) extended from the Edmonton boundary to Bailey's Lane (Stamford Hill). The line, in its present condition, was not fit for the running of engines and cars. A local petition against steam traction was submitted.

On behalf of Edmontond, evidence was given on the state of the line and the engines. Also, it was said, that the service operated was erratic.

The Inquiry was adjourned again until 13 July when evidence was given on behalf of the Company that if steam power was abolished then the tramways would be abolished. The Company could not find the money to buy the new cars and horses, which would be needed if the engines could not be used.

Complaints about the use of steam traction had arisen after the engines had been working for four years. The original complaint was for using steam, in Tottenham, without an agreement. The next was the Wood Green agitation that ended in the matter coming before Board of Trade arbitration, and an award was given in the Company's favour. The liquidation of the Company was attributed to the action of the Wood Green and South Hornsey local boards in closing the lines in their districts for three months and prevented the earning of the debenture interest for the last year.

The first fifteen engines cost under £800 each and the other ten engines £940 each. Details were given regarding the expenditure on the engines and the permanent way. The receiver for the debenture holders said he was prepared to spend £700 or £800, or thereabouts, to put the road in statutory repair. This expenditure was in addition to an annual expenditure of £1,000 or £2,000 - which was practically the amount spent in 1889.

The ordinary capital of the Company was £73,080, the 6% preference shares amounted to £73,020 and the debenture shares to £37,250. No dividend had ever been paid on the ordinary share capital. The last dividend on the preference shares had been made in 1887; in 1888 there had been no distribution; in 1889 the opposition of Wood Green Local Board had even prevented the Company from paying its debenture interest. The Company had exhausted the whole of its borrowing powers and issued the whole of its share capital. Various other people were called in support.

This concluded the evidence; the Inspector announced that he would view the line the next day, with the Surveyors of the various local boards.

Major General Hutchinson, in his report of the inquiry, dated 19 July 1890, made a number of observations which summarised the history of the Company and the condition of its assets to date:

"The North London Tramways, which have a total length of 9 miles 73.71 chains, have been opened for traffic, at various times, between April 1881 and February 1888. Up to April 1885 horse traction only was employed but, since that date, steam traction (with some small exceptions) has been used as authorised by the Acts of 1883 and 1884 and the present powers to use steam, &c. expire on August 2nd 1890".

"The length of tramway, first opened in April 1881, extends from Stamford Hill to Ponders End, a total route length of 5 miles 30.98 chains, of which 2 miles 25.83 chains are in Tottenham, 2 miles 30.84 chains in Edmonton and 54.31 chains in Enfield. This was constructed with Vignole's rails weighing about 42 lbs. to the yard, laid on transverse cross sleepers imbedded in concrete, the paving consisting of square setts of granite, about three inches cube between the rails and about four inches cube outside them".

"After some necessary repairs to the paving and rail joints, this length of tramway was allowed to open for steam traction in April 1885 and it is as to the condition of the permanent way in this portion of the tramways that the principal complaints arise".

"The portions next opened in August 1885, and at subsequent dates up to February 1888 (having a total route length of 4 miles 42.73 chains), were all constructed with girder-rails and larger paving setts; and as to the condition of the permanent-way of these portions, no very serious complaints are made, though there are many places in which the paving setts have sunk and require attention".

"The rolling stock comprises 25 engines and 27 cars (of the bogie type); 15 of the engines were constructed by Messrs. Merryweather, and 10 (newer than the others) by Messrs. Dick, Kerr & Co.; 18 engines and 16 cars are in constant use, the remainder being under repair or on reserve for use on special occasions".

He went on to list the main causes of complaint as being:

"(1) clatter and noise, (2) the emission of steam from various parts of the engine, (3) the emission of noxious vapours, (4) the use of the blast, (5) the showing of fire, (6) vibration in adjoining houses from passage of engines, (7) occasional inattention of drivers, (8) somewhat frequent accidents, (9) bad state of repair of tramway portion of the roads"

"To deal with these seriatim:-
(1) Unnecessary noise and clatter – These can to a large extent be rectified by attention to keeping the shutters of the flaps of the engines properly fastened instead of unfastened as I observed was the case on most of the engines, and by proper attention to the state of the bushes of the side rods.
(2) Emission of steam –– If steam is allowed to issue from the funnel or the cylinder tops so as to be a nuisance, the driver is to blame, but if proceeding from other parts of the engine it must be due to remedial defects. On the two days I was observing the engines, I saw none showing steam in any objectionable quantity.
(3) Emission of obnoxious vapours - This is, I fear, inseparable from the use of steam, but the better the coke employed, the less noxious are the vapours. The Company declare they use none but the best coke, and so long as this is done I do not see what more is possible.
(4) Use of the blast – The occasional use of the blast may be necessary, but then it should only be employed on those parts of the line where no nuisance would be caused thereby.
(5) Showing fire from the engines – This should never be necessary, and must arise from negligence on the part of drivers.
(6) Vibration from passage of engines – This was complained of principally by residents along the Seven Sisters Road, where the tramways are of comparatively recent construction, the rails being of the girder form and the road paved throughout. Short of reconstruction on a different system, I do not see how a remedy for this complaint can be obtained.
(7) Occasional inattention of drivers in not stopping when passing frightened horses – This complaint can only be met by a strict enforcement of the byelaw dealing with the subject.
(8) Somewhat frequent accidents.- The number of these which were brought under notice at the enquiry did not appear to be large considering the length of the tramways. The numbers might, no doubt, be reduced by a strict enforcement of the byelaws and regulations.
(9) The bad state of repair of the tramway portion of the roads – This complaint applies particularly to the condition of the road in the jurisdiction of the Tottenham Local Board, from Stamford Hill along the High Road and High Street to the boundary between Tottenham and Edmonton, and in a less degree to other portions of the roads traversed by the tramways, particularly to a short length in the Seven Sisters Road near Manor House Tavern. The Tramway Company allege that in parts of the High Road in Tottenham and Edmonton one main reason for the state of disrepair complained of arises from the sides of the road having been from time to time been raised, thereby placing the tramway in a kind of hollow between them, the surveyors on the contrary maintaining that the tramway portion of the road has sunk in many places. So far as I could judge, both statements are to a certain extent correct; but whatever may be the

exact cause of the current condition of parts of the tramway portion of the road, it is such to require immediate attention. To place in what the Tramway Company's Engineer calls a state of statutory repair, i.e to make the paving level with the upper surface of the rails, the Engineer thinks an immediate expenditure of about £700, and an expenditure of £1,100 to £1,200 per annum in maintaining such a state of repair will be sufficient. This estimate includes no renewal of rails, or raising the level of any portion of the tramways, it being intended to commence these more extensive works in the Tottenham and Edmonton High Roads in some two or three year's time."

He concluded:

"As a result of this enquiry and from a personal examination of the tramways and rolling stock I have no hesitation in saying that the opposition to the renewal of the power to use steam on the North London Tramways is, in my opinion, based upon substantial grounds and that unless the causes of complaint are at once to a great extent removed, the renewal of these powers should not be granted."

"As it is no doubt impossible for the Tramway Company to find money for the conversion of their mode of haulage from traction by steam to traction by horses, a refusal to renew their power to use steam would practically lead to the closure of the tramway so far as the present Company is concerned, causing for the time a great public inconvenience, 2,000,000 passengers having been carried in 1889, and I would therefore suggest for the consideration of the Board of Trade the adoption of the following recommendations:-

1. That permission to use steam haulage be extended up to 31st October 1890, at the expiration of which period the tramways should again be inspected with regard to the execution of the necessary repairs to the rail joints (most needing it) and to the level of the paving sets, any requisite provision for drainage being effected (for the time being) by means of gully holes and cross drains.

2. That should these repairs have been found on inspection to have been satisfactorily carried out, permission to use steam haulage should then be further extended for a period of two years from 31st October 1890; provided the Tramway Company can give a substantial guarantee of their ability to provide £1,200 a year for maintaining the tramways in a satisfactory state of repair, and that they do so maintain them.

3. That at the expiration of this further period of two years, the Tramway Company should be prepared to commence the relaying of the older portion of the line (viz., that between Stamford Hill and Ponders End), raising the levels of such parts of the tramways as clearly falls within their statutory liabilities, and giving a substantial guarantee that the work of relaying shall be carried on, with all reasonable despatch (say), at the rate of a mile each half year.

4. That at the expiration of the further period of two years, the Tramway Company should be prepared to abandon the use of the 15 engines constructed by Messrs. Merryweather, and replace them by an improved description of engine, or by cars moved electrically, or otherwise.

5. That the Company should at once use every means in their power to diminish as far as possible the causes for complaint in the use of steam haulage as brought forward at the enquiry. As regards complaints Nos. 1, 2, 4, 5 and 7, the remedy is quite within their own competency, and as regards No.3 (the emission of noxious vapours) it can be minimised by the use of the best procurable coke."

"With a view to the due observance of the bye laws and regulations, I would urge upon the *various local authorities the appointment of a joint inspector, whose duty it should be to note and report any breach of them, such legal proceedings being then instituted as may appear desirable."*

Board of Trade Re-inspection

The Board of Trade wrote to all steam tramway operators in the United Kingdom on 7 August 1890 requiring them to provide additional safety appliances on their engines and cars.

"The time has, in my opinion, now arrived when tramway companies using steam power, should, with the object of (if possible) preventing accidents similar in character to some which have recently occurred, be required to provide the following appliances in addition to, or in substitution of, those which already exist."

1. A car brake for every passenger car to be actuated from either platform of the car and to be perfectly distinct in its gearing and means of application from the existing brake. The new brake to be so arranged that it shall be brought into action and shall remain in action upon any accidental severance taking place between the engine and the car.
2. A child or Life Protector - one of these to be fixed in front of every engine.
3. A screw coupling between every engine and car. This may be substituted for the safety chain or chains now in use.

"A period of six months might be allowed for the introduction of these appliances."

The receiver of the Company replied that he had instructed the Company's solicitors to apply to the Court of Chancery for authorisation to incur the necessary expenditure.

In September the local boards of Tottenham, Edmonton and Hornsey jointly appointed an inspector of the tramway for the period until 31 October. He was to note and report breaches of regulations and bylaws of the Board of Trade at a salary of £7 7s 0d a week, including all expenses.

The Board of Trade wrote to the local boards on the 23 October 1890 enclosing a copy of a letter received from the Company solicitors. It stated that Major General Hutchinson had been appointed to make a re-inspection of the tramway but, as the receiver and Manager of the Company would not be in England until 1 November, the Board of Trade had acceded to an application to extend the period for using steam power until 14 November.

Despite the Company claiming a reference for this action under powers in their Act of 1883, the local boards of Enfield, South Hornsey and Wood Green declined to renew their agreement with the Company for the use of steam traction. The Board of Trade had no choice but to appoint another Referee. The reference took place on 27 October at the High Court and an award was made, by consent, extending, so far as it related to Enfield, South Hornsey and Wood Green, the operation of steam traction to fourteen days after the final decision of the Board of Trade was be made. Edmonton Local Board then endorsed its own agreement with the Company to the same effect.

Major General Hutchinson re-inspected the tramway on 10 November, but before his report was made, a deputation representing Middlesex County Council and the local boards of Edmonton, Enfield, Hackney, Hornsey, South Hornsey, Tottenham and Wood Green attended the Board of Trade on 24 November to discuss the subject of steam tramways in their district. A separate deputation of ratepayers also attended and the Company was represented.

The report was issued on 5 December; in a letter from the Board of Trade to the Company it was stated:

"As regards the roadway, the Company would seem to have made some progress in remedying the defects pointed out in Major General Hutchinson's reports but as regards the engines, although the Company allege that they have expended on repairs a sum equivalent to £50 per engine, there can be no doubt that they fail in many respects to comply with the Board of Trade Regulations and are generally in a faulty condition".

"The representatives of the Company expressed their desire to meet the requirements of the Board of Trade but are hampered by their financial position, which will, apparently, only admit of the necessary expenditure if a considerable period of time is allowed for the purpose. The Board of Trade are unwilling, by the immediate withdrawal of the authority to use steam power, to adopt a course which might render it impossible to arrange for a reconstruction of the Company, or the sale of the tramway at a reasonable price. However the annoyance and even danger to the public from the existing condition of affairs were so strongly urged by the local authorities that the Board of Trade feel that, in the interest of the public, no long extension of time ought to be granted. They have therefore decided to grant an extension of the authority to use steam power upon the Tramways for a period of six months from 14th December, provided that the Company deposit with this department a sum of £600, as a guarantee that proper care will be taken to maintain the roadways and the engines in such a state of repair as may be necessary for safety during the period named, which will in no case be further extended to the existing Company".

"I am to add, that the extension of time is granted in the anticipation that, before it expires, the tramway will, either by the reconstruction of the Company, or by some other means, become the property of owners whose financial position will admit of the statutory obligations connected with the tramways being properly and efficiently discharged".

The Company was, however, unable to afford the £600 deposit stipulated and it was agreed that the license to operate be extended from month to month for the six month period upon payment of £100 per month.

Bad Press

Despite another adjudication in its favour, the vitriolic attacks on the Company from some of the local boards, Wood Green in particular, continued in the local press. In the 13 February 1891 edition of 'The Weekly Herald', it was reported from a Wood Green Local Board meeting:

"On some correspondence being read with reference to the agreement with the Company for running the powers within the Board's district, the Chairman said he was bound to repeat what had been said before ... and wished further to say that not a twentieth of what was stated in the letter of the manager was true ...".

The receiver of the Company felt compelled to reply in the 27 February edition of the newspaper:

"Sir, –

I observe, not with surprise, but at least with regret, that the Chairman of the Wood Green Local Board, not content with the efforts of some of the smaller local authorities to damage the Tramway Company, has taken occasion at the recent meeting of his Local Board to make statements which, if they are accurately reported, are incorrect.

1. *The North London Tramway Company does not exist, unfortunately, for the benefit of anybody, except the public and the local authorities. So far as the receiver and manager is concerned he has not received either remuneration or expenses during the time he has occupied that post. I will not further comment on such an observation.*

2. *It is not true that the Company wasted an enormous amount of money before the enquiry by the Board of Trade. That enquiry was held by order of the Board of Trade, and it was the so-called evidence produced by the local authorities that prolonged that enquiry and made it so expensive.*

3. *It is not true the Company spend everywhere except on the roads. The figures produced before the Board of Trade Inspector, and figures that can be produced when necessary to show what has been spent since, prove the exact contrary; and since work was possible on the roads after the frost, from about £30 to £40 a week has been spent upon the roads.*

4. *It is not true that the working expenses include the legal costs, necessitated by the action of the local authorities; and consequently the inference that it is these costs that prevent the Company showing a profit on its working is incorrect.*

5. *It is not true that the public authorities have been vilified, unless stating the truth be considered vilification.*

6. *It is not true that the expense of the men's supper, by which I presume is referred to, is defrayed by the Company. If Mr. Littler had read the local newspaper he would have seen in them the acknowledgement of the subscriptions of a kindly-disposed public towards this entertainment, and I regret to observe that Mr. Litter's name is not among the list of subscribers to the men's enjoyment.*

7. *It is not true that the power of the engines is such that if one stopped they cannot go on to Jolly Butchers Hill.*

May I ask you to give as much publicity to this letter as you have done to Mr. Littler's errors. Possibly your readers in reading his remarks and this dispassionate statement of facts may be able to form an opinion as to the hostility manifested to this unfortunate Company during the past two years.

Yours faithfully,
W. CARRUTHERS WAIN (Receiver)

P.S. Our apparently unpardonable offence has been defending our rights".

An experimental engine

Another barbed report about the Company appeared in the 3 April 1891 edition of 'The Weekly Herald':

"Another bad beginning : Amongst the many misfortunes that in one way and another have befallen the North London Tramway Company there is to be added yet another. To meet the requirements of the Board of Trade the Company have been making arrangements to try a new form of traction and with this view had received on trial a neatly constructed engine, which was covered in with glass and has all the appearance of a car itself. Its fuel is waste petroleum, which is gradually coming into use for driving machinery, not only in small engines but in such as are used on railways and on board some of the warships of the Italian government with great satisfaction.

The engine in question had been brought over from America and a man had been deputed from the makers to attend to its trial working a few days ago. Everything was got in readiness and the machinery was working in the shed preparatory to a start being made when one of the reservoirs containing the oil burst or over-flowed in some way with the result that the flame spread and quickly enveloped the engine, which was pulled away by means of chains from the shed, where it was in dangerous proximity to other cars. The effect of cold water was tried but of course this only increased the flow of oil. Then sand was tried and with better results. The woodwork of the engine, however, was considerably damaged and has necessitated its thorough overhauling and repairing".

The General Manager, E. R. Polden, corrected the factual errors by way of a letter to the editor the following week:

"Sir, –

In your issue dated 3rd inst., there is a report respecting a misfortune which befell an engine in our yard and by which it appears that the engine belongs to this Company. I should like you to correct this error as the engine in question belongs to some gentlemen who received permission to use our line solely for the purpose of trying experiments with the engine on our heavy gradients".

Seeking financial stability: the London Electrical Tramways Company

The Board of Trade had made it clear that, aside from the motive power and infrastructure issues, their greatest concern about the Company was its financial health. Already in receivership, the debenture holders were actively seeking another tramway operator to take over the Company. Their preference was for it to be sold as a going concern to the neighbouring North Metropolitan Tramways Company, but that company had significant reservations about the potential liabilities of doing so.

In April 1891 Middlesex County Council and the local boards received notice of an intended application to be made to the Board of Trade for their approval, under the provisions of the Tramways Act 1870, for the transfer of the undertaking to a new Company to be called The London Electrical Tramways Company Limited. The objectives of the new company were stated as:
i. To acquire the tramway system, equipment and undertaking of the North London Tramway Company as a going concern, together with certain extensions thereof and reparation thereto.
ii. To construct, purchase, lease, lay down or otherwise acquire any tramway or tramways in the United Kingdom and elsewhere, or any running power, rights or easements over same etc.

Behind the new company and the application were two partners, Messrs Charles John Westwood, a civil engineering contractor, and Frederick Charles Winby, a mechanical engineer, with some experience in the construction of tramways. The details behind the application, particularly the financial standing of the new company and the operating experience of the partners, concerned both Middlesex County Council and the local boards through whose areas the North London Tramway operated. The local boards sent representatives to the Guildhall at Westminster to discuss the situation with Middlesex County Council and, in turn, representations were made to the Board of Trade.

Consequently, the Board of Trade notified the interested parties that Major General Hutchinson had been appointed to hold a local inquiry and to report back on his findings. His terms of reference were limited to the question of the financial competency of the company proposing to accept the transfer and their ability to discharge the statutory obligations imposed by the North London Tramway Acts upon the owners of the tramway.

The inquiry took place on 15 May 1891 with the debenture holders of the North London Tramways Company, Middlesex County Council, the local boards, the London Electrical Tramways Company and Messrs Westwood and Winby being represented. A full report of the inquiry appeared in the 'Tottenham Weekly Herald' for Friday 22 May, excerpts of which are given below:

"On Friday morning last, at the Railway Dept of the Board of Trade Whitehall, Mjr. Gen. Hutchinson presided over an inquiry relating to the financial competency of the new company, to be formed for the purpose of taking over the North London Tramway Company. Mr. Burr appeared on behalf of the debenture holders of the N.L.T.Coy., Mr. Page appeared on behalf of the M.C.C., the Hornsey, South Hornsey, Tottenham, Wood Green, Edmonton and Enfield Local Boards and Mr. Hyde was counsel for the London Electrical Tramways Company and Messrs. Westward and Winby".

"Letters were read showing the extension of time granted by the Board of Trade for the use of steam power until the 14th June 1891 and also other correspondence which had come before the various Boards represented".

"Mr. Burr, after making some remarks in reference to the liquidation of the Company, said that on the 20th February the debenture holders entered into a contract with Westward and Winby with reference to the further working of the tramways. He then dealt with the objections to the tramways of the various local authorities through whose districts the tramways ran, and mentioned that the L.C.C. and the Hackney Board of Works had lodged no complaint against the North London Tramway Company. A letter from the M.C.C. suggested that under section 42 of the Tramways Act, the local authority should purchase the tramway and work it. The contract entered into by Messers. Westward and Winby, the contractors, was to the effect that in reconstructing the line they should satisfy the

receivers that the new company was satisfied with a working capital of at least £20,000, or that they were in such a financial position to conform to the statutory obligations incidental to the undertaking, if, with the consent of the defendant, it be transposed".

"Mr. Hyde said The London Electrical Tramways Company was incorporated on the 22nd April 1891 with a share capital of £150,000 in £1 shares and with all the necessary borrowing powers. (A copy of articles of the company and a certificate of incorporation was handed in by the Counsel). As regarded the Company nothing had been done regarding raising the capital, the promoters having waited to see the result of that application. By the 26th February last, Messrs Westwood and Winby rendered themselves personally responsible for all the payments made under the contract and also to satisfy the Receiver as to the existence of the £20,000 working capital. He was prepared to satisfy the Board of Trade also that the money was forthcoming".

Questioning by Major General Hutchinson revealed that the £20,000, which could be deposited with the Board of Trade as surety, was only for the reconstruction of the line and rolling stock *"in accordance with the recommendation of the Board of Trade on 19th July 1890"* but did not make provision for *"altering the mode of motive power"* as Mr Hyde contended *"the mode of working is outside the province of this enquiry"*. Mr Winby stated *"In future the motive power will have to be provided from another fund. It is proposed to adopt an electrical system when the thing is in repair"*.

When asked if it would be necessary to renew the rails, Mr Winby replied *"Well, it would make a better job to put new rails, but it is not absolutely necessary. Some of the rails could be strengthened. The present form of construction is very bad. The original design was bad"*. A lengthy cross examination then ensued about the amount of the line to be relaid, the most appropriate type of new rail and the cost per mile to be allowed .

Mr Winby estimated it would cost about £100 per engine to put them in good order. When questioned by Major General Hutchinson whether this was worthwhile *"considering the short time that they may be allowed to run"* he replied *"Our intention is that the line should be worked on the best principles of electricity. Until we have that power we are unable to say much about it"*.

Mr Winby said that it was intended to float the new company to raise capital of £150,000 if they received the consent of the Board of Trade and the debenture holders of the North London Tramways Company to the takeover. He had already received some guarantees that shares would be taken up but he was not prepared to reveal the extent this was so. Messrs Westwood and Winby were prepared to underwrite the £20,000 (or a larger sum) required to reconstruct the line and was expecting that a profit of about 10 per cent could be made on the undertaking.

"Mr. Page then made submissions on behalf of his clients [the local boards] to General Hutchinson that there was no proof of the financial competency of the new company, and he asked the Board of Trade not give their consent to the sale to a company, which was in the air and which hardly existed at all".

"Mr. E. Eachus, Engineer to the Edmonton Local Board, examined by Mr. Page said his estimate of the cost of relaying the five miles of rails from Stamford Hill to Ponders End was £4,200 per mile. He thought the engines would require £200 spent on each of them".

"Mr. John Edward Worth, Surveyor to the Tottenham Local Board, said his estimate for putting into good repair the line through his district was £4,000".

"Mr. A.B. Greeg, Engineer, said he was appointed by the united Boards to examine the engines of the North London Tramway Company last year. Generally the engines were in bad repair, fifteen manufactured by Merryweather being the worst. The condensers leaked, the side plates were bent and broken, there were no speed indicators on some of them and those existing on the engines were not at work. The coupling rods were in a bad state of repair, the boilers were defective, the governors were not working and in some cases not on the engines at all and the cocks generally were leaking ... To put the engines in repair from £100 to £150 an engine".

"Mr. A. W. Jameson, Surveyor to the South Hornsey Local Board, was then examined. The estimate for relaying the permanent way in his district ... Yes, £2,800. It is a double line and the estimate does not include new rails".

"Mr. Page said ... the question for General Hutchinson was, 'Is the new Company financially competent? Is there satisfactory evidence to that effect?' He submitted that it was not ... It would then, he contended, be as weak as the other company, and would be an equal nuisance to the neighbourhood, and as unsatisfactory to the public, and in the end, would probably come before General Hutchinson again, or some other officer of the Board of Trade, and ask for power – because it could not get on – to transfer itself and undertaking to someone else".

The enquiry then terminated.

In announcing its decision, the Board of Trade refused to sanction the transfer of the line to the London Electrical Tramways Company because it was not satisfied that it was in a financial position to carry out the statutory obligations of the North London Tramways Company. It considered it would not be justified in approving an arrangement which would only have the effect of prolonging the current perilous financial state of the Company and which was seriously and reasonably objected to by the local authorities of the district. Moreover, it declined to renew the authority to run steam trams, which expired on 14 June.

The debenture holders of the Company sent a deputation to the Board of Trade on 2 June to appeal against the decision. However, Sir Michael Hicks Beach, President of the Board of Trade, responded by pointing out that the existing Company had failed to carry out the required works in the stipulated timescale. Six months had elapsed since he gave his original decision, and yet no new company with good financial resources had been formed to buy them out. While the Board of Trade would be willing to grant powers to operate the tramway to any company properly able to fulfil the statutory conditions it was not satisfied that the London Electrical Tramways Company could be floated with any probable prospects of success. Sir Michael gave the debenture holders a fortnight to formulate any new proposals.

To conclude the role of the London Electrical Tramways Company in this history, the Companies Registration Office wrote to it on 21 November 1892 asking why it had failed to file a return. In their reply, Messrs Westwood and Winby stated that the Company had done no work whatsoever and it had been registered purely for the purpose of protecting the name. Subsequently the Company was dissolved and a notice to this effect appeared in the 'London Gazette' dated 11 June 1895.

Seeking financial stability: the North Metropolitan Tramways Company

The clerk to the Enfield Local Board reported he had received a letter from the Board of Trade stating that it had refused to sanction the transfer of this line to the London Electrical Tramways Company or to extend the time for the use of steam traction. If the tramways were to cease operation, the Board might be called upon in future to make up that portion of the tramway setts in its parish, the expense of which was estimated at "about £100". Tottenham Local Board estimated that the cost to it would be £784 12s 0d. Their clerk said the stoppage of the trams would be a great pity, so far as the public was concerned, for over two million people had used them the previous year.

The Board of Trade wrote to the local authorities again on 3 June 1891: *"With reference to the letter from this Department of 28th ult., I am directed by the Board of Trade to inform you that representatives of the debenture holders of the North London Tramway Company have had an interview with Sir Michael Hicks Beach and that the debenture holders are to be called together to consider further their position in the matter. In order to afford time for such further consideration, the Board of Trade have extended till the 28th inst. the authority to use steam power on the tramways".*

Middlesex County Council called a meeting of representatives of the local boards affected by the North London Tramways Company. They agreed:

1. That the authorities will only purchase [the tramway], if at all, in order to secure an efficient service

2. That the authorities will only do so, if at all, on ascertaining first the price, including a sum to be paid to the local authorities to cover the cost of putting the roads in thorough repair, and second that they can secure a responsible tenant who will take a lease to cover the whole outlay with a margin for contingencies such as will absolutely secure the ratepayers

3. That the Board of Trade shall insist on the owners at once making arrangements, temporarily or otherwise, for working by traction, other than steam, from the 28th June

4. That the Board of Trade shall also require the answers in regard to the new proposals to keep the County Council, as representing the local authorities, duly informed so as to avoid loss of time on useless schemes

5. That if the owners bring a scheme, a part of it shall be a deposit with the Board of Trade, of at least £20,000, to be reduced only as and when the Surveyors to the local authorities certify the respective lengths of road in their district as being in proper order

Middlesex County Council then formally wrote to the North Metropolitan Tramways Company (North Met) asking if it would consider operating the lines of the North London Tramways Company. On 24 June 1891 a deputation of the debenture holders of the North London Tramways Company, met with officials of the North Met and put forward proposals for the working of their tramway by the North Met using horse power instead of steam traction. It was considered that there were many common features of the two adjoining systems, which met at three locations: Finsbury Park, Manor House and Stamford Hill. Even though the details of the proposals were not acceptable to the North Met, the prospect of an agreement was enough for the authority of the North London Tramways Company to continue operating steam trams to be extended until 1 August.

Middlesex County Council convened another meeting between the affected local authorities and the North Met on 6 July. Representatives of the North Met outlined their terms for purchasing the North London Tramways Company, explaining that unless all the local authorities were prepared to guarantee them a lease of not less than 21 years or more than 28 years (the period varying in accordance with the amount which it would cost to acquire the undertaking), the purchase was not viable. Considerable expenditure was also required to put the tracks and roads in proper order, to purchase horses and cars to work the line and to acquire additional stabling. The North Met agreed to undertake all necessary repairs within two months and, within 12 months, any reconstruction works the various local boards and Middlesex County Council, as the road authority, considered necessary. It was also agreed that if, at any time in the future, any alternative forms of motive power seemed likely to be successful, the consent of the local authorities would have to be obtained. A resolution to such lease terms was passed by the delegates of the local authorities in Middlesex, guaranteed by deed, to take effect from 25 September 1891. The London County Council also agreed to safeguard the investment by not invoking their option to purchase the North Met. lines in the LCC area until 10 August 1910. These guarantees were subsequently included in the North Metropolitan Tramways Act, 1892.

Until the North Met was able to negotiate a purchase price with the receiver of the North London Tramways Company and complete the legal purchase formalities, it agreed with the local authorities and gave an undertaking to the Board of Trade that it would operate a service of horse cars on the North London Tramways Company routes from 1 August, on behalf of the North London Tramways Company. Initially, a full service could not be operated as there was not sufficient time to obtain the additional stock of horses and cars required. A preliminary agreement between the North Metropolitan Tramways Company and the receiver of North London Tramways Company was made on 29 July to this effect.

Immediately, the notice opposite was printed. It will be noted that no service was to be provided between Stamford Hill and Seven Sisters Corner or between Tramway Avenue, Edmonton, and Ponders End or in Wood Green between the bottom of Jolly Butcher's Hill and the Town Hall.

North London Tramways

**NOTICE IS HEREBY GIVEN, that on
and after SATURDAY next, the 1st of
AUGUST, the above lines will be worked by
HORSE CARS**

**A REGULAR SERVICE WILL BE RUN
between Finsbury Park and Edmonton
and Finsbury Park and Wood Green,
With extra cars on Sundays and Holidays.**

**By Order
Offices of the Company,
Ponders End
29th July 1891**

Winding up

The last North London steam tram journeys operated on the evening of Friday 31 July 1891 with the North Met taking over at midnight.

On Saturday 1 August a farewell 'smoking concert' was held for the employees of the North London Tramways Company at the Golden Lion Hotel in Lower Edmonton. Most of those present were engine drivers and workshop staff, as many of the conductors had been re-employed by the North Met and were on duty. Of the 100 employees of the North London Tramways only twenty-four were taken over.

A call for contributions towards a subscription to support those tramway employees made redundant appeared in the local newspapers the following week:

*"Sir, -
As a result of the long continued and bitter hostility evinced against this Company, its lines were closed for steam traction on the 31st ulto., and I ask your indulgence to permit of the opening in your columns of a subscription on behalf of the unfortunate men who will be thrown out of employment (and whose wives and families will, I am afraid, suffer severely), although they have had to conduct the affairs of the Company under the most harassing circumstances. I shall be pleased to head the list with a subscription of five guineas.*

I trust to the generosity of your readers to assist me in my endeavour to prevent the men and their families suffering, owing to the cruel injustice of the proceedings of the Local Authorities.

*Yours faithfully
W. J. CARRUTHERS WAIN"*

At the beginning of October 1891 the whole of the rolling stock, plant etc. of the North London Tramways Company was offered for sale by private treaty, in lots to suit the purchasers.

This included:

*"15 tramway engines constructed by
Messrs. Merryweather & Sons*

*10 tramway engines constructed by
Messrs. Dick, Kerr & Co.*

*10 bogie cars built by the Metropolitan
Carriage Co., Birmingham*

*17 bogie cars built by the Falcon Engine
& Car Works Co., Loughborough*

*Machinery, sundry stores, including straight
and crank engine axles, rail cleaners, wheel
tyres, gauge lamps, axle boxes, fire bars,
valve castings etc."*

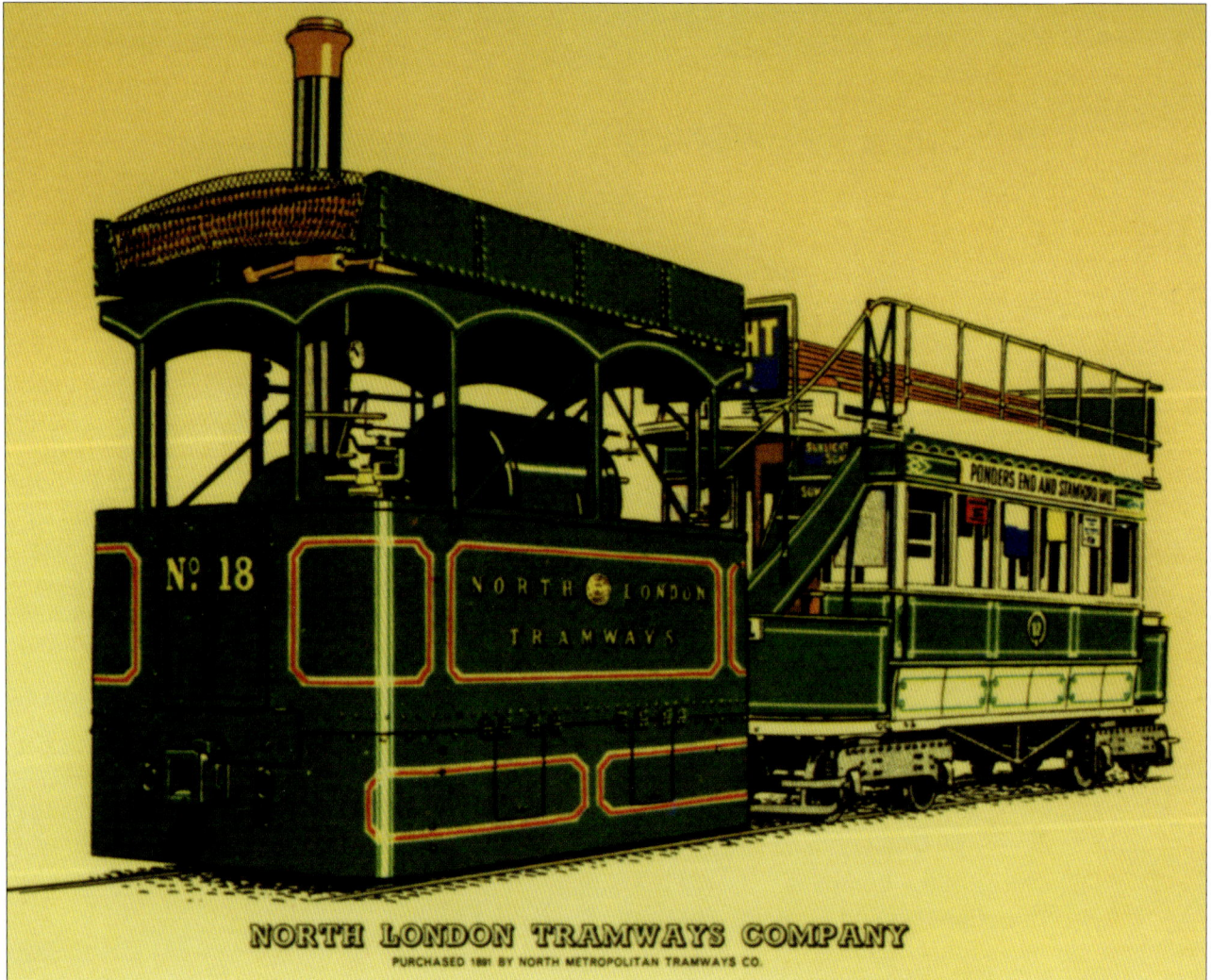

3. Drawing of engine No. 18 in original green livery (it was later painted brown) and trailer No. 17.

"Order to view and full particulars can be obtained from the offices of the North Metropolitan Tramways Company in (the City of) London."

On 18 November Messrs Fuller, Horsey and Cassell, industrial surveyors, valuers, auctioneers and estate agents, of 10 Lloyd Avenue, London E.C.3 were instructed to sell the plant and machinery by auction. The secretary of the North London Tramways Company reported on 23 March 1892 that £1,500 had been received from the auctioneers on account of the sale of plant.

Finally, an indenture dated 12 April 1892 was made between The North London Tramways Company, Arthur Edwin Preston, chartered accountant and Liquidator of the Company, William James Carruthers Wain, civil engineer, receiver and former Chairman of the Company (of the first part), John Shaw Lowe, the plaintiff in the High Court action (of the second part) and The North Metropolitan Tramways Company (of the

third part). The Deed of Assignment, of the same date, sold the North London Tramways Company undertaking, together with its freehold and leasehold properties, as a going concern to the North Metropolitan Tramways Company – for which the latter had to pay into the Court £20,600. This was sufficient to pay off the preference creditors and the first debenture holders.

4. Two steam engines and trailers.

5. A steam tram travelling towards Stamford Hill at the corner of Ravensdale Road.

6. Engine No. 5 and trailer No. 2 outside the Wagon and Horses in High Road Tottenham.

7. Engine No. 11 and trailer 18 in High Road Tottenham.

8. Steam tram outside the premises of W. Hadlow, Auctioneer, Estate Agent and Valuer, Tottenham.

9. Steam tram with trailer No.24 in Tottenham High Road facing the Friends Meeting House.

10. Edmonton New Road.

11. Engine No. 3 and two trailers at Tramway Avenue Edmonton with the Company office in the background. By the 1930s, the ground floor of this building was used as a cafe.

12. Engine No. 2 and trailer No. 6 at Hertford Road, Ponders End.

13. Seven Sisters Corner, Tottenham.

14.   Seven Sisters Road, Tottenham.

15. Engine No.18 and trailer No.17 at the Wood Green terminus near Truro Road and the Nightingale Tavern.

16. Engine No.10 and trailer No.17. There is a board in the centre of the lower deck window stating "To Tramway Avenue only".

Chapter

Three

The North Metropolitan Tramways Company in Middlesex (1891 – 1902)

Background

To understand the history of the tramways originally developed by the North London Suburban Tramway Company and then the North London Tramways Company after 1891, it is necessary to look briefly through the history of the North Metropolitan Tramways Company in the surrounding area before that time.

Finsbury Park

The creation of Finsbury Park as an open space for the residents of North London was the result of agitation by the Member of Parliament for Finsbury (the constituency then including the area immediately north of Seven Sisters Road) and his electorate, who were concerned at the rapidly encroaching urbanisation of the area. The Metropolitan Board of Works Act of 1857 permitted that Board to acquire the land forming part of Hornsey Wood, even though it was mainly in the parish of Hornsey and the County of Middlesex, and it opened this to the public on 7 August 1869. The Great Northern Railway had already opened a station at Seven Sisters Road on its line from Kings Cross in 1861 but it renamed it Finsbury Park following the opening of the park and the area surrounding the station then assumed the same name.

From the City to Islington, Holloway, Highgate and Finsbury Park

The North Metropolitan Tramways Act received Royal Assent on 12 July 1869, prior to the regulations contained in the Tramways Act of 1870. For the north London area, powers were sought and granted to construct and operate double track tramways, by horse power, from Moorgate to the Archway Tavern in Highgate via City Road, Islington, Upper Street, Highbury and Holloway Road and also a branch from The Nag's Head Holloway to Finsbury Park Station via Seven Sisters Road.

As a result of the changes to the regulation of tramways contained in the Tramways Act 1870, the Company applied to the 1870 sessions of both the Metropolitan Board of Works and Parliament to revise various sections of its 1869 Act, to extend the line at the City end from Moorgate to the Bank of England and to include an additional line from The Angel, Islington via Liverpool Road to Holloway Road which passed the well known Chapel Street Market.

However, the Corporation of the City of London refused to allow any tramway to be laid down within the City so the Company had to promote a further bill in 1871 to obtain permission not to construct the section of line between the Bank of England and the City boundary at the junction of Moorgate Street, Finsbury Pavement and Ropemaker Street.

The Board of Trade inspected the section of tramway from Ropemaker Street to Islington Green on 19 July 1871 and passed it fit for operation. The next section, from Islington Green via Upper Street and Holloway Road and connecting with the line in Liverpool Road, opened on 9 December 1871 permitting a service of trams from Moorgate to the Nag's Head Holloway. Soon afterwards, on 18 December, the service was extended along Seven Sisters Road as far as Hornsey Road followed by completion of the route through to Finsbury Park Station (Stroud Green Road) on 21 January 1872. Meanwhile the section from the Nag's Head, Holloway to the Archway Tavern, Highgate had been opened on 1 January 1872, a through service of trams being operated from Moorgate. These routes are illustrated in Figure 4 on page 59.

Horses and stables

Sites for depots and stables were acquired at three different places along these routes: Canonbury (in St Paul's Road between Upper Street and Highbury Grove backing onto the railway), Highgate (on the right hand side of Holloway Road just before Junction Road) and Finsbury Park (at the junction of Seven Sisters Road and Stroud Green Road (see Chapter 6). However, the difficulties in finding sufficient, suitable accommodation for the horses and cars close to the routes in densely populated areas led to the Company exploring a contract arrangement with the London General Omnibus Company (LGOC) for the supply of horses and stabling. On 18 May 1871 the North Met notified the LGOC it was *"willing to give 6½d per mile for horsing the cars on the City Road and Holloway tramways in consideration of the heavy gradient, the price of provender, and difficulties in finding stables, and to let a contract for two years, subject to the right of either party to determine it by three months notice at the end of the first year on payment of £250"*. The LGOC authorised its General Manager to *"to arrange for tenancy of such stables in the Company's old yard at Highbury, on the best terms he can make"*. Arrangements were also made *"for the supply of harnesses and stable utensils at 4s 9d per stud of ten horses"*. This contract was terminated in 1878; on 9 May that year the General Manager of the LGOC recommended to his board of directors that on or before 7 July forty-six additional buses should be put to work with the horses released from the contract (it was reckoned that each horse bus required a team of 10 horses (five pairs) to keep it on the road each day).

From the City to Shoreditch, Stamford Hill, Clapton and Manor House

Construction of the other authorised tram lines then continued. The line from Moorgate to Stamford Hill via Old Street, Shoreditch, Kingsland Road, Stoke Newington Road and Stoke Newington High Street opened on 9 May 1873. Concurrently, a large depot and stables were built at Portland Avenue in Stamford Hill, a through road with access from both Stamford Hill and Clapton Common.

Services along the route from Moorgate to Clapton Pond via Shoreditch, Kingsland Road, Graham Road and Hackney Mare Street commenced on 12 July 1873. Although an extension of this line was constructed from Clapton Pond to Upper Clapton, and authorised for use by the Board of Trade on 14 April 1875, the Company only intended that it should be a link between the route and the Stamford Hill depot and thus allow the unsatisfactory, temporary depot facilities at Hackney to be closed. From 1 July 1875 the only service provided to the public between Clapton Pond and Upper Clapton was that given by cars proceeding from and to Stamford Hill depot. By 1885 it was apparent that a regular service was required so on 20 October the Moorgate to Clapton Pond service was extended to The Swan at Clapton Common.

The Moorgate to Highbury Park line via East Road, North Road, Southgate Road, Stoke Newington Green and Green Lanes opened on 9 May 1874. It was finally extended along Green Lanes to the Manor House Tavern, following a successful inspection by Major Marindin, on 4 September 1883. The depot for this line adjoined The Highbury Park Tavern in Green Lanes at the junction with Riversdale Road and Highbury Quadrant. Highbury New Park is now known as Clissold Park.

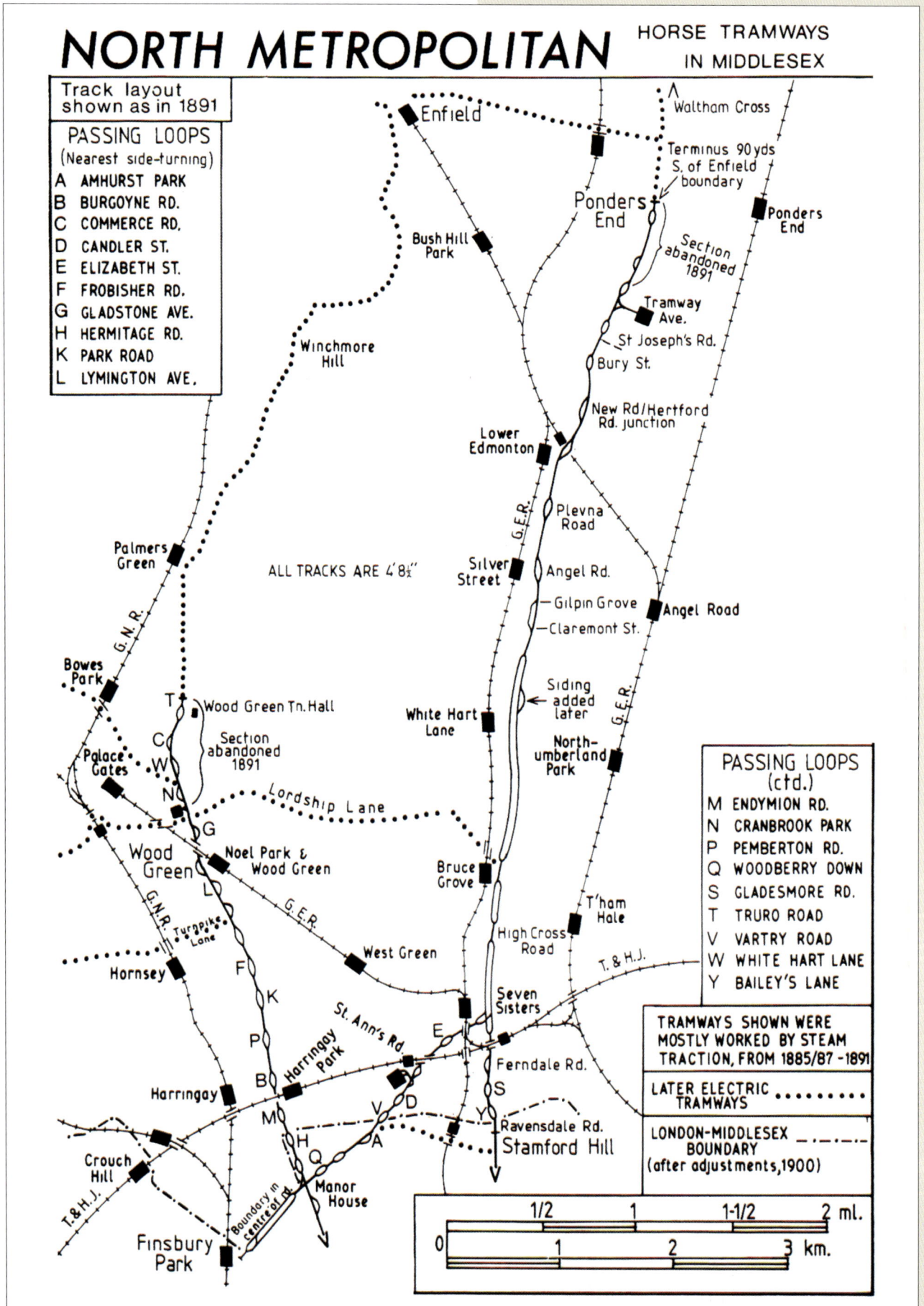

NORTH METROPOLITAN HORSE TRAMWAYS IN MIDDLESEX

Track layout shown as in 1891

PASSING LOOPS
(Nearest side-turning)
A AMHURST PARK
B BURGOYNE RD.
C COMMERCE RD.
D CANDLER ST.
E ELIZABETH ST.
F FROBISHER RD.
G GLADSTONE AVE.
H HERMITAGE RD.
K PARK ROAD
L LYMINGTON AVE.

PASSING LOOPS (ctd.)
M ENDYMION RD.
N CRANBROOK PARK
P PEMBERTON RD.
Q WOODBERRY DOWN
S GLADESMORE RD.
T TRURO ROAD
V VARTRY ROAD
W WHITE HART LANE
Y BAILEY'S LANE

TRAMWAYS SHOWN WERE MOSTLY WORKED BY STEAM TRACTION, FROM 1885/87 - 1891

LATER ELECTRIC TRAMWAYS . . . .

LONDON-MIDDLESEX BOUNDARY (after adjustments, 1900)

ALL TRACKS ARE 4'8½"

Figure 3. North Met horse tramways in Middlesex (1891).

With thanks to Edward Oakley

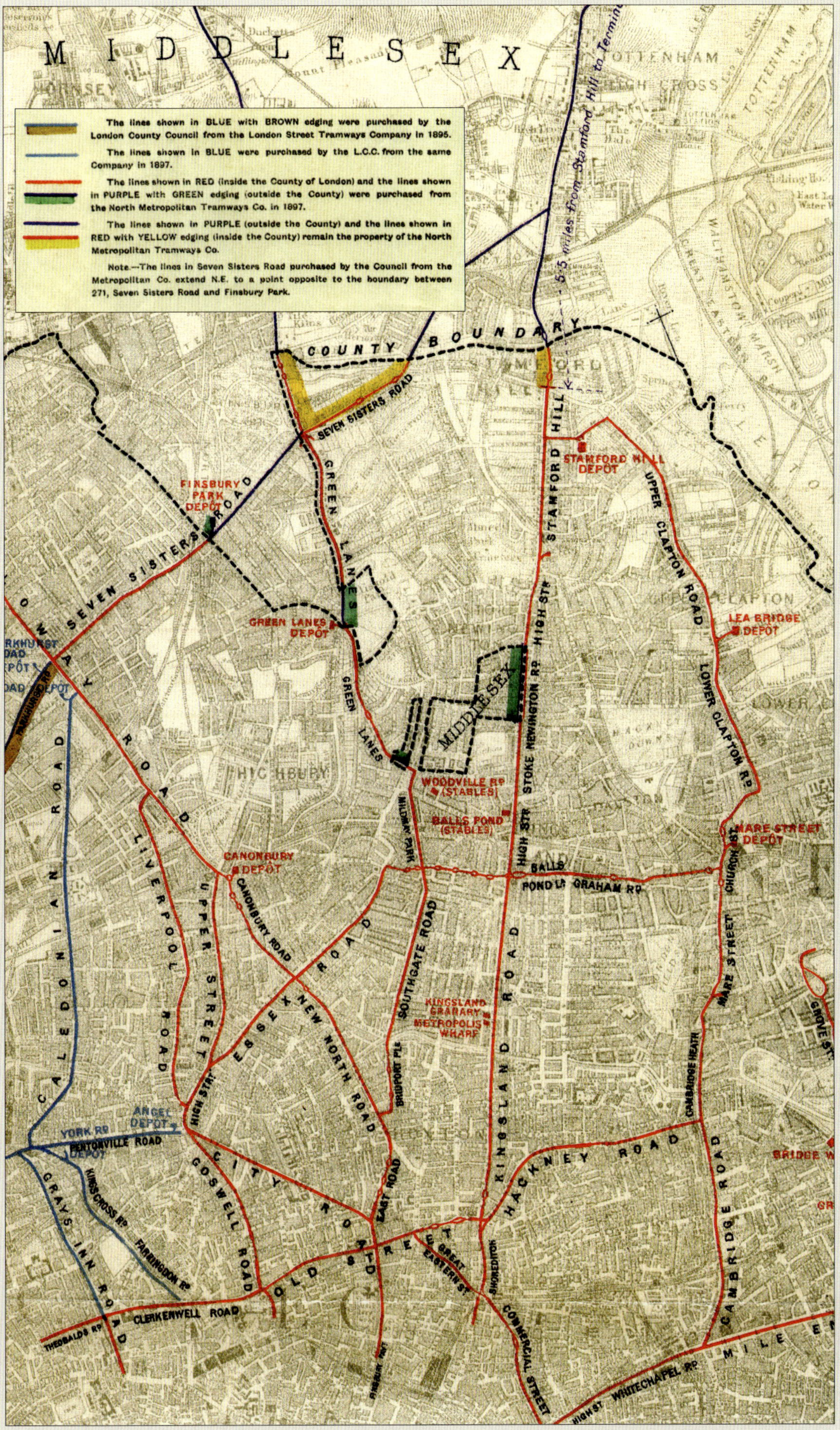

Figure 4. North Met horse tramways sold to the LCC in 1897.

Services operated in 1897 were as follows:-

	Length	Frequency	Journey time	Thro' Fare
Edmonton (Tramway Ave.) – Stamford Hill	5½ miles	every 14 mins	55 minutes	4d
Edmonton (Tramway Ave.) – Finsbury Park	6½ miles	every 14 mins	65 minutes	5d
Wood Green (bottom of Jolly Butcher's Hill) – Finsbury Park	2¾ miles	every 8 mins	28 minutes	2d

Purchase by London County Council

Arising from the Local Government Act 1888, the London County Council came into being on 1 January 1889 with a remit, amongst other things, to take over all the functions of the former Metropolitan Board of Works and also with powers to acquire (but not operate) all existing tramways within the new county boundary.

When the LCC commenced negotiations to purchase the lines and depots of the North Met in its area, the Company was concerned about the future of its newly acquired lines in Middlesex. A separate company, entitled the Metropolitan Tramways and Omnibus Company Limited (MT&O) was incorporated on 21 November 1894 with the apparent intention that it would work those parts of the North Met's horse tramways in Middlesex, after the LCC purchased the company's lines in the County of London.

However, the negotiations with the LCC were satisfactorily completed on 14 October 1897 with the LCC agreeing to lease back to the North Met to operate not only its own lines and depots but also those of the adjacent London Street Tramways Company which had been purchased by the LCC These routes are shown in Figure 4 on page 59. The leases of each route had different expiry dates, the last of which was in 1910.

The depot at Finsbury Park was used for services operated by the North Met in both London and Middlesex so ownership was only partly assigned to the LCC.

Operations: 1897 – 1902

In anticipation of the North Met having to sell its lines and depots in the county of London to the LCC., the MT&O built a horse tramway depot at Wood Green, behind the Three Jolly Butchers public house, in 1895. Once it was clear that the

LCC would be leasing back the purchased lines to the North Met to operate, the MT&O agreed to lease the Wood Green depot to the North Met from 2 June 1897.

Now with responsibility for operating the former London Street Tramway routes as well as its own, the North Met received permission to connect the tracks of the two systems at The Nag's Head, Holloway, from Parkhurst Road across Holloway Road to Seven Sisters Road. On 22 February 1898 a through service of trams commenced from Euston Road to Finsbury Park via Hampstead Road, Camden High Street, Camden Road, Parkhurst Road and Seven Sisters Road. At the same time, the tram service from Kings Cross to Holloway Road was also extended to Finsbury Park, thus restoring the former through service along Caledonian Road.

From 2 April the service from Euston Road to Finsbury Park was extended to the Manor House Tavern in rush hours and, shortly afterwards, through to Wood Green at all times, thus replacing the separate service from Finsbury Park to Wood Green.

The double deck horse cars based at Wood Green depot at this time seated 46 passengers, 10 each side downstairs inside and 26 upstairs outside. Two services were operated from the Nag's Head Wood Green; one to Euston Road via Finsbury Park and the other to Moorgate Street via Manor House and Stoke Newington. A round trip from Wood Green to Moorgate and back took 2½ hours. An average day's work for a driver or conductor was five round trips plus one journey off in the middle – giving a spreadover working day of 15 hours. For this, the conductor's pay was six shillings a day.

Local newspapers reported an accident at dusk on Christmas Day 1898. Two cars, travelling in opposite directions, arrived at the passing loop near Snell's Park. One failed to brake in time and collided with the other, causing an advertisement board to be knocked off one and the front platform to be damaged and a handrail broken on the other. The driver of the car travelling towards Edmonton also found his brake to be damaged and, being afraid to take the car over the Angel Bridge, he pulled the car off the track resulting in a lamp standard being smashed.

By the beginning of 1899, combining its original routes with those of the North London Tramway and the London Street Tramway gave the North Metropolitan Tramways the opportunity to operate the following services in and around North Middlesex:

Finsbury Park – Caledonian Road – Holborn

Finsbury Park – Highbury – Moorgate

Finsbury Park – Tottenham – Edmonton

Wood Green – Manor House – Finsbury Park – Camden Town – Euston Road

Wood Green – Manor House – Green Lanes – Southgate Road – Moorgate

Manor House – Green Lanes – Essex Road – Aldersgate

Stamford Hill – Shoreditch – Holborn

Stamford Hill – Shoreditch – Moorgate

Stamford Hill – Shoreditch – London Docks

Stamford Hill – Tottenham – Edmonton

Clapton Pond – Hackney – Shoreditch – Bloomsbury

On 25 August 1900 the service from Edmonton to Stamford Hill was withdrawn and replaced by one between Bruce Grove, Tottenham and Aldgate via Hackney.

The frequency of the service which could be operated for the increasing numbers of passengers was restricted by the long lengths of single track between the passing loops and this resulted in overcrowding of the cars. Agreements were reached with a number of the local authorities to double the tracks: from Manor House along Seven Sisters Road to Tottenham High Road and from Manor House along Green Lanes to Wood Green (February 1898), all the single track sections in the Tottenham Urban District Council area (November 1899) and Stamford Hill to Seven Sisters Corner (May 1900). However, it is thought that much of the work was not undertaken at this time as disputes with the local authorities over road widening are recorded five to seven years later in connection with the electrification of the tramway.

Fares

In 1897 the end to end fares of the routes taken over from the North London Tramway were given as 5d from Edmonton (Tramway Avenue) to Finsbury Park, 4d from Edmonton (Tramway Avenue) to Stamford Hill and 2d from Wood Green to Finsbury Park.

By 1898 the fare from Wood Green to Moorgate was reduced to 2d one way or 3d return. The workmen's cars, run in the early morning and early evening, charged a single fare of 1d.

However, in August 1899 it was decided to abolish the 3d return fares. The maximum fare of 2d single was charged for journeys between Tramway Avenue, Edmonton to Finsbury Park or from South Tottenham to the London Docks or from Wood Green to Moorgate Street.

In July 1901 the 2d fares on the Edmonton route were increased to 3d and the intermediate 1½d fares to 2d. Increases to the Wood Green route fares were deferred.

Labour Relations

Relations between the Company and their employees were not as good as they might have been.

On Tuesday, 6 September 1898, some of the horse keepers employed at the Stamford Hill depot came out on strike as a result of the depot manager discharging three men. It appears that on the previous Saturday a man was 10 minutes late for work and was suspended for two days, resulting in eight shillings being deducted from his wages. The man protested strongly about this and was discharged. Two other men were discharged under similar circumstances and on Thursday morning all the horse keepers at Stamford Hill refused to work unless the three men were reinstated. The depot manager would not agree to this and, consequently, all the men left the yard after first feeding and watering the horses. As a result 64 cars which would have operated on the services in the London area could not run and 200 other men could not work. Following consultations between officials of the Company and the horse keepers, two of the discharged men were reinstated that morning and it was agreed the case of the third man would be reconsidered. The horse keepers then resumed work.

The following Wednesday, 14 September, delegates of the horse keepers and stable employees of the Company attempted to form a Union, similar to that of the tramway operating employees (drivers and conductors) and were dismissed by the Company. It was decided that the 24 men employed at the Wood Green depot stables should come out on strike the following morning. As the result of the strike the drivers and conductors had to fetch the horses from the stables and harness them to the cars themselves. As the cars were leaving the depot some of the strikers, who knew the animals well, called the attention of police officers to the unfit condition of some of them from sore shoulders and withers (necks). These horses had to be taken back to the stables.

Other grievances raised were the alleged overbearing manner of the yard foreman at Finsbury Park, being dismissed without notice and without any appeal to the head office and dismissal, without any apparent reason, after six months' work as they then received four shillings for a $19\frac{1}{2}$ hour day instead of the three shillings and sixpence earned by new employees.

On the Thursday evening the Traffic Manager of the Company interviewed the strikers, following which all but two or three returned to work.

An electric future

The fundamental problem of operating tramways at this period was the motive power. Horse power was both slow and expensive – especially in the numbers of horses required, their feed and the stable hands and vets needed to look after them. As the history of the North London Tramway (Chapter 2) illustrates clearly, there was strong public objection to the use of steam power, particularly the smoke and noise from it, in public streets.

At the Berlin Exhibition of 1879, Werner von Siemens had first demonstrated the capabilities of a small electric locomotive and then began public services on a short line in Berlin during 1881. Although his original concept, using the two running rails as the power conductors much like a model railway today, had clear disadvantages, further experiments in America and Germany during the next decade, developing an overhead electric cable flexibly connected to the locomotive or car by an under-running trolley arm, showed a way forward.

Also pertinent to the subsequent history was the passing of the Light Railways Act of 1896. Although it was clearly intended that this Act was to simplify the promotion of light railways to serve rural districts and boost rural economies at a time of agricultural depression, the preamble of the Act did not define a 'light railway'. Since the procedure to promote a light railway was much simpler than that for a tramway, requiring only for an application to be considered by three commissioners of the Board of Trade rather than for a separate Act to pass through Parliament, and avoiding the right of veto held by local authorities under the Act of 1870 (although they could petition the commissioners) and requiring only a quarter of the general district rates to be paid, the imprecise wording of the Act of 1896 was soon used for the development of urban tramways – including those in Middlesex. Colloquially referred to as 'tramways', the subsequent extensions to the North Met system were, technically, 'light railways'.

Seeing the opportunities which would be opened up by electric powered tramways in suburban London, the North Met used its otherwise dormant subsidiary, the MT&O to take the lead on discussions with Middlesex County Council about both the electrification of the existing horse tramways owned by the North Met in Tottenham, Edmonton and Wood Green and extensions to them. An application to the Light Railway Commissioners for various route extensions to the existing tramways in April 1898 was unsuccessful. However, a further attempt in November 1898 was granted and the Company obtained powers to construct lines, with the consent of the local authorities, from Edmonton to Waltham Cross, from Ponders End to Enfield and also from Wood Green to both Enfield via Winchmore Hill and to Bruce Grove via Lordship Lane. At an inquiry held at Enfield on 22 February 1899, the construction of the lines from Edmonton (Tramway Avenue) to Waltham Cross and to Enfield was approved.

However, in January 1900, Middlesex County Council approved a policy that it should identify roads suitable for building light railways along but, while remaining the owner of such light railways or tramways, would lease them to a company to equip and operate. During subsequent discussions held between the MCC, the Board of Trade and the Light Railway Commissioners it was agreed any

approved lines in Middlesex would only be in the name of the county council.

Even prior to this policy being agreed, the MCC and the MT&O had made joint applications to the Light Railway Commissioners in May and November 1899 for electrified extensions to the existing North Met horse tramways, although not affecting those horse tramways. The two applications were successfully heard together in March 1900 and became the County of Middlesex Light Railway Order 1901. Powers were given, amongst others, for the lines from Tottenham to Wood Green and from Wood Green to Friern Barnet (New Southgate Station). A further application in May 1901 included the lines from Wood Green to Enfield and from Friern Barnet to North Finchley.

On 1 October 1901 the MT&O became a full member of the British Electric Traction Company (BET) group of companies. It was renamed Metropolitan Electric Tramways Limited (MET) on 12 October 1901, this name being registered on 15 January 1902.

In November 1901 the LCC informed the Company that it proposed to directly operate all the lines in the County of London, and convert them to electric traction, upon expiry of the individual route leases between 1906 and 1910.

The on-going negotiations between the MT&O / MET and the Light Railways Committee of the MCC resulted in an agreement by December 1901 that the North Met would sell its lines and assets in Middlesex to the MT&O by way of an exchange of shares which gave the latter a controlling interest in the former. The Council's parliamentary committee had found the prospects of directly purchasing only part of the North Met, a statutory company that was still operating services in the County of London, too complex. It was also agreed that the Council would grant a lease to the MT&O to operate these lines until 1930 providing that it constructed the proposed new lines, electrified all the routes and paid 45 per cent of the net profits of the lines worked in Middlesex to the MCC.

HIGHBURY STATION.

17. Horse tram and horse buses at Highbury Station. *A.A. Jackson Collection*

The valuation put, by representatives of the MT&O, on the purchase of the 7½ miles of the North Met lines in Middlesex, including depots, horses, rolling stock, reconstruction and electrical equipment was 'about £300,000', although the price eventually paid was only £220,000. The gross profits of the horse tramways were estimated 'at about £66,000 a year' but the Light Railways Committee of the MCC report stated *"Experience has shown that when a tramway has been converted from horse traction to electric traction it is a fair and moderate estimate to reckon that the gross receipts will be one third more in the case of electric traction"*.

In September 1902 permission was received from the Board of Trade for the Metropolitan Electric Tramways (MET), as the MT&O had been renamed, to purchase the North Met's lines in Middlesex. Consequently, service alterations were introduced on 1 November to divide the routes between LCC and MCC ownership. The service from Wood Green to Euston Road was split at Finsbury Park while that from Moorgate to Highbury via New North Road was extended to Finsbury Park resulting in the withdrawal of the short working between The Nag's Head, Holloway,

and Highbury. Additionally the service from Wood Green to Moorgate via Stoke Newington was split at Manor House.

By now, the LCC had obtained powers to operate tramways itself. On 1 April 1906 it took over the direct operation of the remainder of the North Met's horse tramway routes in its area, with the intention of electrifying them.

HIGHBURY. — Upper Street.

18. Horse tram in Upper Street, Highbury. *A.A. Jackson Collection*

SEVEN SISTERS CORNER, **SOUTH TOTTENHAM.**

19. Horse tram at Seven Sisters Corner.

20. Horse car approaching Coombes Croft House, Tottenham High Road.

21. The Swan public house, High Cross, Tottenham High Road (1892).

22. The Friends Meeting House, Tottenham High Road.

23. Passing the Grammar School, Tottenham High Road.

24. The Tottenham – Edmonton boundary at Snells Park. Tottenham High Road is in the foreground, Edmonton Fore Street is to the rear of the tram.

25. Wood Green High Road with Lordship Lane to the right.

Electric Trams at Finsbury Park.

26. Finsbury Park terminus, with horse tram in background, and horse tram depot behind the electric trams.
A.A. Jackson Collection

1618 SEVEN SISTERS CORNER. TOTTENHAM N.

27. MET electric tramcar No. 28 operating between Finsbury Park and Seven Sisters Corner. The horse tram service (on the right) has been cut back, but continued to operate to Edmonton (1904).

28. Farewell journey of the last horse tram passing the Central Library in Fore Street, Edmonton (1905).

Chapter
Four

The Metropolitan Electric Tramways in North Middlesex (1902 – 1933)

Incorporation

The background to the split of the North Met's horse tramway system into the London County Council (LCC) area and the Middlesex County Council (MCC) area and the Company's intention to electrify the latter (through its subsidiary, the Metropolitan and Omnibus Company Limited (MT&O) and extend it with new lines leased from MCC is detailed in Chapter 3.

On 1 October 1901 the MT&O became a full member of the British Electric Traction Company (BET) group of companies. It was renamed Metropolitan Electric Tramways Limited (MET) on 12 October 1901, this name being registered on 15 January 1902.

In January 1903 the MET agreed to pay for the promotion of the North Metropolitan Tramways Bill 1902, which formalised the purchase and authorised the electrification of the North Met's lines in Middlesex. On 12 May 1903 the Company applied to the High Court for permission to amend their Memorandum of Association to include the operation of 'Light Railways' as well as 'Tramways'. The alteration was granted and registered at the Company Registry on 27 May.

In October 1903, the Company signed a lease for new head offices on the second floor of Evelyn House, 101 Finsbury Pavement, London E.C.2, adjacent to the LCC's Moorgate tram terminus. However, in November 1908 it moved the head office again to the Electrical Federation Offices, Kingsway, London and then sub-leased the former offices to the LCC for a period of three years.

Electric power supply

The North Metropolitan Electric Power Supply Company Limited (North Met EPS Company) was incorporated by Special Act of Parliament in 1900 and authorised to construct and operate electric power stations in Middlesex and Hertfordshire and to supply electricity in those counties and also in Essex, not only for tramway traction purposes but also for general power and lighting. All the issued shares of the North Met EPS Company were acquired by the MET following an Agreement dated 17 June 1903 between the MET, the North Met EPS Company and the MCC.

In October 1903, an agreement was entered into between the MCC and the MET and also between the MCC, the North Met EPS Company and the MET for the supply of electricity to work the tramway system. The MET also completed the purchase of 1,710 shares in the North Met EPS Company from the BET parent company.

The Engineer of the North Met EPS Company prepared the plans for the power station, which was to be located at Brimsdown, east of Enfield alongside the River Lea and near the Great Eastern Railway line from Liverpool Street to Cambridge, but an architect was engaged to design the power station buildings. In December 1903, a contract was entered into with the Brush Electrical Engineering Company Limited as the general contractor for the supply and erection of buildings and plant for the power station, although various parts of the work were to be sub-contracted. A dock for two barges was also constructed on the Lea Navigation so that construction materials and later coal could be delivered directly to the power station.

Earlier, in September 1903, a contract had been entered into with the British Electrical Engineering Company Limited for the supply and erection of plant for sub-stations at Edmonton depot, Wood Green depot and a new depot to be built at Finchley (see Chapter 6). The sub-station buildings were owned by the MET while the equipment inside was owned by the North Met EPS Company and connected to Brimsdown Power Station by high tension cables laid in duplicate. The high tension current of 10,000 volts was converted by rotary converters into continuous supply at 550 volts at which voltage it was fed into the overhead wires of the tramway.

Construction works – upgrading the horse tramways

In November 1902, the tender of Hadfield's Steel Foundry Company Limited of Sheffield was accepted for the special track work at junctions in Tottenham, Edmonton and Wood Green while the order for 2,050 poles to support the overhead wires was placed with John Spencer Limited of Wednesbury in Staffordshire, subject to satisfactory arrangements being made for delivery and an option being obtained for a further quantity. The cast bases of the poles were supplied by John Forster and Company Limited of St. Helens and W. Lucy and Company of Oxford.

The electricity supply to the lines was divided into half–mile sections; the section boxes and equipment were supplied by the British Thompson-Houston Company Limited and R. W. Blackwell and Company Limited. The tender of British Insulated Wire Company was accepted for the supply of high tension cables, that of Callander's Cable and Construction Company for the low tension cables and that of Thomas Noakes and Sons Limited of London for the supply of frogs for the junctions in the tramway overhead wires. The overhead wires were erected by the Company's own staff, at a height of 25 feet, and later tested at least twice a week by means of an attachment to the trolley pole of a special car.

In March 1903, the MET Company entered into a contract with Dick, Kerr and Company Limited for the reconstruction of the $8\frac{1}{2}$ miles of largely single tracked horse tramways in Tottenham, Edmonton and Wood Green as a double track electric tramway. The works included lowering the roadway under railway bridges at Noel Park, Wood Green, Harringay and St. Ann's Road, Tottenham.

Before any of the reconstruction works could commence, the Company had to negotiate with each of the local authorities along its lines.

Excluded from the North Met's agreement with the LCC in 1897 had been the line from Finsbury Park to Manor House, since only one half of the width of the road was transferred to the County of London in 1889 with the South Hornsey district. A dispute with the LCC then arose in November 1902 after the North Met agreed to sell the right of beneficial user of that line to the MET, subject to the approval of the Board of Trade and its shareholders. Following the breakdown of negotiations between the LCC and the MET, the LCC applied to the High Court in November 1903 for an interim injunction to prevent the Company from electrifying this section of the line, despite the Board of Trade having given its approval to the transfer of this tramway to the Company. A satisfactory conclusion was finally reached in July 1904 when the LCC agreed to stay its action against the Company, not to purchase the line until 1910 and to set up a joint committee to negotiate the details of the matters still outstanding.

The negotiations which took place with Wood Green Urban District Council (UDC) were lengthy and the Council was particularly adamant that the Great Eastern Railway bridge at Noel Park Station in the High Road should be widened before the single tram track could be replaced with double track. The Council even refused an offer that the Company would carry out improvement works to Jolly Butcher's Hill instead. By June 1904 the Company had to agree to pay to widen the bridge in order that work could continue on relaying the line for electric traction. For this it had to purchase a strip of land from the Great Eastern Railway for road widening and pay for altering the staircase approach to the station platforms. In return the Council undertook not to exercise its rights to purchase the lines in their area, under Section 43 of the Tramways Act 1870, until 1930.

Under the agreement made between the Company and Tottenham UDC, the Company was under an obligation to widen Seven Sisters Road near St. Ann's Station by acquiring a number of forecourts. By June 1904, although the single tram track had been replaced by double track, the Council refused to allow the Company to use the extra track because not all the widening of the road had taken place. Again unable to open the line for electric traction, the Company was forced to negotiate the purchase of the remaining frontage forecourts.

The negotiations which took place between the Company, Edmonton UDC and Middlesex County Council regarding the proposed widening of Hertford Road were terminated when it became clear the MCC was unwilling to commit itself to the cost, for the time being, because of the state of the money markets. To overcome this difficulty, and in order to commence the works, the Company suggested to Edmonton UDC that an arrangement be made, similar to that between the Company and Tottenham and Wood Green UDCs. This would mean that the agreed road widening would be undertaken at the expense of the Company on the condition that the Council would not exercise its rights to purchase the lines in their area until 1930.

In June 1903, the company gave notice of its intention to commence the reconstruction of the tramways between Finsbury Park and Wood Green and between Manor House junction and Seven Sisters Corner, Tottenham. Operation of the horse tram services had to be suspended while the reconstruction of each section took place but was provided up to each side of the works. As the reconstruction progressed, the horse car services were reinstated until each section had been inspected by the Board of Trade and approved for operation by electric traction.

A dispute over poles in Tottenham

An unexpected dispute between the Company and Tottenham UDC occurred in January 1903 when the Engineer for the Company submitted plans to the Engineer for the Council regarding overhead equipment for the lines running through Tottenham. The Council's Engineer objected to the plans:

*"He could not advise the Council to sanction the proposed arrangement of side poles and span wires as they had a most primitive look …
As the main thoroughfares of Tottenham lent themselves to the erection of ornamental centre poles, he suggested that the Company took advantage of the situation and give an artistic effect to their proposed system".*

The Company replied that the extra cost of the centre pole system would be over £5,000 and suggested the Council pay the difference. The Council then had second thoughts and decided that the roads in some locations of the district were not wide enough to make the centre pole practicable and consequently passed a resolution stating which roads should have centre poles and which should have side poles with brackets. The term 'side pole' in this context meant poles situated on the pavement but the overhead wires were to be supported by a bracket from one side pole and not by a span-wire stretched across the road between two side poles.

The Company informed Middlesex County Council of the position and it, in turn, referred the matter to the Board of Trade for arbitration. Meanwhile, in March 1903, Members of Tottenham UDC and its Engineer, at the invitation of the Company, inspected the Croydon Corporation Tramways, where the side bracket system was in use, the London United Tramways Company at Brentford and Hounslow, where the span-wire system was used, and also systems in Leeds and Bradford.

The Board of Trade wrote to the Council asking for its observations. The Council decided to rescind its previous decision and passed another resolution that centre poles were to be used 'where practicable' although the 'Rosette' system, of a metal casting fixed to the wall of a building to support span-wires stretched across the road instead of side poles, should be used along the High Road at Bruce Grove and High Cross and also along Seven Sisters Road until the road widenings were completed. Following the inspections at Leeds and Bradford, the Council decided that span-wire construction was best suited for the new line along Lordship Lane, with the type of pole used by the London United Tramways.

However, once the Company had installed the centre-of-the-road poles to the Council's specification, the Council realised the obstruction they were causing to traffic. When, on 26 April 1907, Tottenham UDC urged the North Met EPS Company to proceed with the installation of electric street lighting in the district, the electric supply company replied that it was unable to do so because of the negotiations taking place between the Council and the MET about moving the centre poles. The Engineer to the Council had informed the MET that the Council was unable to bear the cost of removing the centre poles and substituting them with side poles; he suggested the Company should do this work at its own expense!

Further negotiations took place in July 1911, at which it was suggested that while the Company should remove the centre poles and substitute side poles at its own cost, the Council should, at its cost, reinstate the road and pavements where disturbed by the removal of the centre poles. Both parties agreed to this and it was made a statutory obligation under an Act obtained by the Company in 1913, under which it had to carry out its part of the work within one year from the date on which the Act received the Royal Assent. A draft agreement between the Company and the Council was approved in July 1914.

Rolling stock delivered 1904 – 1905

For both the electrification of the former North Met horse tramways and the opening of the MCC's new light railways, the MET initially ordered 150 cars and spare parts for them from the Brush Electrical Engineering Company Limited, on the understanding that the Company should not be called upon to accept delivery before September 1903, and then only as required.

The cars were of two types. **Type A cars** were double deck, open top bogie cars fitted with Robinson-type rectangular staircases which resulted in no overhanging canopy above the driver. This design can be seen in the photographs on pages 110 – 112. These cars were numbered from 71 to 130 and were favoured by the County Council. At a later date, many of these cars were fitted with top covers.

Type B cars were double decked open top bogie cars fitted with normal staircases, a canopy over the driver and longitudinal seating inside. Type B/1 cars were almost identical but were partly fitted with cross seating inside. These were numbered from 1 to 70 and were favoured by the Company (see photographs on pages 105 – 106). These cars were allocated to Wood Green depot for the opening of the system by electric traction. Some of these cars were also fitted with top covers at a later date.

Both Type A and Type B cars were mounted on Brush maximum traction trucks and were fitted with British Thompson Houston Company (BTH Company) B18 type controllers and two GE58 type motors of 37½ h.p. each. The trolley poles and trolley heads were also supplied by the BTH Company as was the electric rheostatic brake system. The hand brakes were by Brush and the lifeguards were of the Tidswell and Wilson-Bennett types. The seating material inside the cars differed; some were fitted with rattan seats, some with shaped wooden slats and others with cushions.

Subsequently 20 four-wheeled single decked cars were also ordered from Brush as the Board of Trade inspecting officer had refused to allow double deck cars to be used on the steeply graded routes to Alexandra Palace. These cars became Type E and were numbered 131 to 150 (see photographs on pges 112 –113). They were delivered in

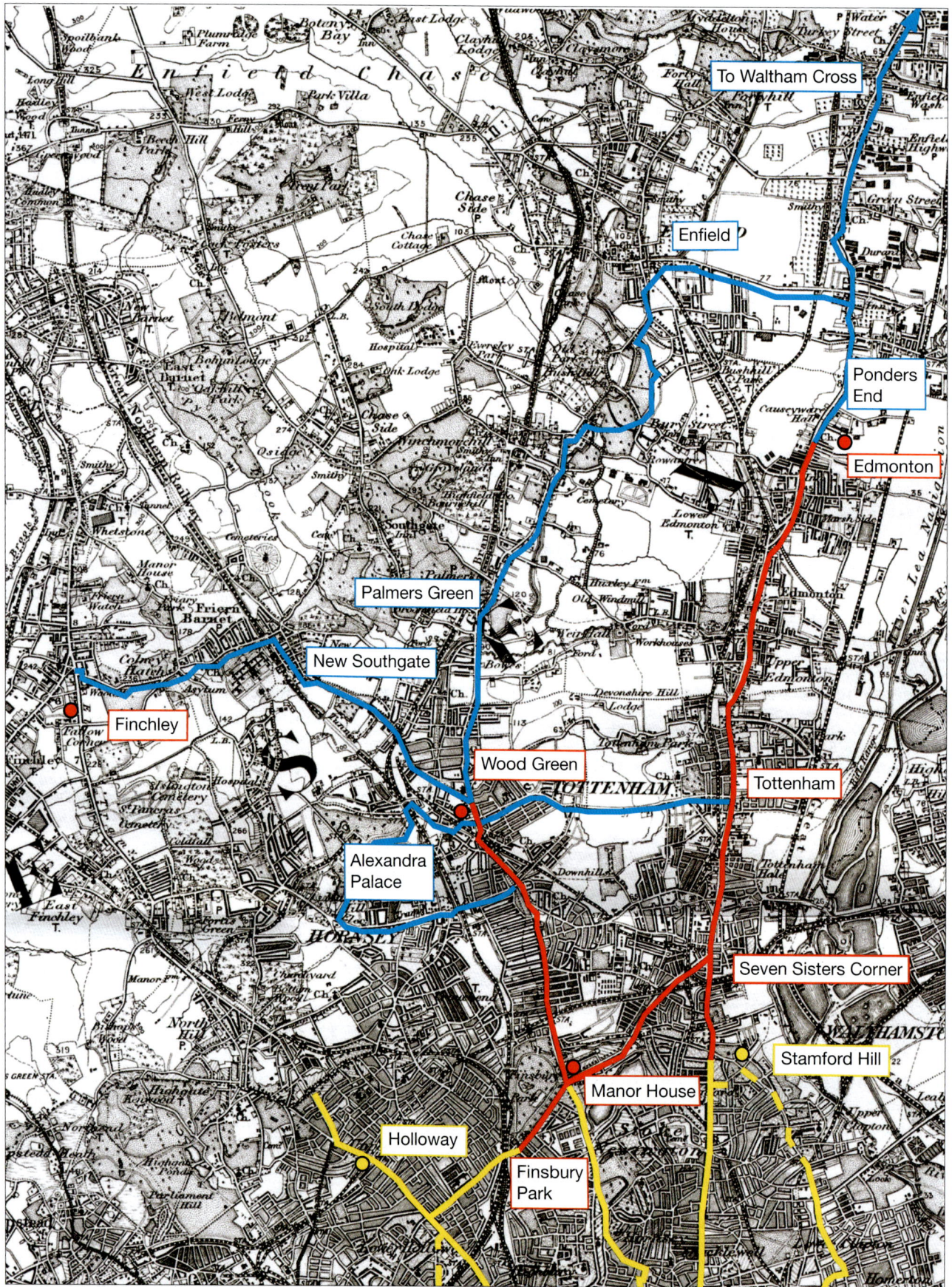

Figure 5. Development of MET routes in north Middlesex.

Former North Met horse tram routes electrified by the MET
Former North Met horse tram routes electrified by the LCC
MCC electric 'light railways' built and operated by the MET

● **MET depots**
● **LCC depots**

sections to and assembled at Edmonton depot in August 1905. In 1907 four of these cars, being surplus to requirements, were sold to a BET-owned system in Auckland, New Zealand.

The Type C and Type D double decked cars were delivered from 1906 onwards (see page 84).

Advertisements

At a meeting with the Company in February 1904, the MCC objected to any advertisements appearing on the tramcars and stated it required the name of the Council to be shown. The Company suggested it was prepared to allow the name of the Council to appear on the cars to be used on the Council's light railways and to abandon the scheme to display advertisements on those cars provided the Council paid the Company a sum in respect of the advertising revenue foregone. It was reported that the London United Tramways received an average net rent equal to £27 10s 0d for each running car for advertisements.

Further negotiations followed and in February 1905 the Company suggested that, in the event of the Council refusing to allow advertisements on the outside of its 'light railway' cars, it should be allowed to deduct 55 per cent of the sum equivalent to £27 10s 0d for each running car from monies due to the Council while at the same time crediting the Council with whatever revenue was derivable from advertising inside the cars. The cars of the Company tramways were to be included in the same arrangement. Middlesex County Council then reconsidered its position and decided to allow the Company to show advertisements on both the outside and the inside of all the cars, passing a resolution to this effect on 26 October.

In June 1906, a Mr R. Frost was employed by the Company as advertising agent to obtain advertising for display on the cars.

The first electric services

A map of North Middlesex at this period, showing the localities mentioned in the text, is included as Figure 5 on page 76 opposite.

Such was the progress in reconstructing the former horse tram lines, that an inspection on behalf of the Board of Trade was arranged for 20 July 1904. The Inspector consented to the lines from Finsbury Park to Wood Green and to Tottenham (Seven Sisters Corner) being opened on the understanding that the Company dealt with points he had raised in his report, within the specified period, in respect of car equipment and fittings.

The horse cars ceased to run on these lines after the evening of 21 July 1904 and the public service of electric cars commenced the following morning with 24 cars. On the same day, representatives of the Company, local dignitaries and the press travelled by a special train from Liverpool Street Station to Brimsdown, near Enfield, where the new power station had been built. The party subsequently drove to view the reconstruction works at Edmonton depot and continued their journey to Wood Green depot which was also inspected. Here the horse tramway depot had been adapted by raising the roof and enlarged to accommodate 62 electric cars. The invited guests then travelled by special cars from Wood Green to Finsbury Park and Seven Sisters Corner.

Services were operated from Wood Green to Finsbury Park commencing at 5 a.m. and running at 15 minute intervals until 7 a.m., then increasing to a 6 minute frequency and, gradually, to a 2 minute frequency. The last car from Wood Green was at 11.49 p.m. and the last from Finsbury Park at 12 minutes after midnight. On the Seven Sisters line, the first car left the Corner for Finsbury Park at 7.20 a.m. and the last at 11.50 p.m. with departures returning from Finsbury Park between 7.02 a.m. and 11.38 p.m.

Horse cars continued to run from the City via Stamford Hill to Tottenham (Seven Sisters Corner) and from Seven Sisters Corner to the depot at Edmonton (Tramway Avenue). However, as reconstruction of the horse tramway commenced again at Tottenham and proceeded northwards towards the Edmonton boundary at Snells Park, the horse tramway service was progressively cut back.

The first of Middlesex County Council's new light railways, that between Tottenham (Bruce Grove) and Wood Green via Lordship Lane, was built by W. Griffiths & Company Limited under a contract awarded in October 1902. After completion it was inspected on behalf of the Board of Trade on 6 August 1904 and opened for public service on 20 August as a through route from Bruce Grove to Finsbury Park via Lordship Lane, Wood Green and Green Lane, the Finsbury Park service no longer using Jolly Butcher's Hill in Wood Green. To celebrate the opening of the first of the authorised light railways, a reception was held by Middlesex County Council in Bruce Castle and its grounds. The celebrations commenced at 3 o'clock with the official first tram, followed by other cars, departing Bruce Castle at 4.30 p.m. for a run over the line via Wood Green to Manor House.

A further part of the reconstructed horse tramways, from Stamford Hill through Tottenham to the Edmonton boundary at Snells Park, was inspected on 19 August 1904. The section from Seven Sisters Corner to Snells Park was opened for public service on 24 August as part of an extended through route from Finsbury Park. A three track layout was constructed at Snells Park, the boundary between Tottenham and Edmonton, but a direct connection with the new Wood Green line could not be made at Bruce Grove until the railway bridge at Bruce Grove station was rebuilt.

Delays in reconstructing the tramway in Edmonton and Tottenham

By September 1904, the Company was receiving complaints from Edmonton UDC and the public, regarding the unsatisfactory nature of the connection between the new electric services and the remaining section of the horse tramway and the fares that were being charged. Passengers travelling from Edmonton (Town Hall) to Bruce Grove were being charged two separate 1d fares instead of the previous total of 1d because no through tickets were being issued. The Company stated that the issue of separate tickets on the two services was only of a temporary nature, pending the reconstruction of the tramways for electric traction in the district of Edmonton. From the Company's point of view, it would have been preferable to close the whole of the horse tramway in Edmonton completely during the period of reconstruction but it was desirable to continue the operation of that line for the convenience of the public. It agreed there was a gap of considerable distance between the temporary terminus of the electric cars in Tottenham and the horse cars in Edmonton but stated that the contractors were getting on with the reconstruction work. The work along Fore Street was being finished first and, when completed, the electric cars could run right up to the horse cars.

On 3 November 1904, the Board of Trade granted the Company permission, by letter, to extend its public service between Finsbury Park and Snells Park as far as Angel Road in Edmonton for an initial period of three months. To enable the Company to operate over the reconstructed double track in the Edmonton district before the completion of the road widenings, temporary crossovers were laid.

The main cause of the delay in completing the reconstruction of the line through to Edmonton (Tramway Avenue) was the reconstruction of two bridges – the Angel Bridge in Edmonton over

Pymmes Brook and the New Road Bridges over the Great Eastern Railway at Lower Edmonton station. A compromise was reached regarding the latter whereby the tramway company contributed towards the cost of strengthening these bridges while the railway company undertook to carry out the work with as little interference as possible to the operation of the new electric cars.

The Engineer of the Company prepared a report dated 19 October 1904 about the reconstruction of the Angel Bridge since, by virtue of Section 10 of the North London Suburban Tramways Order of 1879, the Company was responsible for the maintenance and repair of the bridge and, under an Agreement dated 28 June 1904 made with Edmonton UDC, the Company had undertaken to pay for the widening of it. The horse tram line over the bridge was laid as single track and until it was reconstructed the tramways in Edmonton could not be permanently worked as part of the whole electrified system. The reconstruction had to be undertaken without interference to other traffic and required the removal of the existing hump in the bridge structure and the laying of double track. To have laid a temporary additional track would only have delayed the situation in the long term.

On 4 December, the old railway bridge at Bruce Grove station was removed and replaced by a wider bridge; even so, there was still insufficient clearance for double deck cars to pass underneath it and, therefore, no connection was made between the line from Wood Green with the one along Tottenham High Road.

On 12 April 1905, the section of the reconstructed tramway between Seven Sisters Corner and Stamford Hill was finally brought into use, having been inspected the previous August. An additional service was then introduced between Stamford Hill and Angel Road in Edmonton.

By the beginning of June, the electric cars were running out of passenger service beyond the Angel Bridge to the depot at Tramway Avenue, Edmonton. The reconstruction work was sufficiently advanced for them to do so but the Board of Trade would not allow passengers to be carried until the Angel Bridge had been rebuilt and other road-widenings carried out. Consequently, a small number of horse trams had to be retained in service to operate along Fore Street and Hertford Road in Edmonton until the work was completed. The line in Edmonton from the Angel Bridge to Tramway Avenue was inspected by the Board of Trade representative on 5 July and on the evening of 18 July the final horse trams made their last journey on the truncated route. The following morning the full service of electric cars commenced operation between Tramway Avenue and both Stamford Hill and Finsbury Park.

In August, work finally commenced to lower the roadway under the railway bridge at Bruce Grove Station to permit the operation of double decked cars. An Agreement with the Great Eastern Railway in November also permitted the level of the station booking office to be dropped in consequence of the lowering of the roadway and footpaths. However, a dispute then arose between the Company and Tottenham UDC about the tracks which would connect the two lines at Bruce Grove. The Company wanted to lay a crossover in the High Road to enable it to run through cars between Stamford Hill and Wood Green via Bruce Grove but the Council insisted that the crossover should be in Bruce Grove itself. The Company considered it would be practically impossible to carry out the works in the way suggested by the Council because the track in the High Road was still single at this point. However, agreement was reached and by the end of December a junction had been made allowing a new service of single decked cars from Wood Green along Lordship Lane to Tottenham, Bruce Grove, High Road and Stamford Hill to commence at the beginning of January 1906.

From 11 April, this service was extended to commence from Alexandra Palace and Wood Green Station Road. In May 1908, the single track along the High Road at Bruce Grove Station was

granted on 1 November 1904 and Company employees had, therefore, trespassed when erecting them. When the actions were heard in 1907, the first action was dismissed and for the second the owners of the private roads were awarded twenty shilling damages in respect of a technical trespass committed by the Company. The owners of the road then appealed against the judgements given. Meanwhile, these proceedings had been brought to the attention of Finchley UDC who had inserted a clause in their General Purposes Bill in respect of the adoption of private streets in its area. Royal Assent to this Bill was received in 1908, whereupon the Council took steps to declare Woodberry Grove a public highway.

Included in the Middlesex County Council Light Railways Act 1901, was the grant of powers to construct a line from Wood Green to New Southgate. It had originally been intended that the line should continue to North Finchley via Woodhouse Road but it had not been possible to reach agreement with Finchley and Friern Barnet UDCs over plans to widen the roads and pavements within the deadlines. The new line from Wood Green to North Finchley was, therefore, opened in stages.

The first part from Wood Green along Bounds Green Road to The Ranelagh public house in Bounds Green, a distance of one mile and one furlong, was inspected on behalf of the Board of Trade on 23 November 1906 and opened for public service, using single deck cars, on 28 November. The service was extended to New Southgate Station on 10 May 1907, after a successful inspection on 7 May.

Eventually, agreement was reached, and powers granted, to extend the line to North Finchley and on 11 June 1908 the MCC placed a contract with Dick, Kerr & Company Limited for its construction. The completed line was successfully inspected on 7 April 1909 and public services commenced the next day. From 21 February of the next year, the full service of double deck cars commenced between Finsbury Park and North Finchley via Wood Green,

at which time the line in North Finchley was extended over the High Road to terminate outside the Tally Ho Corner public house, adjacent to the terminus of the tram service from Golders Green.

The new line from Wood Green to Enfield was also opened in stages. A contract was placed with Dick, Kerr & Company Limited for the construction of the section between Wood Green and Winchmore Hill on 12 July 1906. The section from the top of Jolly Butchers Hill in Wood Green to the Kings Arm Bridge in Palmers Green, a distance of 1 mile 1 furlong in length, was inspected on behalf of the Board of Trade on 4 June 1907 and opened for public service on 7 June. It was extended to the Green Dragon Hotel in Winchmore Hill, a distance of 1 mile and 5 furlongs on 1 August, after a successful inspection on 23 July.

Another contract was made with George Wimpey & Company Limited on 9 July 1908 for the section between Winchmore Hill and Enfield. It had been intended that the route from Winchmore Hill would ascend the steep Bush Hill, passing the gates of Old Park and then descend into Enfield Town. However, negotiations with the owners of the Red Ridge Estate permitted Ridge Avenue to be constructed as a new and more level 60-foot wide road between Winchmore Hill and the Edmonton to Enfield (Village Road) highway, which was also widened to 60 feet. This section, a distance of 1¾ miles, was successfully inspected on 21 June 1909 and the public service commenced on 3 July – although the official opening did not take place until 10 July. The line terminated at Enfield Market Place in a trailing point facing towards Southbury Road, although the intended connection with the Southbury Road route was never constructed.

The Board of Trade inspection of the new line from Tramway Avenue in Edmonton along the Hertford Road to the Middlesex – Hertfordshire boundary at Freezywater took place on 26 November 1907. On 11 December the public service commenced at 3 p.m., preceded by the official first car of dignitaries at 2 p.m. The remaining 300 yards of the line to Waltham Cross High Street was inspected on 15 January 1908. The extension did not open to the public until midday on 16 April, when a special car with 'Hertfordshire County Council' painted on the sides made the journey from the county boundary to the terminus and back (a similar car is illustrated on page 114). As 17 and 20 April were the bank holidays of Good Friday and Easter Monday, the service between Finsbury Park and Edmonton (Tramway Avenue) was extended to Waltham Cross to enable passengers to make the through journey without changing cars. However, after the Easter holidays the service returned to being a separate 'shuttle' route between Tramway Avenue and Waltham Cross.

The delays in the construction of the final MCC light railway, that along Southbury Road between Ponders End and Enfield Town, required an Extension of Time Order from the Board of Trade. This became the final order, of any kind, made for tramway construction in North Middlesex. The MET had proposed that this line should be worked experimentally as a rail-less trolleybus route, but the MCC would not agree. The County of Middlesex Light Railways (Extension of Time) Order 1909 was confirmed and extended the period allowed for the construction of the Southbury Road Light Railway until 31 December 1910. Questions had already been raised by local people as to whether the narrow and congested entrance into Enfield Market Place, which was about 19 feet wide, was suitable for a single track tramway and a petition had been organised against it. Under pressure, Middlesex County Council decided the track should be laid but the service to be operated should be truncated at a point some 200 yards short of the entrance to the town at the Great Eastern Railway Station. While the MCC stated that this short section of line was for service purposes only and not for passengers, Enfield UDC approved it subject to the following conditions:

1. *No stopping places to be fixed along it*

2. *The speed not to exceed 4 mph*

3. *Regulations for the safety of the public to be made to the satisfaction of the Council.*

In fact this connection between the line from Wood Green and the line from Ponders End was never constructed and the connecting point for it, at the terminus of the line from Wood Green in Enfield Market Place, remained in position, but unused, until the end of tramway operation.

The line along Southbury Road from Ponders End to Enfield, a length of 1 mile, 3 furlongs and 1 chain, was officially inspected by the Board of Trade on 6 February 1911 and opened for public services on the morning of 20 February. The official opening did not take place until 2.30 p.m. that afternoon when a single deck Type E car was used for the purpose. Initially, only single deck cars were used for this 'shuttle' service but they were replaced by double deck cars in June.

Although there was a triangular junction at Ponders End off the main line to Waltham Cross, only the side from Edmonton into Southbury Road was used regularly. The opposite side of the triangle out of Southbury Road facing towards Waltham Cross was rarely used, except for a period during the First World War for munitions-workers' services.

Operations 1904 – 1912

During the evening of 3 November 1904, two trams, travelling in opposite directions along Tottenham High Road, collided with each other opposite Factory Lane in Bruce Grove where the double track became single. The cars struck each other with considerable force and both were damaged at their front ends.

On 9 November, a traction engine, drawing a

van, was turning out of White Hart Lane into Tottenham High Road when a tram collided with the van, knocking it onto a centre pole of the overhead and practically wrecking it. The front part of the car was also badly damaged and the driver had to complete the journey to Snells Park using the controller at the rear, as the front controller was so damaged it could not be used.

A fatal accident took place in Edmonton during the last days of horse tram operation when a man who was standing between the temporary tracks watching the men at work relaying it saw a car approaching. As he went to step on the footpath his foot slipped and he fell back between the horses and the car.

In 1906 the Company applied to the Board of Trade for permission to increase the maximum speed of the tramcars in certain areas, subject to the approval of each local authority, from 10 mph to 12 mph. Although Edmonton UDC dismissed the application, Hornsey UDC agreed to it. Stops were arranged every 160 to 200 yards and were either indicated by enamel stop signs or by circles painted on the poles. The average speed, including stops, was now 8 mph.

In 1908 the average daytime service interval for each route was about every five minutes - which was increased during the morning and evening rush hour periods to provide a car up to every minute. Some services commenced at 4.30 a.m. and finished at 1.30 a.m.

Particulars of the car depots at this time were:

	Edmonton	Finchley	Wood Green
Width	137ft 0ins	173ft 6¼ins	83ft 8½ins
Length	217ft 6ins	148ft 7½ins	473ft 0ins
No. of tracks	10	15	7
No. of pits	10	15	6
Capacity of depot	60 cars	60 cars	87 cars

The MET became increasingly concerned about the rapidly multiplying number of buses being operated by the London General Omnibus Company and many smaller 'pirate' companies in the area served by its tramways. In January 1912 the BET formed another subsidiary, known as the Tramways (MET) Omnibus Company Limited, to operate buses in those areas without tram routes and to act as feeders into them. An order was placed with the Daimler Company for 350 buses to be fitted with 40 h.p., 4-cylinder, sleeve valve 'Night' type engines. However, during the course of the year an agreement was reached between the MET and the London General Omnibus Company whereby the 'General' would operate these buses on behalf of the MET but for the same purpose.

Additional rolling stock 1906 – 1912

Between 1906 and 1912 the Company purchased another 166 tram cars, manufactured by the Brush Electrical Engineering Company Limited. Each type of car is illustrated, both as new and as subsequently rebuilt, on pages 114 – 123.

Type C, numbered 151 – 165 - open top, double decked bogie cars built in 1906 and rebuilt (as Type C/2) 1912-1916 as covered top cars fitted with open balconies.

Type D, numbered 166-190 – open top, double decked, four-wheeled cars built in 1906. Following the First World War they were fitted with plough carrier electrical pick ups to operate over LCC tracks.

Type D/1, numbered 191 – an open top, double decked, four-wheeled car which had been built by Brush as a demonstration car for Leicester Corporation Tramways but not accepted by them. It was sold to the MET and later fitted with a plough carrier.

Type C/1, numbered 192-211 – double deck bogie cars fitted with top deck covers (but with open balconies) built in 1908 and fitted with plough carriers between 1912 and 1916. Some were rebuilt with fully enclosed top decks and, together with the later rebuilds of the Type G cars, were the only covered top trams able to pass under the railway bridges at Turnpike Lane, Hornsey on the Muswell Hill route.

Type F, numbered 212-216 – double deck bogie cars with enclosed top decks built in 1908 and fitted with plough carriers from 1912.

Type G, numbered 217-236 – open top, double decked bogie cars built in 1909 and fitted with plough carriers from 1912. Rebuilt between 1928 and 1930 with fully enclosed top decks and fitted with windscreens from 1931.

Type H, numbered 237-316 – double deck bogie cars with enclosed top decks built between 1909 and 1912. By 1912 some were fitted with plough carrier electrical pick ups to operate over LCC tracks and subsequently all were adapted.

Fares 1903 - 1912

In October 1903 an agreement was entered into with the Bell Punch and Printing Company Limited for the supply of tickets and ticket punches. The agreement also gave the Bell Punch Company the right to arrange for advertisements to appear on the tickets.

In December 1903 the Board of Trade agreed to insert a clause in the various Light Railway Orders of the MET and the MCC to the effect that the lowest fare should be 1 penny (1d). In support of their application, the MET undertook that every penny stage would not be less than two miles in length and that cheap Workmen's Tickets would be issued every day, except Sundays, bank holidays, Christmas Day or Good Friday, on every car completing its journey by 8 a.m. for the whole length of the routes:

Stamford Hill to Edmonton
Finsbury Park to Wood Green
Tottenham (Bruce Grove) to Wood Green

The two-journey tickets were available for a second journey, either way, on any car at any time, with the same exceptions:

Single journey of any distance – 1d.
Two-journey ticket – 2d.

From the start of the electrified services the ordinary fares were stated as:

Wood Green to Finsbury Park – 1d.
(a reduction from 1½d.)
Tottenham (Bruce Grove) to Wood Green – 1d.
Stamford Hill to Wood Green – 2d.
Stamford Hill to Bruce Grove – 1d.
Edmonton (Tramway Avenue) to Brereton Road (opposite the Spurs football ground) – 1d.
Brereton Road (opposite the Spurs football ground) to Stamford Hill – 1d.
Seven Sisters Corner to Westbury Avenue – 1d.

For its own light railway sections, the MCC recommended that the following fares and stages be adopted:

Penny Stages:
Edmonton (Tramway Avenue) to Southbury Road
Southbury Road to Green Street
Green Street to Bell Lane
Bell Lane to Putney Road
Putney Road to the county boundary.

Two penny stages:
Edmonton (Tramway Avenue) to Putney Road
Putney Road to the county boundary.

Three penny stages:
Edmonton (Tramway Avenue) to the county boundary.

Although, at the time of their introduction, protests were received about the location of the stages, rather than the fares, the Council decided to let them stand and for them to be reviewed a month or so later.

On 28 February 1907, the Stores Sub-Committee of the BET wrote to the Company informing them of arrangements which had been made with the Bell Punch Company for supplying tickets to all associated companies, resulting in a saving to the Company. Part of the arrangement was that the Company would be released from its existing agreement with the Bell Punch Company.

In 1908 the longest through route was from Finsbury Park to Waltham Cross, a distance of 9$\frac{1}{4}$ miles, with a maximum fare of 6d.

By October 1909, the Company had obtained a petrol-driven vehicle, kept at Wood Green depot, which was used as a ticket punch van to distribute ticket stocks and ticketing equipment between the depots and offices and to collect the cash taken by conductors.

On 1 January 1910, fares were reduced on the two single deck routes running to Alexandra Palace because of a drop in receipts. It was hoped that more passengers would use the services. The fares from Wood Green Station and the foot of Muswell Hill to Alexandra Palace were reduced to $\frac{1}{2}$d, as was the fare from Wood Green Station to Wood Green High Road.

In May 1912, the Company agreed to amend its Bye Laws so as to come into line with the LCC and permit the carriage of dogs in the cars.

Relations with the LCC tramways 1904 – 1912

The background to the London County Council becoming firstly the owner and then the operator of tramways in London has been described in Chapter 3. The LCC finally took over the direct operation of all the North Met's horse tramway routes in its own area on 1 April 1906 as a prelude to electrifying them.

Unlike the MET, and most other tramway systems in the UK, the LCC chose not to install overhead electric power supply but supplied the current from a conduit laid under the road between the rails. Tramcars made contact with the power in the conduit by way of a removable 'plough' fitted in a transverse 'carrier' underneath them. When cars changed from one power supply to the other, the ploughs could be inserted or removed at special pits installed in the middle of the road between each pair of tracks. Examples are illustrated on pages 88 and 151.

In December 1906, the MET and the LCC entered into an agreement whereby the LCC agreed not to purchase that part of the Company's tramway at Stamford Hill within its area until 1930. In return, the Company granted the LCC permission to run trams over a short section of these tracks in order to gain access to the new LCC Stamford Hill tram depot at the end of Egerton Road. Thus a short section of trackwork north of Stamford Hill Crossroads had to be electrified by both the overhead system for the Company cars and the conduit system for the LCC cars.

The LCC opened its route from Stamford Hill to St. Leonards Church in Shoreditch, using electric traction on the conduit system, on 6 February 1907. It included a section of side conduit track, installed along Kingsland Road in Dalston where the conduit equipment was fitted below the offside rail (which was slotted), although at points and crossings it was installed in the normal position in the centre of the running track.

The LCC built another electric car depot in Holloway on the site of a former football ground off Pemberton Gardens which it purchased in December 1905; it opened on 28 November 1907. On the same day, three electric cars using the conduit system were introduced into the timetable of horse cars operating between Highbury Station and Highgate. This service was increased to six electric cars on 2 December and the horse cars on this route were withdrawn entirely on 6 January 1908. Additional LCC electrified lines were opened between the Nag's Head in Holloway and Finsbury Park on 9 July 1908 and from Stamford Hill to Hackney via Clapton on 23 September 1909.

By the Agreement of 1902, the LCC had the right to purchase the section of the Company's tramway along Seven Sisters Road between Finsbury Park and Manor House from 10 August 1910, subject to three months' notice, at a price to be settled by arbitration in the event of disagreement, in accordance with Section 43 of the Tramways Act 1870. They gave this notice to the Company on 11 August 1910. Since this was a key section of its profitable network, the Company was anxious at least to retain running powers along it and tried to negotiate with the LCC for the same terms that had been agreed for the Harrow Road and Paddington Tramway in West London. The Company assumed that the LCC would require the line and the junction at Manor House to be reconstructed so that power could be obtained from the conduit system

as well as the overhead wires. The Company also suggested that the LCC should apply for powers to construct a loop line at Finsbury Park so the terminating Company cars did not interfere with the eventual through running of the Council's cars at this point. This was agreed by the Council.

In May 1911, the LCC's Tramways and Improvements Bill was passed by the Committee of the House of Commons but, when the bill came before the House of Lords Committee in August 1911, the Commissioner of Police opposed it and the Finsbury Park loop line was rejected. By October 1911, negotiations for the purchase of this section of tramway by the LCC were no longer proceeding satisfactorily for the Company. At first it considered depositing a Bill in Parliament with a view to obtaining compulsory running powers over this tramway following its purchase by the LCC. However, meetings with Middlesex County Council, Hornsey UDC and Islington Borough Council suggested that, since the boundary between the LCC and the MCC ran along the centre of Seven Sisters Road, the Company should instead deposit a Bill in Parliament to acquire a strip of land forming part of Finsbury Park and to construct a new tramway just inside the park between the Manor House junction and a point near the existing terminus. Immediately before the parliamentary debate on the Second Reading of the Company's Bill to this effect on 11 March 1912, the Company received a letter from the LCC which caused it to withdraw the Bill.

The letter stated that the Chief Officer of the Council's tramways had been authorised to negotiate with the Company regarding through running arrangements after the purchase by the Council of the Finsbury Park tramway which was to take place on 17 July 1912. An agreement was subsequently reached for the joint operation of a through service between Euston Road and Enfield Town:

1. *The mileage to be run by each party to be in proportion to the length of track in each party's area.*

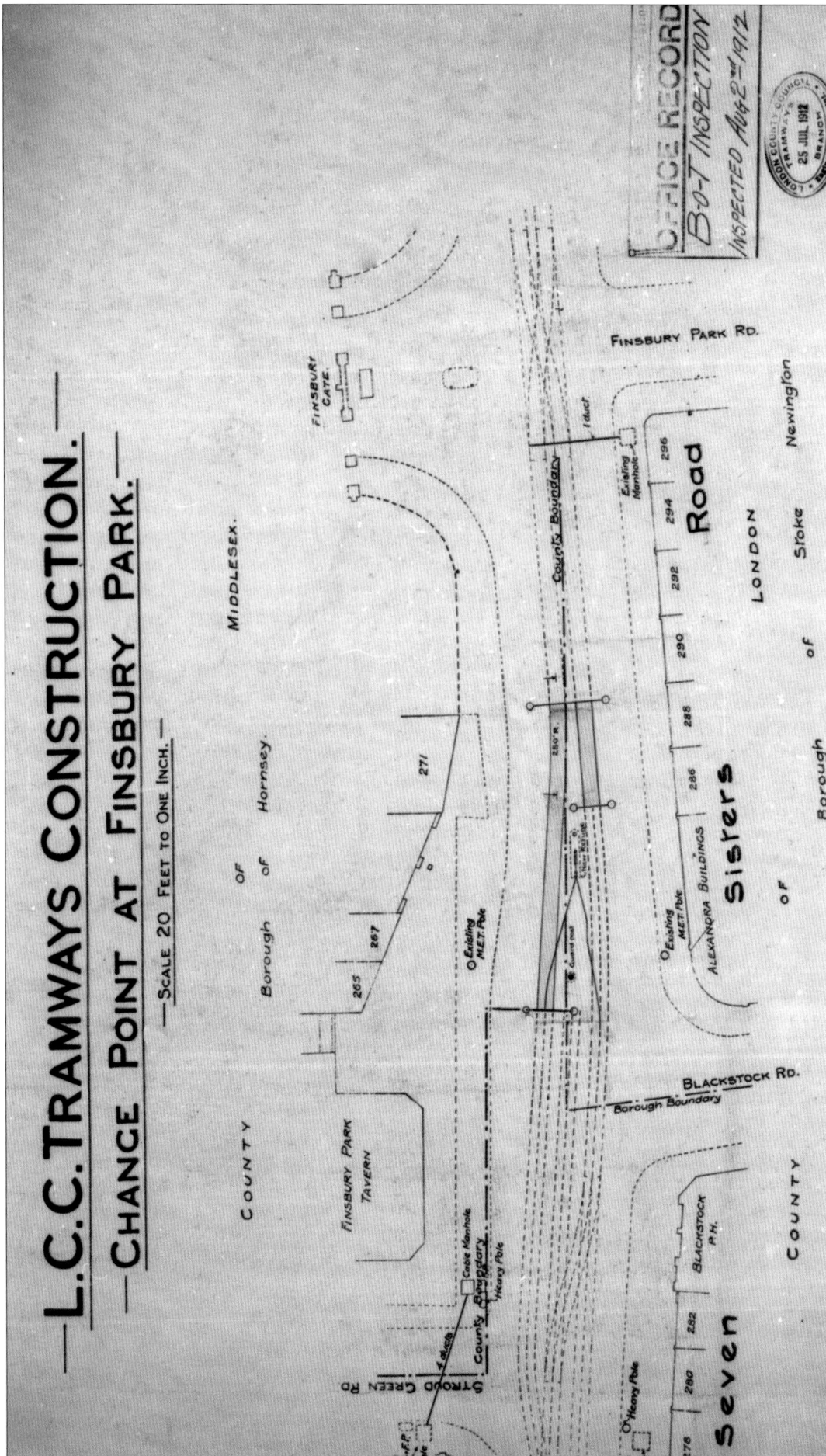

**Figure 6.
Plough
change point
at Finsbury
Park (1912)**

2. *The receipts from all through running cars to be pooled and divided between the two parties in the following manner. Each party to receive the proportion calculated by multiplying the number of car miles run, by the receipts per car mile earned by each party during the year ended 8th December 1911 on the proportion of the through route belonging to each party.*

3. *The Company and the Tramways (MET) Omnibus Company Limited to undertake not to run any omnibus, without the Council's consent, over any portion of a route on which a through tram service is in operation.*

4. *The Company to pay 6½d per car mile for all miles run by their cars, (other than through cars) over the Finsbury Park Tramway. The Council, in consideration of this payment, to maintain and renew the tramway, pay all taxes leviable on the same and supply the Company with electricity free of charge.*

5. *The through running arrangements to continue in force for twelve months and thereafter for further periods of twelve months, subject to three months notice before expiration of each twelve monthly period.*

The arbitration to settle the purchase price of the Finsbury Park Tramway was heard in March 1912, when the Company agreed to the withdrawal of the value of the offices at Manor House from its claim against the LCC. The Arbitrator then adjourned the hearing of the arbitration to enable the Company and the LCC to attempt to come to an agreement on the purchase price once more.
This was achieved on 12 April; the LCC took over the line from 1 August and joined its own routes to it at Finsbury Park.
On 30 May 1912, the LCC wrote to the Company asking whether it would be prepared to lease the tramway from Stamford Hill to Seven Sisters

Corner to it on similar terms to those by which the LCC had leased another section of tramway to it at Highgate Archway, as part of the MET's North West Middlesex network. Although discussions took place, nothing came of the idea.
The LCC was under an obligation to reconstruct the tramway between Finsbury Park and Manor House and additionally to install the conduit electric power supply system by 2 August 1915. However, the agreed through service of cars, jointly operated by the LCC and the MET from Euston to Enfield Town via Finsbury Park, Wood Green and Palmers Green, was able to commence much earlier, on the morning of 1 August 1912, with the cars changing from the conduit power supply to the overhead power supply at Finsbury Park after the LCC installed a temporary conduit plough change pit opposite Blackstock Road for this purpose (see Figure 6 opposite). Because of the shortage of time before the joint service started, and since the MET did not have any cars fitted with plough carriers to operate over the LCC conduit system, 15 of the new LCC cars (numbers 1590 – 1604) were delivered to the MET and operated by it from Wood Green depot until the company's own cars could be hurriedly fitted with plough carriers.
On 3 August, the LCC route from Manor House to Mildmay Park (Balls Pond Road) was reopened to the public on the conduit electric system after conversion from horse traction. At the time, this was an isolated LCC route because the LCC tracks from Balls Pond Road to Essex Road and Balls Pond Road to Baring Street via Southgate Road were not reopened until 26 November. In the intermediate period, the cars travelled into service from Holloway depot via Nag's Head Holloway and Finsbury Park to Manor House.
Following the success of the through joint service between Euston and Enfield Town, and spurred on by the ever increasing competition from omnibuses, further meetings took place between the MET and the LCC in December to discuss

additional through routes. Although the concept had been initially handicapped by the Company's lack of cars fitted with plough carriers for working on the LCC's conduit lines, it soon adapted some of its covered-top bogie cars for the purpose.

Relations with the LCC tramways 1912 – 1914

The LCC decided to use route numbers across its tramway system from 1 January 1913, although some of its cars had shown route numbers before this date. It allocated odd numbers to routes north of the River Thames, commencing with the Hampstead services and continuing in a clockwise direction. To avoid duplication of route numbers, the MET used even numbers, commencing with the Stamford Hill Routes and continuing in an anti-clockwise direction. It was agreed that through running joint routes should be numbered in the LCC series.

The MET numbered its routes:

10	Stamford Hill – Edmonton
12	Stamford Hill – Ponders End
14	Stamford Hill – Enfield Wash
16	Stamford Hill – Waltham Cross
18	Stamford Hill – Bruce Grove – Wood Green – Finsbury Park
20	Finsbury Park – Edmonton
22	Finsbury Park – Enfield Wash
24	Finsbury Park – Waltham Cross
26	Enfield Town – Ponders End
28	Finsbury Park – Muswell Hill
30	Alexandra Palace (West) – Turnpike Lane (The Wellington) (single deck service)
32	Alexandra Palace (East) – Wood Green (single deck service)
34	Finsbury Park - Wood Green – North Finchley

The through route from Tottenham Court Road to Enfield Town was numbered 29 and 31.

Two additional through services started on 1 March 1913. Number 59 was from Edmonton Town Hall to Holborn via Finsbury Park and Caledonian Road and operated entirely by MET cars; consequently the MET local routes 20 and 22 were withdrawn. Number 27 was from Seven Sisters Corner to Euston via Finsbury Park and operated entirely by LCC cars.

While both the MET and the LCC wanted to counter omnibus competition by introducing more through routes between their systems, the Company had to inform the LCC that it had no more cars already fitted with top covers, which the LCC preferred to use, although it was pursuing a policy of rebuilding its earlier cars in this manner. The Council reluctantly agreed to the Company using open top cars on the through routes but did not wish for any section of its lines to be served only by open top cars. To avoid such a situation occurring between Smithfield and the Angel Islington when a new through route was introduced between Smithfield and Waltham Cross on 23 June 1913, only half of the MET route 24 journeys were extended from Finsbury Park to Smithfield and were renumbered 79. By now the MET had sufficient top-covered cars for this, permitting the LCC service to be halved. As the MET rebuilt more cars with top covers for operating over the LCC conduit lines, the LCC route 23 and the MET route 24 were gradually phased out and replaced by additional MET trams on route 79.

On 13 September, the LCC route 27 was extended at peak hours from Seven Sisters Corner to the Tottenham – Edmonton boundary at Snell's Park, where there was a third track which could be used as a terminal stub.

On 23 November, the LCC route 21, which operated from Holborn via Caledonian Road to Finsbury Park, was extended via Wood Green to North Finchley (Woodhouse Road), although the MET route 34 continued to operate between Wood Green and North Finchley, but only as far as Woodhouse Road.

MET route 28, which was operated with four-wheeled open top cars between Muswell Hill and Finsbury Park via Manor House, was renumbered route 51 from 15 August 1914 and diverted at Manor House to operate over LCC tracks via Green Lanes to Bloomsbury. However, from May 1916 and for the duration of the Great War, it was decided to revert to the previous operation of the route in two parts by the Company and the Council each in its own area. The through service was restored on 7 July 1920.

There was a difficulty in operating through services across Stamford Hill, caused by the LCC using the side, rather than centre, conduit along Kingsland Road in Dalston.

The Great War 1914 -1918

Following the outbreak of the Great War on 4 August 1914, 379 employees left the Company to join the colours in the period up to 30 September; this was 24 per cent of the workforce at that time. Although recruitment of replacement staff was stepped up, it became difficult to maintain the advertised services until agreement was eventually reached with both the licensing authorities and the trades unions to employ women as conductors.

Alexandra Palace and its grounds were closed to the general public by the government for the duration of the war. Troops were stationed at the Palace for a short time and from 14 September 1914 it became a reception centre for Belgian refugees. On 29 March 1915 it became an internment camp for Austrian and German civilians; a large area being closed off with barbed wire. As a result of these activities, the tram services were cut back. The service to the western end of the Palace and park was withdrawn altogether, leaving just that to Muswell Hill, while on the eastern side there was

only provision between Wood Green and Wood Green Station. At the end of the war, various Government departments took over the Palace as offices and remained there until 1922. However, after bitter protests and arguments, the park was reopened to the public on 27 March 1920. The two tram services were reinstated on 30 March, in time for the Easter holidays. The Company still had to pay the MCC rent for the lines during this period and submitted a claim to the Government which included damage to the tracks and loss of revenue. In 1921, the War Losses Commission awarded the MET compensation in respect of loss and damage to the Alexandra Park lines from 1914 to 1920.

From the winter of 1914/15 reductions were made to the Sunday services. One result of this was that only route 10 from Edmonton served Stamford Hill. On weekdays, route 24 was withdrawn and was replaced by short workings, operated by the LCC, on route 79 between Finsbury Park and Waltham Cross.

Air raids by Zeppelin airships began in the summer of 1915 and immediately a complete blackout was enforced at night. After a while, restricted lighting was permitted in the tram cars, lower power electric bulbs being substituted for the standard type.

The LCC was also finding that the shortage of manpower and of materials, such as motors and other spare parts for its cars, was causing it operational difficulties. During 1915 the LCC Class E/1 cars, which had been on loan to the MET since 1912, were due for their triennial overhaul and sent to the LCC's Charlton Works for that purpose. Subsequently, these cars were not returned to the MET but re-allocated to the LCC's Norwood depot and replaced on a one-for-one basis by a mixture of cars from other LCC depots.

The installation of the conduit system between Finsbury Park and Manor House was completed by 30 April 1915, from which date through cars changed from the conduit to the overhead power supply at a new change pit in Seven Sisters Road, near the Manor House junction. The temporary change pit at Finsbury Park was then removed. Short working MET cars, turning back at Finsbury Park, continued to use the overhead wires from Manor House.

Recognising the greater ties of the MET with the Underground Group of companies, it was decided on 7 May 1915 to move the registered office of the Company, as soon as convenient, to Electric Railway House, Broadway, Westminster, SW1. Some years later, as 55 Broadway, this building became the London Transport headquarters. From 30 June 1916, responsibility for selling advertising space on the cars was taken over by the advertising department of the Underground Group, who then acted as the advertising agents of the Company.

During 1916, when British steelworks were prohibited by the government from rolling tramway rails, the Company ordered a small quantity of replacement rails from the United States of America.

In February 1917 the Company made an application to the Ministry of Munitions for, and was granted, a certificate proving that the tramways facilities afforded by the Company's system were important for the purpose of carrying on munitions work. This enabled the Company to have a higher priority in obtaining labour and materials, by then in short supply, to maintain its services. Each day it had become necessary to provide transport for the significant numbers of workers employed at the munitions factories established in the Lea Valley to the east of Enfield.

After considerable difficulties with the licensing authorities, the Company began employing women as conductors to replace men who had joined the armed forces. By early 1917 it was employing 160 conductresses. However, women could not be employed as drivers of the cars because the Commissioner of Police, who was the licensing authority for the Metropolitan area, had refused to give his permission on the grounds

that the tramway unions seemed to be strongly opposed. Despite the desperate shortage of drivers to transport workers to the munitions factories, it was not until 13 April 1918 that the Director of General National Labour Supply wrote to the Company to inform it that it had been tentatively agreed no objection would now be raised to women being employed as tramcar drivers in the Metropolitan Police area.

In order to further overcome war-time shortages of labour, particularly drivers, the Company applied to the Board of Trade to tow unpowered passenger trailers, converted from the Type D, four-wheel, open top trams, behind other cars in the districts outside the northern boundary of the County of London – specifically to the munitions factories of the Lea Valley. However, authorisation was not granted until mid-1919 – after the end of the war and when staff recruitment was returning to normal.

Wartime difficulties for the LCC tramways also continued to mount and by February 1917 it was estimated that about one seventh of the Council's fleet of tram cars was out of use, principally due to lack of skilled maintenance personnel. The trams were hard pressed to carry all the available traffic, particularly because omnibus services were even more restricted by a shortage of operating personnel. Unable to utilise all of its own fleet because of its own staff shortages, the Company returned the 15 Class E/1 tramcars on loan from the LCC.

In order that each undertaking could give the best possible service within its own operating area with limited resources, adjustments were made to the through routes between them. These service changes, from 2 May 1917, included route 21 operating between Holborn and Manor House only while route 34 was restored to operate between Finsbury Park and North Finchley (Tally Ho Corner). Further changes took place on 23 March 1918 when the MET extended route 21 back to Wood Green and withdrew the section of route 18 between Finsbury Park and Wood Green, except for

At the end of the war, in November 1918, the following services were being operated:

No	Operation	Route	Operator	Depot
10	Daily	Edmonton – Stamford Hill	MET	Edmonton
	Rush hours	Ponders End – Stamford Hill	MET	Edmonton
12	Daily	Ponders End – Stamford Hill	MET	Edmonton
14	Daily	Enfield Wash – Stamford Hill	MET	Edmonton
16	Daily	Waltham Cross – Stamford Hill	MET	Edmonton
18	Daily	Bruce Grove – Wood Gn – Finsbury Pk	MET	Wood Green
21	Rush hours	Wood Green – Holborn	LCC	Holloway
26	Daily	Enfield Town – Ponders End	MET	Edmonton
27	Daily	Seven Sisters – Tottenham Court Rd	LCC	Holloway
	Rush hours	Snells Park – Tottenham Court Rd	LCC	Holloway
29	Daily	Enfield – Tottenham Court Rd	MET	Wood Green
31	Weekdays	Palmers Green – Tottenham Court Rd	MET	Wood Green
32	Daily	Wood Green Station – Wood Green	MET	Wood Green
34	Daily	N Finchley – Wood Gn – Finsbury Pk	MET	Wood Green
39	Rush hours	Manor House – Aldersgate	LCC	Holloway
41	Daily	Manor House – Moorgate	LCC	Holloway
43	Daily	Stamford Hill – Holborn	LCC	Stamford Hill
45	Weekdays	Stamford Hill – Moorgate	LCC	Stamford Hill
47	Daily	Stamford Hill – London Docks	L.C.C	Stamford Hill
49	Daily	Stamford Hill – Liverpool St	LCC	Stamford Hill
51	Weekdays	Manor House – Bloomsbury	LCC	Holloway
59	Daily	Edmonton – Holborn	MET	Edmonton
75	Weekdays	Stamford Hill – Holborn	LCC	Stamford Hill
79	Daily	Waltham Cross – Smithfield	MET	Edmonton
83	Rush hours	Stamford Hil – Moorgate	LCC	Stamford Hill

weekday rush hours, reducing it to a shuttle between Wood Green and Bruce Grove. At the same time, the Company took over the operation of route 29 completely, while the Council became the sole operator of route 31, which it withdrew on Sundays until 26 November.

As a result of increased costs of operating the system in war-time conditions, the Company approached the MCC and the LCC for their comments on a scale of increased fares which it had drawn up in conjunction with the London General Omnibus Company. These were approved by the councils and introduced on the Great North Road routes in North West Middlesex on 3 October 1917 and for the remainder of the northern section of the Company's system at the end of that month. It was also decided that there were too many different ticket denominations in use and that ordinary tickets above the value of 3d should be withdrawn; passengers wishing to travel beyond the 3d stage should be issued with two tickets of a lower denomination, to the correct value.

In October 1917, the Company decided to transfer the management of the traction sub-stations at Enfield, Finchley and Wood Green depots to the North Met EPS Company.

On 20 April 1918, the Board of Trade's Tramways Committee sent a circular letter to all tramway undertakings in the south of England, calling upon them to reduce, at once, their coal consumption at the power stations by 15 per cent. The Company responded to this call to curtail the car mileage by withdrawing services on Sunday mornings. As so many complaints were received about this action, and the withdrawal of the services had not resulted in any significant reduction in coal consumption by the North Met EPS Company, the Sunday services were reinstated on 16 June. Other service changes occurred on 12 May 1918, when route 27, worked entirely by the LCC, was extended from Snells Park to Edmonton on Sundays and on 27 October, when the operation of route 59 was transferred from the LCC to the MET.

The LCC were using covered top Class E and E/1

cars on all their services in the area while MET open top cars were still seen on all routes, including those in the LCC area, except the 79.

The Post War Era

With the cessation of hostilities, the Company again looked towards providing the public with the cheap, comfortable and efficient service it had come to expect. Being a large undertaking with its own workshops and resources, the condition of the cars and track of the MET's system in Middlesex had not deteriorated to anything like the degree that had befallen some of its neighbours. For the two years following the war there were shortages of materials and high prices of essential commodities but, when the opportunity arose, priority was given to relaying the entire track.

Slowly, the services returned to normal. The Sunday service was restored to Route 16 between Stamford Hill and Waltham Cross in August 1919.

In October 1919 the Company agreed that future purchases of required materials would be made through the purchasing agents of the Underground Group of companies.

Operations: 1919 – 1933

As men returned from military service, motor buses again began competing in strength on the through routes from districts north of Stamford Hill to the City and the West End and the tram services were again revised. From 8 December an 'EX' (extra) service commenced operation at rush hours between Finsbury Park and Tottenham Court Road. This was extended to start from Bruce Grove, and numbered 27A, from 9 January 1920 and then became an all day operation on weekdays from 14 April.

The operation of through services across Stamford Hill was still prevented by the LCC using the side, rather than centre, conduit along Kingsland Road in Dalston. The intense competition from motor buses finally forced the LCC to relay the conduit in the centre of the track and install a change pit at Stamford Hill, thus permitting joint services with the MET to commence in June 1920. In preparation, the LCC equipped its Class E double decked cars at its Stamford Hill depot with trolley poles to use the MET's overhead electric system. However, LCC cars only requiring access to the depot continued to use their conduit ploughs for power north of the new change pit.

On 2 June, the LCC route 49 from Liverpool Street to Stamford Hill was extended to Edmonton Town Hall with a weekday daytime frequency of every four minutes, increasing to every three minutes during the rush hours. The overall journey time was 50 minutes. On Saturday afternoons these journeys were extended further to Waltham Cross commencing at 2.04 p.m., as they were on Sundays from 11.02 a.m. Route 49 was entirely operated by LCC cars but, in consequence of its operation, the local MET routes 10 and 16 were withdrawn. At the same time, the MET took over the operation of routes 59 and 79, route 27 was withdrawn between Bruce Grove and Edmonton Town Hall between the rush hours and route 27A was withdrawn completely. However, on 25 August, route 27 was re-extended to Edmonton Town Hall all day on weekdays.

Cars operating the LCC routes 43, 45 and 47, which continued to terminate at Stamford Hill, frequently obstructed the through cars on route 49. This was resolved by laying a double track siding ending in a single track, which was opened for use on 28 August 1920, on the eastern side of the main line.

The LCC route 21 was re-extended from Wood Green to North Finchley on a daily basis from 27 October and the MET route 34 was consequently withdrawn from the LCC area. As a result of these reorganisations of routes, the LCC took over additional mileage on routes 29 and 31 but from 9

February 1921 the LCC returned the entire operation of route 31 to the MET as the Company had fitted sufficient of its uncanopied, open top cars with plough carriers for the purpose. Of the joint routes now operating in the MET's North Middlesex area, numbers 21, 27 and 49 were worked by the LCC and numbers 29, 31, 51, 59 and 79 by the MET.

As a result of the Coal (Emergency) Supplementary (No.3) Directions of 1921, from 9 May 1921 the frequency of tramway services was again cut by 25 per cent to reduce the amount of coal being burnt at the Brimsdown Power Station.

The rush hour route 39, between Aldersgate and Manor House and worked by the LCC, was extended on 12 December via Wood Green to Bruce Grove. It replaced part of the MET's local route 18 and became an all day operation on weekdays from 29 March 1922. At this time, another new rush hour route, numbered 25 and worked by both MET and LCC cars, was introduced between New Southgate Station and Tottenham Court Road.

Route 49 was extended to Waltham Cross at all times, except the weekday slack hours, on 15 October 1922. Seriously affected by omnibus competition, route 49 was revised from 3 December 1923 to operate between Liverpool Street and Ponders End with an extension to Waltham Cross only on Saturday afternoons and on Sundays. Further changes from 9 July 1924 resulted in route 49 operating only between Liverpool Street and Edmonton although it still continued to Ponders End in rush hours.

In October 1923, routes 25 and 31 were withdrawn and route 27A was re-introduced during weekday rush hours between Tottenham Court Road and Tottenham (Snells Park). However, route 27A was again short-lived, lasting only until 3 December although the MET now took part in the operation of route 27.

During 1923, the LCC was able to realise its plans to construct a new line from the Stamford Hill terminus via Amhurst Park to connect with the MET line in Seven Sisters Road and, in turn, its

own tracks at Manor House. The line was operated on the overhead electrical system from the start and an additional change pit from the conduit system was installed at Stamford Hill. Although services were scheduled to commence on 23 March 1924, the opening was postponed until 1 April because of a strike. The service was provided by extending the existing route 53 between Aldgate and Stamford Hill. Half the frequency continued along the new line to Manor House and Tottenham Court Road (as route 53) and the other half continuing to Wood Green via Tottenham and Bruce Grove (as route 71). Route 71 was linked to route 39 a few months later creating a through route from Aldgate to Aldersgate via Lordship Lane; the whole of which was numbered 71. Although the combined route was well into the MET's area of operation, it was only operated by LCC cars from their Hackney (route 71) and Holloway (route 39) depots while route 53 was operated by both their Holloway and Stamford Hill depots.

For the operational reasons of late running and consequential irregular frequencies, this long through route number 71 was split at Bruce Grove on 4 March 1925 (except on Sundays) and the number 39 reallocated to the western side. With the expanding LCC housing estates along Lordship Lane and increasing numbers of passengers using the line, route 71 was again extended from Bruce Grove to Wood Green on 16 January 1928 so that both routes 39 and 71 served Lordship Lane. In 1931, the through route from Aldgate to Aldersgate via Lordship Lane (numbered 71) was reinstated on weekdays and the route number 39 was again withdrawn. Other routes operated by the MET serving Lordship Lane at this time were the 18 between Bruce Grove and Wood Green on weekdays and the 34 between Bruce Grove, Turnpike Lane and Muswell Hill every day. Route 18 had various rush hour terminals at its western end over the years – including New Southgate, North Finchley and, latterly, the new Piccadilly Line station at Wood Green.

Another through route came into being on 29 November 1928 when LCC route 41 from Moorgate was extended from Manor House along Green Lanes to Wood Green, continuing to Alderman's Hill in Palmers Green during rush hours. The service to Wood Green was withdrawn in 1931, apart from the rush hour journeys to Alderman's Hill which were extended through to Winchmore Hill in 1932. Route 41 was only operated by LCC cars.

Fares

The costs of operation had increased substantially during the war and, to off-set these, the Company received approval for further increases in fares. These came into operation for all routes via Manor House on 14 January 1919 and on the rest of the system on 1 February. These fares were still not enough to cover the costs of operation and another increase was authorised to take effect from 22 June 1920. A joint meeting of the three tramway companies of the London & Suburban Traction Group and the London General Omnibus Company of the Underground Group decided to introduce a penny fare for one stage throughout their systems from 1 December 1921.

Modernisation of the MET

The ever closer ties of the MET with both the other tramway companies in the London & Suburban Traction Group and that group with the Underground Group were symptomatic of having to control financial expenditure tightly while facing severe competition from independent bus companies in the years immediately before and after the Great War and the economic downturn of the recession of the late 1920s.

At a meeting of the London Underground Group it was decided that the London General Omnibus Company, which was already operating and main-taining the buses of the Gearless Motor Omnibus Company and the Tramways (MET) Omnibus Company, should acquire the shares and take over the management of these undertakings from 1 January 1922. During the course of that year, the Tramways (MET) Omnibus Company's fleet of buses was modernised with 210 new vehicles.

While the General Manager, C. J. Spencer, was an advocate of modern tramways, there were many with responsibilities for public transport who were not. Faced with a lack of dividends, responsibilities for road maintenance, having to offer very cheap workmen's fares in the morning rush hours, an aging fleet and expiry of the lease to operate the Middlesex County Council's light railways at the end of 1930, the BET, as principal shareholder in the MET, decided, in November 1928, that it was not prepared to make a long term commitment to its tramways in London and would dispose of its shareholdings in the London & Suburban Traction Group and, therefore, the MET.

The Underground Group took over the MET by purchasing the BET's shares in the London & Suburban Traction Group in January 1929. Immediately it formulated plans, requiring substantial capital expenditure, to modernise the existing cars with top deck covers for those still open, new seating and improved lighting, enclosure of the driving platforms and fitting more powerful motors.

The depot facilities were not overlooked, including, amongst other equipment, high-pressure car washing machines installed at Wood Green depot in 1927, Finchley depot in 1928 and Edmonton depot in 1929. A vacuum cleaning plant was also installed at Finchley depot in 1929 for the car interiors, particularly the new seat cushions.

Overshadowing all these events was the knowledge that the Company's lease to operate the Middlesex County Council's light railways expired at the end of 1930. Discussions had commenced in 1924, but without much enthusiasm on either side until the MET was taken over by the Underground Group. While the MCC did not wish to operate the

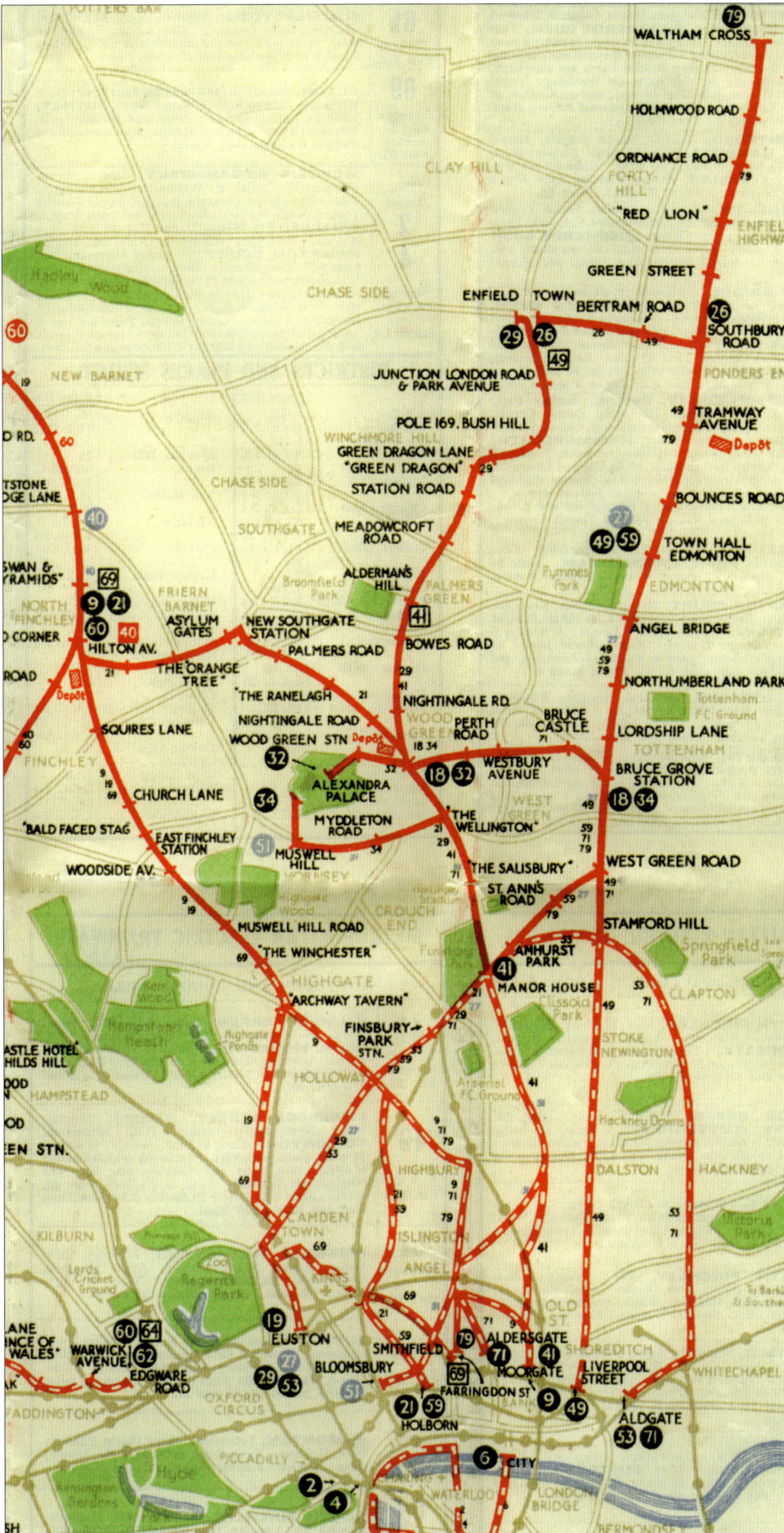

Figure 7. Section of MET map of routes showing north Middlesex and north London (1931).

tramways directly, although it threatened to do so, it was seriously committed to its heavy investment in the tramway infrastructure. In February 1929, the MET stated its terms that they would sell its part of the undertaking to the MCC for £1.2 million or alternatively would accept a 42 year lease if the Council would assume full financial responsibility for the maintenance, repair and reconstruction of the track and roads and a 'reasonable' rent. In July the MCC's Tramways Sub-Committee agreed, by five votes to four, to grant a new lease to the MET. Hard bargaining between the representatives of the two parties still followed and reduced the annual rent to £6,222 12s 10d for the Company to operate the Council's lines and depots for a period of 42 years from 1 January 1931, although the Company was still responsible for the cost of maintaining the track and paving and had to renew 24 miles of the track within the next three years. It is clear that the Council had noticed the new owners' recent investment in improving the rolling stock and services.

The LCC rebuilt its Kingsway Tramway Subway, including the two underground tram stations at Holborn and Aldwych, to accommodate double decked cars and reopened it in January 1931. The subway emerged underneath Waterloo Bridge onto the Victoria Embankment from where the trams ran to Westminster and across the Thames on the Westminster Bridge to South London. To the original two cross-river routes (33 and 35) the LCC then added route 31. In October, the LCC diverted its route 33 from its original terminal at Highbury to Manor House and rerouted route 51, which covered the same roads between Bloomsbury and Manor House, into the Aldersgate terminus.

The Piccadilly Line of the Underground Group was extended from Finsbury Park to Cockfosters in stages between September 1932 and July 1933. Included in the works were direct connecting passageways and escalators for passengers between the underground station platforms and covered tramway stations built on the surface at Manor House and Turnpike Lane. Such a connec-tion was much appreciated by the passengers. The tram station at Manor House was used by tram routes 27, 53, 59 and 79. That at Turnpike Lane was used by the through tram routes 39 and 51 and the terminating single deck route 34 to Muswell Hill and Alexandra Palace.

Rolling Stock 1919 – 1933

In 1920, two of the Type E single deck trams (Nos. 145 and 150) were loaned to the South Metropoli-tan Electric Tramways Company (SMET) system in South London, initially based at Penge depot to work the short 'shuttle' service between Crystal Palace and The Robin Hood public house. In this they were not entirely satisfactory and returned to the MET in 1923.

An additional Type G double decked bogie car, fitted with a plough carrier and numbered 317, was built in 1921 by the MET's Hendon Works and rebuilt in 1929 with a fully enclosed top deck. The Hendon Works also built six cars to replace one Type A and five Type B cars which had been scrapped following accidents.

Between December 1921 and April 1922 tests were carried out with sliding trolley heads, in place of trolley wheels, for the overhead electrical con-tact. It was found that the sliding heads de-wired less frequently than the wheels but, in the event of this happening, it was not so easy to replace on the overhead wire. It was also established that the cast iron skids had a considerably longer life than the trolley wheels and the maintenance costs of them was less.

Following a visit by the General Manager to the USA, where a large number of one man cars were in use, one of the MET's Type E single decked cars (No. 132), which had been damaged in a collision with a steam wagon, was rebuilt for one man operation in 1922. Extended platforms were fitted at each end by shortening the saloon so that it only seated 30 passengers. The driver sat behind a windscreen in the body of the car. The entrance was fitted with a sliding door and a folding step, working in conjunction with each other and operated by the driver with a lever. The car could not be operated when the door was open. An electrically operated 'Automatic' ticket machine was fitted at one end of the car and tickets were issued by the driver by pressing a button. Passengers boarded and alighted at the front-end of the car and paid their fare on entering. The rear door was locked. Also fitted was a 'Road Guide' display, supplied by Road Guides Limited, showing passengers where they were and the route ½ mile ahead, which was driven off one of the axles. This car was subsequently sold to the associated London United Tramways and placed in service in the Kingston area, where it operated on route 77 from Richmond Park Gates to Tolworth.

Following agreement to raise the maximum permitted speed of the MET system from 16 mph to 20 mph in 1926, the Company decided to design and build two modern tramcars. Entering service in March 1927, No. 318 (nicknamed 'Bluebell') was built at the MET's Hendon Works and allocated to Finchley depot but was confined to the north west Middlesex area routes of the MET as it was not fitted with conduit equipment. Number 139 (nicknamed 'Poppy' and temporarily renumbered 319), the other experimental car, was built with a body from the Chiswick Bus Works on bogie trucks from Brush. It entered service from Finchley depot in April 1927 but was transferred to the London United Tramways in November 1927 (where it was given the number 350).

The Feltham Cars

Using the experience gained from the standards of the experimental cars, the MET began to modernise its fleet of older cars from 1929 onwards. However, future developments were concentrated on two further experimental cars (numbered 320 and 330), also allocated to Finchley depot, which were to form the basis of a new standardised fleet of 54 Feltham cars. Another experimental car, but with a central entrance (No. 331), was added in 1930. A further 46 Feltham cars were built at the same time for the London United Tramways although they had different electric motors and controllers to the MET cars.

The new Type UCC cars were generally known as the Feltham cars after the site of the Union Construction Company works where they were built. Numbered 319, 321 to 329 and 332 to 375 the first of these luxury cars, fitted with both overhead and conduit electrical systems for working in the LCC area, were delivered to Finchley depot from December 1930 to operate route 40 in the MET's North West area between Cricklewood, Golders Green, North Finchley and Whetstone. As more Felthams were delivered, the lowest numbered cars were transferred to Wood Green to operate that depot's share of route 21 between North Finchley, Wood Green and Holborn; route 21 being jointly allocated to Finchley and Wood Green depots.

Later, these cars also operated the MET's share of route 29 between Enfield, Wood Green and Tottenham Court Road but operating problems were encountered here because the new cars were more powerful and faster than those used by the LCC from their Holloway depot on the same route.

The author recollects:

I first saw the Feltham tramcars and travelled on them in 1931, when they started operating on route 21 between North Finchley and Holborn via Wood Green. I was walking along Seven Sisters Road when one overtook me. People were standing looking at the new type of tram car as it passed. At the time I was living near Finsbury Park and my paternal grandparents lived near Turnpike Lane so I usually waited for a Feltham car to come along for this journey when I visited them. The Felthams were in complete contrast to the old single deck Type E cars I rode on to Alexandra Palace.

In London Transport days, I remember seeing the experimental car number 330 (by then renumbered 2167) turning from Lordship Lane into Jolly Butcher's Hill on a rush hour service from Bruce Grove to Winchmore Hill.

The boys from all LCC schools in the area were taken once a week to Finsbury Park to play football on the ash pitch backing onto the railway. We could only travel free on the LCC cars and would have had to pay if we used a MET one.

My father was in the Territorial Army so once a year we went, as a family, from Islington to the drill hall at Beresford Square in Woolwich for a children's Christmas party. Our journey was by tram, including a ride on an LCC single decker through the original Kingsway Tramway Subway (before it was enlarged to accommodate double deckers) as far as Westminster where we changed onto a double decker.

Management

From the inauguration of the MET system there was no overall general manager. Mr A. L. Barber was Secretary, Mr A. H. Potts was Chief Engineer and Mr W. E. Hammond was Traffic Manager – although it was A. L. Barber whose name appeared with the legal lettering on the side of the cars until he retired in 1913. A. H. Potts was then promoted to General Manager and Engineer until his retirement in 1918.

The Traffic Manager, W. E. Hammond, retired in December 1918. He had first joined the London Tramways Company, which operated horse trams in south London, in 1872 before moving to the North Metropolitan Tramways Company in 1882 and remaining with that company until it was taken over by the MET in 1902.

The new Manager of the London & Suburban Traction Group, which included the MET and the London United Tramways of west and south west London, was Mr C. J. Spencer, who was formerly General Manager of the Bradford Corporation Tramways. He took up his duties on 1 November 1918, subsequently and additionally taking on the same role for the South Metropolitan Electric Tramways in the Croydon area on 24 June 1919. From 28 January 1921, following a scheme of reorganisation covering the Underground Group of companies and the tramway companies associated with the London & Suburban Traction Group of companies, C. J. Spencer was appointed General Manager of the combined undertaking.

The Metropolitan Electric Tramways Limited

29. Enfield Town terminus showing the connecting tracks to the Southbury Road terminus (left) which were never used.

30. Tally Ho Corner at North Finchley showing the original terminus of route 21 (left) in High Road North and cars on routes 40 and 60 in Ballards Lane (right).

16184 ELECTRIC TRAM TERMINUS.   WOOD GREEN N.

31. Original terminus of the Finsbury Park to Wood Green route on Jolly Butchers Hill. The tram depot is to the left. The terminus was later moved to Lordship Lane. *A.A. Jackson Collection*

32. Wood Green looking towards Station Road. The library on the right hand corner no longer exists.
A.A. Jackson Collection

33. Wood Green High Road with Lordship Lane to the right. The shops on the right were demolished to make way for the Underground station buildings. *A.A. Jackson Collection*

34. Wood Green after the opening of the Underground station with Lordship Lane on the right.

35. Lordship Lane in Tottenham.

LORDSHIP LANE, TOTTENHAM.

36. Bruce Grove Station terminus in Lordship Lane during the period when it was used by through services to Alexandra Palace.
A.A.Jackson Collection

37. Seven Sisters Road in Holloway looking towards the Finsbury Park railway bridges and showing an open top MET tram and an enclosed LCC one.
A.A. Jackson Collection

Examples of types of car used in north Middlesex.

38. 'Type B', Series 1 – 35. Car No. 2 in original condition at Hertford Road, Edmonton. Track into Tramway Avenue Depot in the foreground.

39. Car No. 7 at the Enfield Town terminus.

40. Car No. 14 at Finsbury Park terminus. This shows the first electric route to be opened to Wood Green and Seven Sisters Corner on 22 July 1904.

41. Car No. 15 at the "Wellington" public house in Wood Green. Turnpike Lane is to the left.

Wood Green, High Road, Wellington Corner

42. Car No. 19 at the Stamford Hill terminus. The board on the side of the car shows the destination 'Angel Bridge, Edmonton'.

Stamford Hill N.

43. Car No. 20 at the Finsbury Park terminus.

Finsbury Gate, Finsbury Park.

44. Car No. 4 rebuilt with top cover as 'Type B/2' at Golders Green (not on the north Middlesex section).

45. Car No. 9 at Stonebridge Park depot (not on the north Middlesex section).

46. Car No. 11 at Ballards Lane terminus, North Finchley (not on the north Middlesex section) to show variation of design in rebuilt cars.

47. 'Type B/1', Series 36 – 70. Car No. 53 at the Enfield Town terminus.

48. Car No. 68 at the Stamford Hill terminus.

49. 'Type B/1' Car at Bruce Grove Station on the Stamford Hill route about to turn right into Tottenham High Road, under the very low railway bridge.

50. 'Type A', Series 71 – 130. Car No. 73 at Enfield Town in original condition. These cars were owned by Middlesex County Council.

FIRST TRAM RUN FOR PUBLIC. ENFIELD July 3RD 1909.

51. 'Type A' Car at the Muswell Hill terminus in Priory Road.

52. Car No. 78 at Wood Green with Lordship Lane to the right.

53. Car No. 78 at Enfield Town.

54. Car No. 78 at Priory Road, Hornsey.

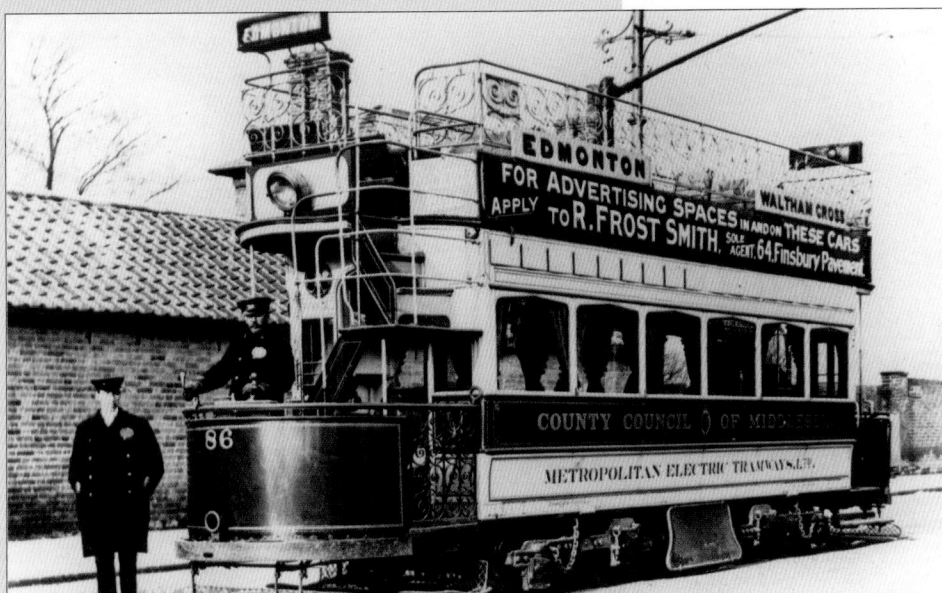

55. Car No. 86 at the Waltham Cross terminus. When this route was first opened it ran as a shuttle service between Edmonton Tramway Avenue and Waltham Cross only, except at holiday periods.

56. 'Type A' Car 117 rebuilt with top cover at Stonebridge depot (not on the north Middlesex section).

57. 'Type E', Series 131 – 150. Single deck car No. 138 showing the entrance to Alexandra Park from Priory Road, Muswell Hill.

58. 'Type E' car No. 141
leaving the eastern
terminus of Alexandra
Palace.
A.A. Jackson Collection

59. 'Type E' car No. 138
at Turnpike Lane tram
station where the
Alexandra Park services
later terminated.
A.A. Jackson Collection

60. 'Type C', Series
151 – 165. Car No. 156
at Wood Green.

61. 'Type C', Series Nos. 159 – 163. Car lettered for Hertfordshire County Council. This illustrates the delivery of the car body when new and still awaiting its trucks and electrical equipment.

62. Car No. 152 rebuilt with top cover as 'Type C/2'.

Above: 63. Car No. 157 rebuilt with top cover as 'Type C/2' illustrating variations in design of the rebuilt cars.

Left: 64. 'Type D', Series 166 – 190. Four wheel cars Nos. 182 and 171 at Turnpike Lane, Wood Green.

65. 'Type C/1', Series 192 – 211. Car No. 198 opposite Mayes Road, Wood Green.

66. 'Type C/1' car No. 198 in rebuilt form at the junction of Turnpike Lane with Wood Green High Road. Underground station with tram station and connecting subways under construction in the background.

67. Car No. 279 at the Manor House tram station looking towards Finsbury Park, July 1932. This shows the direct connection from the tram station to the Underground station.

68. 'Type F', Series 212 – 216. Car No. 215 at the Waltham Cross terminus, looking towards the Cross.

69. 'Type G', Series 217 – 236. Car No. 229 in original open top form at Kings Cross Bridge, Grays Inn Road. On the left is Euston Road and on the right is Pentonville Road.

70. 'Type G' car No. 234 near Winchmore Hill.

71. 'Type G' car No. 225 rebuilt with top cover at Islington High Street, Angel crossroads.

72. 'Type G' car No. 232 in its final form fitted with windscreens. Near Angel Islington July 1932.

73. 'Type H', Series 237 – 316. Car No 245 (as built with top cover) at Grays Inn Road, near Kings Cross.

74. 'Type H' car No. 258 at the Waltham Cross terminus.

79. Feltham car No. 370 at Finchley depot.

80. Upper deck of Feltham car taken inside Finchley depot.

74. 'Type H' car No. 258 at the Waltham Cross terminus.

75. 'Type H' car No. 291 at the Holborn terminus, Grays Inn Road with a modern Feltham car behind.

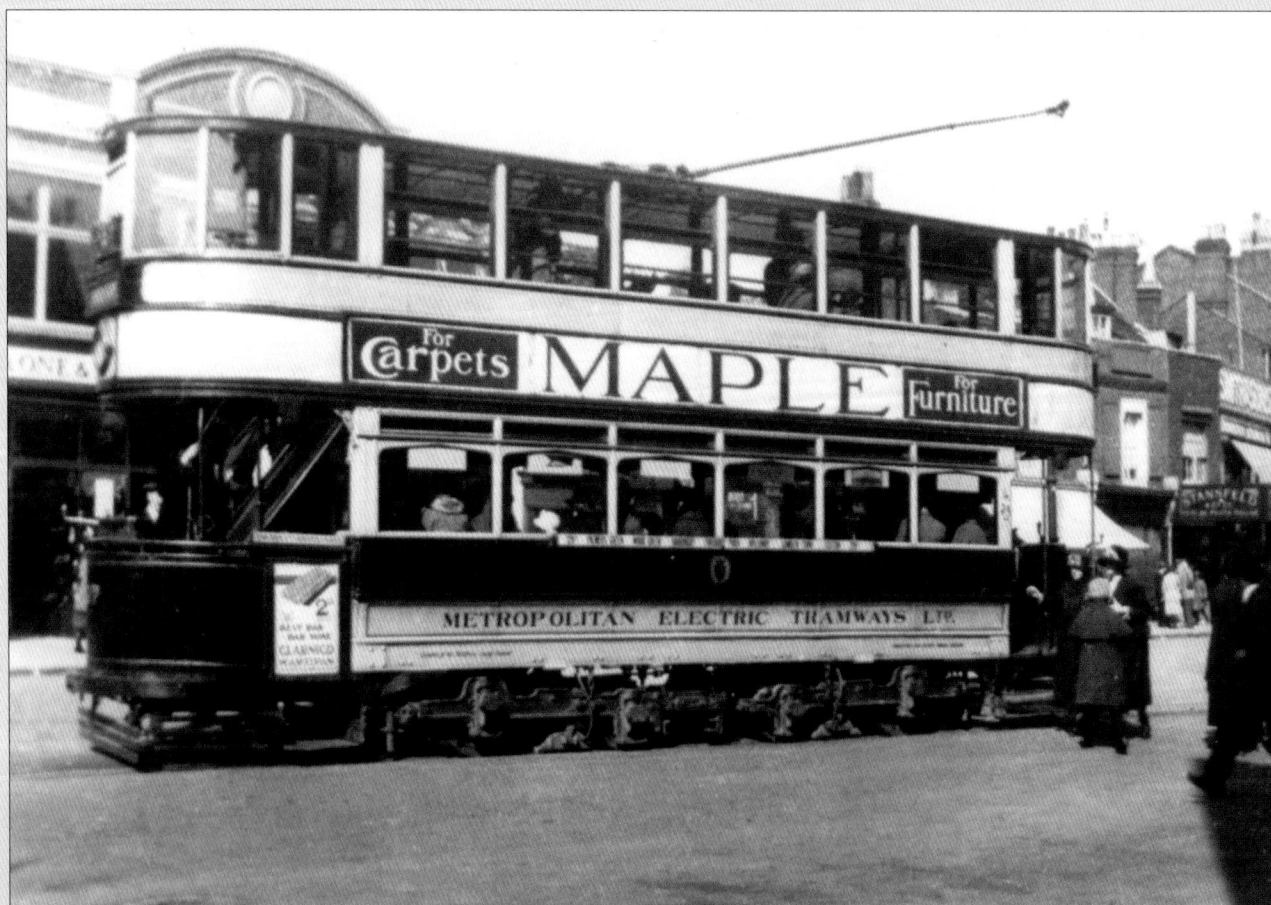

76. 'Type H' car No. 316 at the Enfield Town terminus.

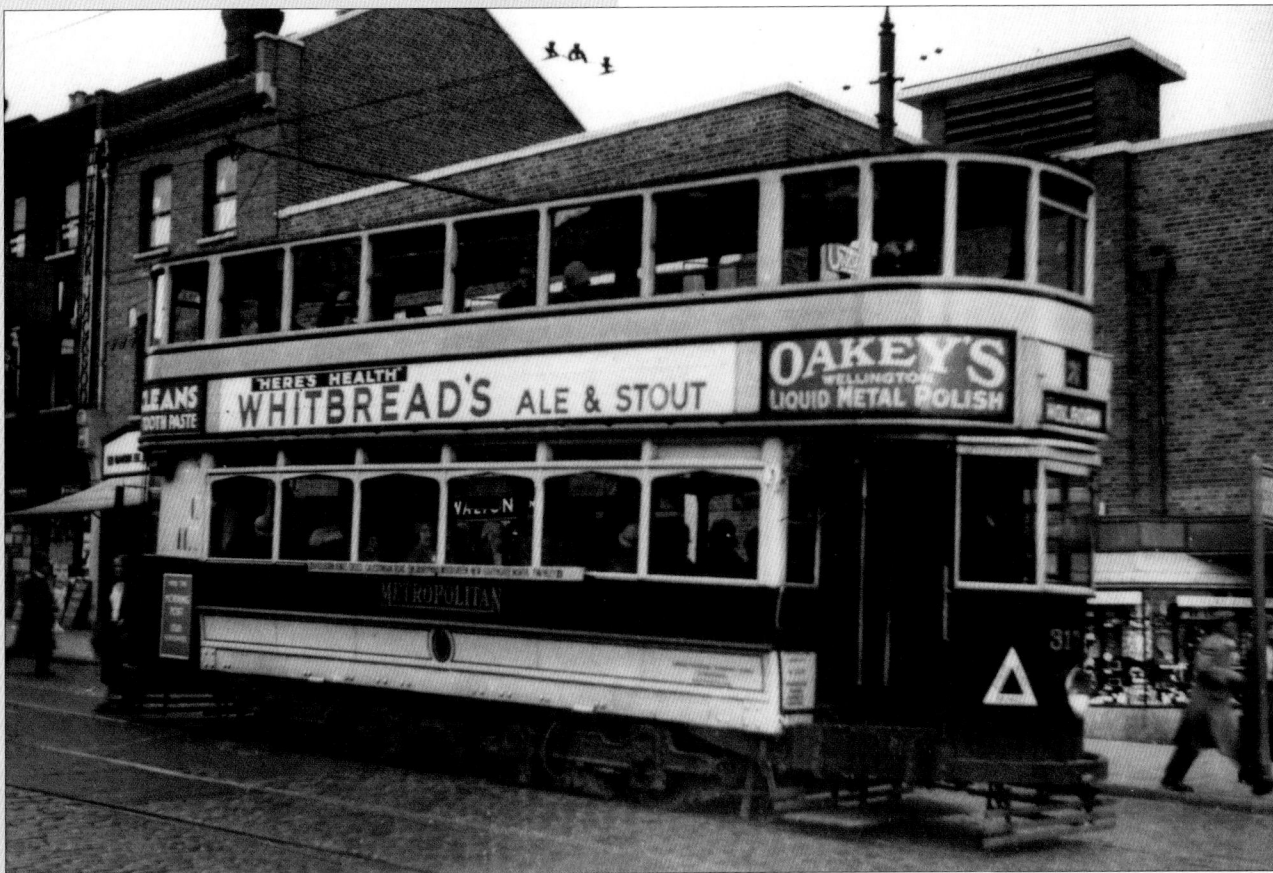

Above:
77. 'Type G' car No. 317.
Built as an open top car
in 1921, fitted with top
cover in 1929, and later
with windscreens.
Seen at Jolly Butchers
Hill, Wood Green with
the Underground station
behind the tram.

Left:
78. Six 'Type H' cars were
built at Hendon Works in
1925 to replace one
'Type A' and five 'Type B'
cars which had been
scrapped.Numbered 2,
12, 22, 31, 46 and 82 in
a second series,
Car No. 22(II) is shown
at Cricklewood Lane
(not on the north
Middlesex section).

79. Feltham car No. 370 at Finchley depot.

80. Upper deck of Feltham car taken inside Finchley depot.

81. Car No. 330 was the second experimental Feltham built 1929. Originally allocated to North Finchley depot it was later transferred to Wood Green depot.

82. The lower deck of car No. 330 showing the reversed stairs and the space for the conductor's seat. Note the swing-out bracket for the ticket machine.

83. Feltham Car No. 344
and 'Type H' car No. 291
at the Holborn terminus.

84. Feltham car No. 345
at Grays Inn Road near
Holborn Hall.

85. Feltham car No. 354
at Green Lanes,
Manor House.

LCC tram routes operating over MET tracks in Middlesex

86. LCC Car No. 1052 at Enfield Town terminus on route 29.

87. LCC Class E/1, Series 552(II) – 601(II). Car No. 589, used on route 29, shown inside Holloway depot.

88. LCC Class E/1, Series 1227 – 1426. Car No. 1272 on route 41 at Green Lanes, Stoke Newington. Brownswood Road is on the left.

89. LCC Class E/1, Series 1477 – 1676. Car No. 1612 on route 53 at the Manor House tram station.

90. LCC Class E/1, Series 552(II) - 601(II). Car No. 590 on route 71 at Lordship Lane, Wood Green.

Chapter
Five

Tramways of London Transport in North Middlesex

(1933 – 1938)

The London Passenger Transport Board

The London Passenger Transport Board (LPTB) was formed on 1 July 1933 as a statutory authority to operate all of London's public passenger transport with the exception of the suburban services of the main line railways, which were to be co-ordinated. Among the many companies compulsorily purchased were the Underground Group, the London & Suburban Traction Group and subsidiaries – including the progressive Metropolitan Electric Tramways and their operating lease of the Middlesex County Council light railways system – and all other tramways systems, underground railway and bus services in the London area.

Insofar as the MET tramways of north Middlesex were concerned, London Transport soon decided to renumber certain tram services in north London because they used the even numbers which were, by then, generally allocated to the LCC routes south of the Thames.

Route 18: Bruce Grove – Wood Green and extended in rush hours to Enfield became 39A
Route 26: Ponders End – Enfield Town via Southbury Road became 49A
Route 32: Wood Green (Piccadilly Line) Station – Alexandra Palace East became 37
Route 34: Bruce Grove – Alexandra Palace via Muswell Hill became 39.

The 34 operated in two sections; a double deck service daily between Bruce Grove Station and Muswell Hill and a single deck service operating each afternoon just between Alexandra Palace and Muswell Hill but extended in rush hours to Turnpike Lane tube station.

The standard Feltham cars were renumbered in sequence between 2066 and 2119 while the experimental cars 320, 330 and 331 became 2166, 2167 and 2168 respectively.

Soon after the formation of the LPTB, the modern bogie cars Nos. 39 – 62 of the former Walthamstow Corporation Tramways were transferred to the LCC's Holloway depot to operate on route 29 as, unlike the ex-LCC cars, they were able to keep pace with the MET's Feltham cars on the same route.

The author recollects:

Any LCC cars short working to Finsbury Park used a crossover between Stroud Green Road and Station Road. This was a congested part of Seven Sisters Road but, towards the end of the tramway operation, these short workings were moved beyond the railway bridges at Finsbury Park nearer Nag's Head, Holloway. Here there was a crossover between Isledon Road, near the Astoria cinema and Coleridge Road where the trolleybuses on short workings also terminated.

After the withdrawal of route 29 I remember seeing the ex-Walthamstow Corporation trams terminating at Finsbury Park on route 27 and, later still, on route 53. Following abandonment of this route they were transferred from Holloway depot to operate in East London.

A regular pull-up for tramcar crews was at a snack bar along the wall by the Co-operative store in Seven Sisters Road, between Hornsey Road and Sonderburg Road, where the conductors had their billy cans filled with tea.

The end of the tramways in north Middlesex

That London Transport so rapidly adopted a policy of replacing its trams with trolleybuses might appear surprising in view of the recent investment by the MET in track renewals and new cars. However, in the overall context of the general physical condition of the tramways the LPTB inherited from other

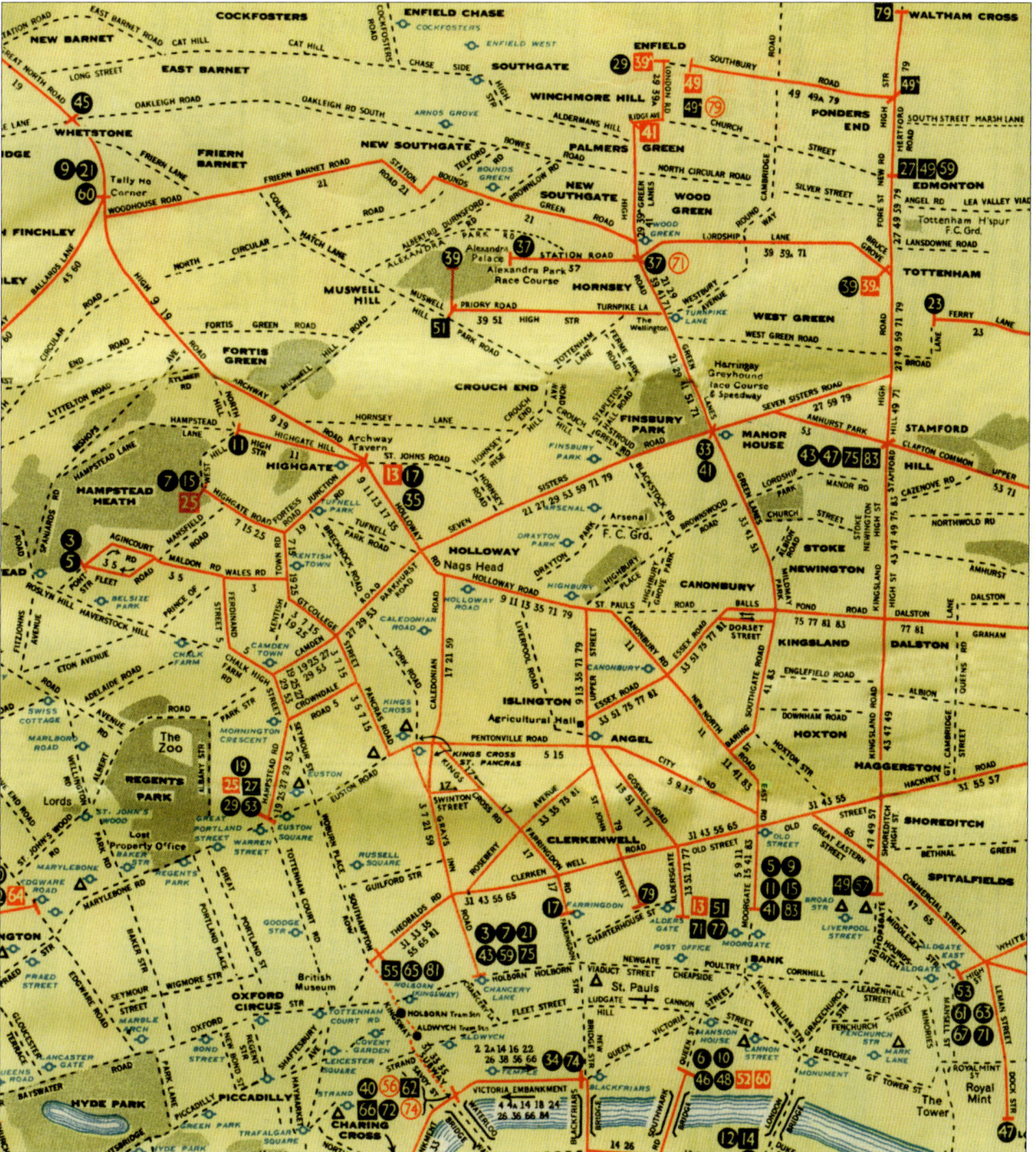

Figure 8. Section of London Transport map of tramway routes showing north Middlesex and north London.
Map No.1 Winter 1934 – 35.

companies and local authorities other than the LCC, the decision is more understandable because of the heavy investment by then required in those parts of the combined system and the probable lack of return on much of the required investment, even if it had been available. In addition, there was the complication of the dual power supplies – by conduit electrical system in most of the LCC area and by overhead electrical system elsewhere – with the operating costs of the conduit system being substantially more than those of the over-head system.

Trolleybuses first began replacing MET tram routes in the north west Middlesex area. On 2 August 1936, one of the main routes operated by Feltham cars, the 45 (previously 40) between Cricklewood and Whetstone was abandoned. While a sufficient number of Feltham cars were retained at Finchley depot to operate route 21, the remainder (including the experimental car 2167) were transferred to Wood Green depot for use on routes 29 and 39A.

The experimental Feltham car 2168 (previously 331) with a central entrance could not be fitted with conduit equipment to be used on former LCC routes and was sold to Sunderland Corporation with whom it saw regular service until 1952.

A copy of the last destination and number blind contents for MET Type F, G and H cars based at Edmonton depot is shown as Figure 9 (right).

The author recollects:

At this time I had little information about which tram services were operated, other than a London Transport Tramways Map. Aware that there were tram routes along streets in west London, I travelled out to Shepherds Bush and found the former LUT route 7 to Uxbridge was also being operated by Feltham cars.

As I did not have time to ride on this route that day I decided to return as soon as I could – but

Figure 9. Contents of Edmonton depot destination blind (1938).

Reproduced (below left) are the contents of almost certainly the last destination blind produced for Type F, G and H cars based at Edmonton depot, including some destinations no longer used by then on a regular basis.

The number blind (below right), also for Type F, G and H cars and marked 'Edmonton depot', includes route numbers for all ex-MET routes at that time.

EDMONTON DEPOT L P T B APRIL 30 1938	OCT. 16 1936 EDMONTON DEPOT SERVICE NOS,
SPECIAL	17
SEVEN SISTERS CORNER	19
PUTNEY RD	21
ALBANY RD	27
SNELLS PARK	
NAGS HEAD	29
MANOR HOUSE	37
FINSBURY PARK	39
BRUCE GROVE	
TRAMWAY AV	39A
TOTTENHAM CT RD	45
EDMONTON TN HALL	49A
WORKMAN	51
HOLBORN	
WALTHAM CROSS	64
SMITHFIELD	59
ENFIELD VIA EDMONTON	60
PONDERS END	
SPURS GROUND	62
CAMDEN TOWN	64
	66
HIGHBURY	69
ANGEL ISLINGTON	79
KINGS CROSS	
	XTRA

when I got back I found the route had been abandoned the previous week – on 14 November 1936.

The first tramway routes to be abandoned in the MET's north Middlesex area were the single deck tram services to the east and west sides of Alexandra Palace on 23 February 1938. They were replaced by single deck buses operating a through route along the south side of the Palace, something which had been denied to Middlesex County Council for the tramway. It also resulted in the total abandonment of the reserved track section to the Western terminus although the reserved track section from the Muswell Hill entrance was rebuilt for use by the buses. At the same time, route 51 was diverted from Hornsey and Muswell Hill to terminate at Wood Green Underground Station and the double deck section of route 39 was cut back to terminate at Turnpike Lane Underground Station. A double deck replacement bus service was introduced between Muswell Hill, Hornsey High Street and Turnpike Lane Underground Station.

On 6 March, route 21 between North Finchley, Wood Green and Holborn was converted to trolleybus operation which brought an end to tramway operations from Finchley depot and also resulted in the withdrawal of route 51 between Wood Green and Aldersgate. In part replacement of route 51, operation of the former LCC route 41 was reallocated to cars based at the former MET depot at Wood Green and extended from Manor House to Winchmore Hill as an all day service. At the same time, the remaining Feltham cars at Finchley depot were transferred to Wood Green for Route 29, displacing the Holloway depot allocation of cars on that route. Also, route 27 began to operate on Sundays.

This was only a temporary respite for on 8 May routes 29 from Tottenham Court Road to Wood Green and Enfield, 39A from Bruce Grove to Wood Green and Winchmore Hill and 41 from Moorgate to Manor House, Wood Green and Winchmore Hill were replaced by trolleybuses.

That evening I made my way to Wood Green to travel on the last tram to Enfield Market Place. While waiting there, another young fellow came up to me and started talking about trams. His name was John Barrie, one of the early members of the Light Railways and Transport League, and he gave me a copy of the 'Modern Tramways' magazine, although he did not travel on the last tram to Enfield when it arrived. This was the first time I was aware of the newly-formed League and its dissemination of information about tramway developments; until then I had had to find out any information about trams myself.

The last tram to Enfield Market Place was a "G" type car and full, but I managed to find a seat upstairs at the rear of the car. Nothing untoward happened until we reached Enfield terminus when it fell prey to souvenir hunters – both those already on the tram and others waiting for it to arrive. All the lights went out. Upstairs the tram was fitted with a hatch at one end to allow maintenance staff to climb out and inspect the trolley pole. Someone thought it was a good idea to climb out onto the roof and a number of others followed, I decided to look out and saw some were sitting round the trolley pole and holding onto it. Others were sitting on the roof with their legs over the side and that is how the last tram left Enfield Market Place, very late, escorted by a police car in front and followed by a number of private cars. However, along Village Road in Enfield, the police stopped the tram and turned everyone off.

I then had to walk back home to Finsbury Park. Passing Wood Green depot in the early hours I saw the new trolleybuses lined up ready to go into service later that morning. A farewell

133

ceremony for this last tram from Enfield should have taken place at the depot but the car was running so late that the ceremony was cancelled and the car was sent on directly to the Edmonton depot in Tramway Avenue.

I subsequently travelled on this car again while it was based at Edmonton depot. The damage caused by the souvenir hunters had been patched up to allow further service. I recall that it was noticeable that someone had wrenched off one end of the parallel hand rails, which ran along the ceiling, from its fittings and split the wood.

Continuing walking from Wood Green to Finsbury Park, I noticed permanent way staff were locking the points in position at Manor House, which meant that trams could no longer turn left from Seven Sisters Road into Green Lanes towards Wood Green. Consequently, trams on the Kingsway Subway route 33, which still terminated at Manor House, could not travel directly to and from Holloway depot via Seven Sisters Road but had to operate via Islington Green and follow the Subway route 35 along Upper Street and Highbury into the depot. The previous procedure had been somewhat complicated in that they had arrived at Manor House using the conduit power supply, put up their trolley pole and shed the plough in Green Lanes to cross Seven Sisters Road onto the crossover outside the Manor House public house, reversed to turn right into Seven Sisters Road then picked up another plough at the change pit, lowered their trolley pole again in order to travel to Nag's Head Holloway. Here they crossed Holloway Road into Parkhurst Road, reversed on the crossover there and then took the left hand curve into Holloway Road to approach Holloway depot. It was the only time this curve was used.

The last day of operation of the Feltham cars in north London was also 8 May 1938.

I saw the Feltham cars in service for the last time in north London, immediately before they were transferred to the south London depots at Streatham (Telford Avenue) and Brixton, after operating the Saturday morning rush hour journeys. I walked along Seven Sisters Road towards Manor House and Wood Green and saw them travelling, out of service, south along Seven Sisters Road towards Nag's Head, Holloway. I noted ex-MET cars numbered 2066 to 2073, 2078 to 2082, 2084 to 2088, 2092, 2095, 2097 and 2098, 2100 and 2101, 2104, 2106, 2110, 2113 and 2116 together with 2143 – a former LUT car which had operated on route 7 between Shepherds Bush and Uxbridge until that had been abandoned earlier. This journey to South London was made through the Kingsway Tramway Subway, the only time these cars were permitted to use the Subway because of very tight clearances; photos taken at the Holborn end of the Subway on this occasion are shown on page 145. After the departure of the Felthams for south London, they were replaced on service by former MET cars of types "G" and "H" for the remainder of the day.

On 16 October the tramway routes from Edmonton to Ponders End, Southbury Road and Waltham Cross were abandoned. Route 49 was cut back to operate only between Liverpool Street and Stamford Hill while routes 59 from Holborn to Holloway and Waltham Cross and 79 from Smithfield to Waltham Cross were abandoned. All these routes were converted to trolleybus operation. Route 49A from Ponders End via Southbury Road to Enfield was converted to motor bus operation.

I travelled on the last tram to Waltham Cross. On this occasion, as the tram approached the stub terminus in Waltham Cross High Street I could see milling crowds in the road. The public houses had turned out. The tram started to cross onto the stub when a detonator someone had placed on the track went off. That was the signal for the tram to be vandalised. The tram continued on into the crowd and cleared the point ready for the return journey to Edmonton depot, which it eventually reached.

A report appearing in the local paper the following week stated that when the last tram arrived at Edmonton depot so-called souvenir hunters had started stripping the interior of the tram, including unbolting the seats from the floor. As these people walked the length of Tramway Avenue from the depot to the Hertford Road they found police waiting for them and had to appear at the Magistrates' Court the following Monday.

This left just one purely ex-MET route, the 27, operating from Edmonton Town Hall to Tottenham Court Road until 5 November 1938 – although former LCC routes continued to operate in parts of Tottenham for a little longer. Although route 27 had latterly been a joint service operated by the MET's Edmonton depot and the LCC's Holloway depot, for the last days of operation it was provided entirely by ex- MET cars. The tram track between Edmonton Town Hall and the depot at Tramway Avenue had to remain in place for these cars even though it was not officially used by passenger services.

The final service operated by ex-MET cars was route 27 between Edmonton Town Hall and Tottenham Court Road. The conversion of this route to trolleybuses took place on 5 November 1938. It was a miserable day, raining and cold, so I did not attend the abandonment of this route or travel on its last tram.

Although this was the end of MET operations, it was not the end of the tramways in Tottenham. Former LCC route 71 still operated between Wood Green Underground Station via Bruce Grove and Stamford Hill to Aldgate and a short section of MET track along Seven Sisters Road from Amhurst Park to Manor House was used by former LCC route 53. Route 71 was abandoned on 5 February 1939, and replaced by an extended trolleybus route from Stamford Hill, leaving just route 53 to be replaced by trolleybuses on 5 March.

A local resident of Edmonton wrote a letter to the Tottenham and Edmonton Herald at this time:

"In 1898, 40 years ago, I commenced as a conductor on the North Met Tramway Company. The trams were, of course, horse drawn and carried 46 passengers, 10 each side inside and 26 on the open top deck. My journey was from Nag's Head, Wood Green to Moorgate terminus. The journey took 2½ hours return and the fare was 2d all the way or 3d return. Workmen's cars were run in the early hours. My average days work was five journeys, 12½ hours with one journey off, making a spread over of 15 hours. We were paid 6 shillings per day, which was very good pay in those days ... In 1904 I assisted in coupling the last pair of horses to draw a tramcar from Wood Green depot."

Former MET tramcars in London Transport days

Above:
92. North Finchley tram station after the introduction of trolleybuses.

Right:
93. 'Type G' car No. 2276 at North Finchley tram station.

Left:
94. 'Type E'
single deck car
No. 2303 at the
Alexandra Palace
west terminus.

Below:
95. 'Type E' car
leaving the
Alexandra Palace
west terminus
on the reserved
track section.
A.A. Jackson
Collection

Above:
96. 'Type E' car No. 148 (in MET livery, but in the ownership of LPTB) on the reserved track at Alexandra Palace.

Right:
97. 'Type G' and 'Type E' cars at Turnpike Lane.

98. 'Type G' car No. 2269 at Turnpike Lane tram station on route 51.

99. The LPTB soon transferred ex-Walthamstow Corporation cars to Holloway depot to operate route 29 as they had a similar top speed to the ex-MET Feltham cars. Ex-Walthamstow car No. 42 at Jolly Butchers Hill, Wood Green in Walthamstow livery.

100. Feltham car No. 2070 at the Enfield Town terminus of route 29.

101. 'Type H' car No. 2246 at Southbury Road, Ponders End on route 49A.

102. 'Type F' car No. 2260 at Southbury Road, Enfield on route 79.

103. 'Type G' car No. 2271 at Southbury Road, Ponders End on route 79.

Above:
104. 'Type C/1' car No. 2294
at Southbury Road, Enfield
on route 79.

Right:
105. 'Type H' car
No. 2178 at Snells Park,
Edmonton showing
the three-track layout
used to terminate
short-working journeys.

106. Experimental Feltham car No. 2167 at Bruce Castle, Bruce Grove on route 39.

107. 'Type H' car No. 2179 at the Nag's Head, Holloway on route 79.

108. 'Type H' cars Nos. 2185 and 2235 at Grays Inn Road, Kings Cross on route 59.

109. Feltham car No. 2115 at the Holborn terminus of route 21.

Former MET tramcars at the Kingsway Subway

The Feltham cars only used the Kingsway Tramway Subway on one occasion – Saturday 8 May 1938 – when they were transferred from north London to south London depots.

110. Feltham car at the Bloomsbury entrance to the Kingsway Subway.

111. Feltham car at the Bloomsbury entrance to the Kingsway Subway.

112. Feltham car at the Bloomsbury entrance to the Kingsway Subway.

The end of the tramways in north London

Only four tram routes were now left operating in north London. Three of them operated to Blooms-bury, into the Kingsway Subway and then via the Victoria Embankment, Westminster and across the River Thames to south London.

Route 31 had been cut back from Hackney and diverted to Islington Green, from where it now operated to Wandsworth

Route 33 operated between Manor House and West Norwood

Route 35 operated from Highgate Archway to Forest Hill

The fourth route was not strictly geographically part of this history. Tram route 11 from Moorgate to Highgate Village via Highbury, Nag's Head Holloway, Holloway Road and Highgate Archway was a survivor as it should have been abandoned in 1938. London Transport wanted to replace it with trolleybuses but the local authorities and the residents objected to the proposed operating procedures at the terminus. Eventually properties on the corner of High Street and South Grove were purchased and demolished to make way for a turning circle, enabling the trolleybus conversion to take place on 9 December 1939.

The author recollects:

Highgate Village was served by the LCC tram route 11 until its eventual closure on 9th December 1939. It was very much a village, unlike the hurly burly at Highgate Archway and the Nag's Head at Holloway. In the High Street, the butcher had livestock on the premises adjoining his shop at Christmas time. Route 11 was popular, particularly at weekends, because at the southern end

of the High Street was Waterlow Park and from the terminus it was an easy walk along Hampstead Lane to Kenwood House. Further along, where it became Spaniards Road, were to be found the well-known Spaniards Inn and, beyond that, Hampstead Heath.

Only the LCC's powerful HR/2 type trams were allowed to operate route 11 because of the very steep hill leading up to the Village. I have stood at Highgate Archway both watching these trams waiting to ascend the hill and riding on them. A brakesman, in addition to the driver and conductor, would board the rear platform here and place his hands on the hand brake in case of an emergency on this steep section of the route. At weekends I have seen the trams not only full with seated passengers but with passengers standing the full length of the interior to the door.

The three subway routes survived until after the Second World War. Route 31 was converted to motor bus operation on 30 September 1950 and routes 33 and 35 were finally abandoned in favour of buses on 5 April 1952. This also meant the end of tramway operation through the Kingsway Subway and the closure of the ex-LCC Holloway depot, the last in north London, to trams.

The author recollects:

Between 1949 and 1952 I used the all night Subway route 35 between Highgate Archway and Bloomsbury as far as the Nag's Head at Holloway twice a week. Having arrived at Highgate Archway I waited for the tram which stood at the terminus until it was time to depart. It then crossed over to the tram stop outside the Archway Tavern. Loadings varied; sometimes just a few passengers, at other times it could be full. Usually the tram car was an ex-LCC E/3 type but occasionally an HR/2 type was used.

My most memorable ride on this journey was on an HR/2 type tram. It ran non-stop from the Archway terminus to the Nag's Head at a good speed down the slight gradient, only slowing down once - for the junction leading to Holloway depot.

In the period between the pre-war and post-war tramway abandonments London Transport had changed its policy and decided to use motorbuses on all services, which of course sealed the eventual fate of the trolleybuses.

The Feltham cars in south London and Leeds

The author recollects:

I found both the MET and LUT Feltham cars operating from Streatham (Telford Avenue) and Brixton depots on the south London all day routes 8, 10, 16, 18 and 20 and the rush hour routes 22 and 24. The former LUT Felthams had not needed conduit system plough carriers in west London and had to have them fitted before they could be used on the ex-LCC routes in south London.

In the early 1940s, before I was called up in 1942, I went to Wallington in Surrey one Sunday afternoon. On the return journey I arrived at West Croydon to catch a number 16 or 18 tram back to Westminster. As it was late in the evening, a reduced service was operating and there was a large crowd waiting at the stop. Eventually, a Feltham car arrived. Being wartime the blackout was in force and the tram had dimmed lighting inside and out. The headlamp of the tram was fitted with a mask which pointed the light down towards the road. Passengers wishing to board a tram at a stop and holding a torch during blackout time were advised to

refrain from waving it in the air in case they blinded the tram driver. It was suggested the torch was pointed down towards the ground.

Although the official capacity allowed on board a Feltham car was 64 seated passengers and 10 standing on each platform, this tram already had many passengers standing on the platform. I managed to find space standing right on the edge of the rear platform holding onto the hand rail attached to the rear drivers' cab with my right hand. The tram driver (in the front cab) was waiting for the conductor to press one of the buzzers to give him the signal to start the tram but he wasn't able to get to one because of the number of passengers (at least 140) on board. However there was a buzzer by the rail I was holding onto. I called over to the conductor "Shall I press the buzzer?" and he replied "Yes". The conductor allowed me to continue giving the driver the signal to start.

Travelling along the main road towards Norbury I managed to turn round with my back to the rear driver's cab. The buzzer was then on my right. This enabled me to see better the passengers wishing to alight or board all the way to Streatham High Road. Most of the passengers alighted in Streatham and Brixton and there was no longer the need for me to be on the platform pressing the buzzer so I went upstairs to my favourite seat at the front.

At Westminster, with only a few passengers still aboard, I left the Feltham to continue its journey along the Embankment to Blackfriars Bridge and then return south. I then waited for a route 35 Kingsway Subway tram to Nag's Head Holloway - which was reasonably full but not to the same extent as the Feltham.

Although the programme of tramway abandonment was halted during Second World War, it was resumed in phases afterwards. The Feltham cars had a good reputation as modern vehicles and were still less than 20 years old. Leeds City Transport arranged to borrow the former MET car number 2099 on trial and transported it to Leeds in December 1949. Both the MET trolley poles collecting overhead electric power and the LCC conduit ploughs were removed and replaced by a Leeds bow collector and the car was repainted in London Transport colours. The trial proved satisfactory in that it showed these cars could be allocated to all the Leeds routes except the one to Beeston. The Leeds Transport Committee decided to purchase all 92 of the remaining Feltham cars from London Transport for £500 each, considered a bargain. The cars were delivered to Leeds between August 1950 and October 1951 and entered service there after a full overhaul at the City Transport's Kirkstall Works. Leeds requested that the ex-MET cars should be delivered before the ex-LUT ones and this was achieved as each phase of the London tramway abandonment progressed. However, not all the ex-LUT cars delivered to Leeds entered service there. Sixty eight were in service by May 1952 when the work was halted although a further 15 were refurbished in 1955-56.

The author recollects:

I was able to renew my acquaintance with the Feltham cars when I travelled to Leeds on business and socially with friends. However, Leeds also decided to abandon their tramway system despite earlier modernisation of a number of their routes. The last day of operation, 2nd November 1959, saw both Feltham cars and Leeds Corporation's own trams still in service until the afternoon when all were withdrawn.

Only two standard Feltham cars still exist today, both in a static condition. One is in the London Transport Collection (at their Acton depot rather than on display at their Covent Garden Museum in central London) and the other is at the Seashore Trolley Museum in Kennebunkport, Maine, USA.

The experimental Feltham car 2168 (previously 331) with a central entrance, which was sold to Sunderland Corporation in 1936 since it could not be fitted with conduit equipment to be used on former LCC routes, saw regular service there as their car number 100 until 1952; it was withdrawn in 1954.

The author recollects:

Although I was not able to ride on this car in London, I did so in Sunderland - both while on business there and on League visits. This car was purchased by J.W. Fowler for preservation and subsequently donated to the Crich Tramway Museum where it has been restored to running order and occasionally operates in service.

Little else survives as a reminder of this progressive transport system, which served the public of London and north Middlesex so well from 1881 until 1938, other than some of the depot buildings described in Chapter 6.

Former LCC Kingsway Subway routes

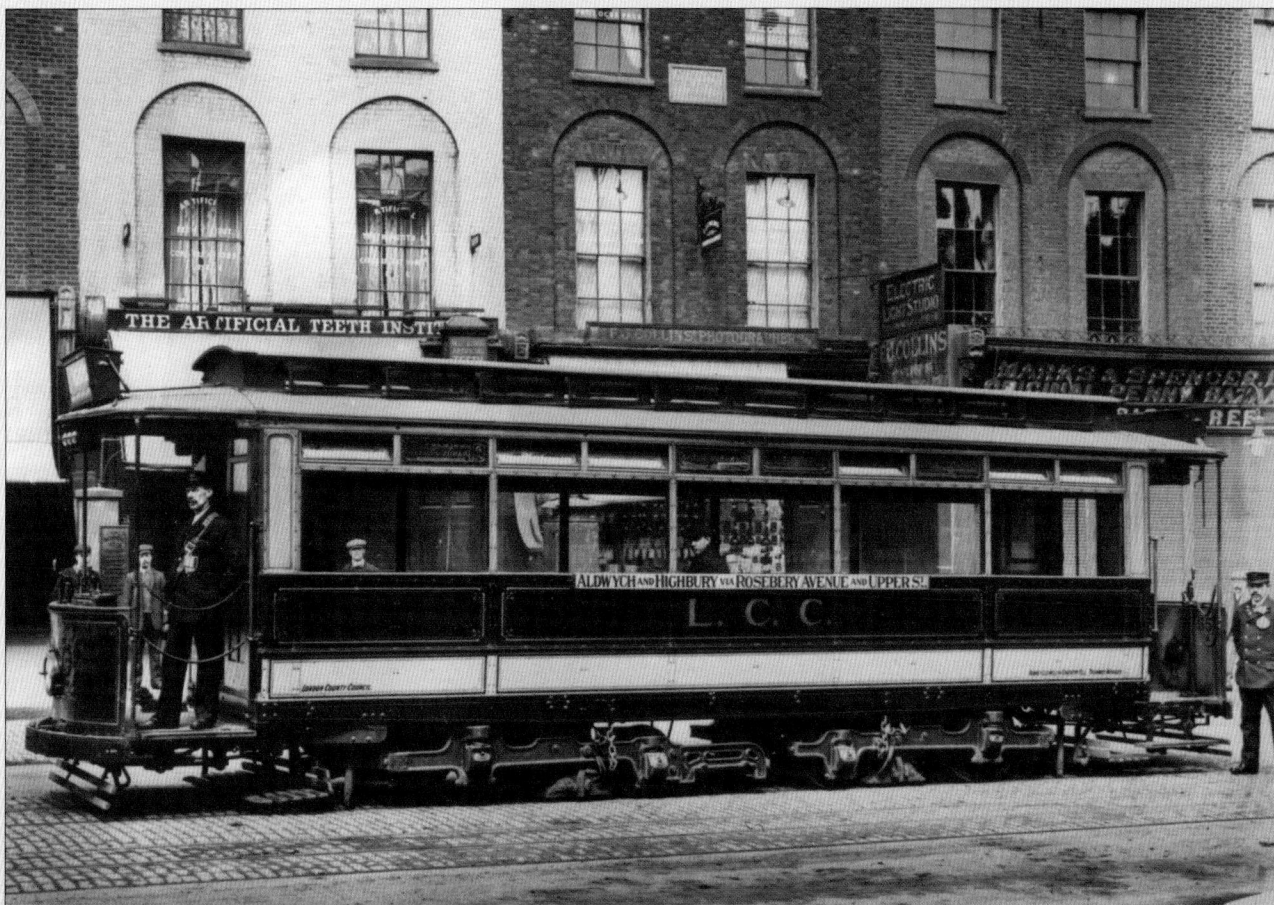

113. A single deck LCC car used on the original Kingsway Subway route between Aldwych and Highbury from 1906 until 1930 when the subway was rebuilt to use double decked cars. *A.A. Jackson Collection*

114. Ex-LCC 'Type E/3' car No. 1929 at Holborn Kingsway tram station on a southbound working of route 33.

115. Car on route 35 leaving the south exit of the Kingsway Subway. Both the Victoria Embankment entrance to the subway and Waterloo Bridge are being rebuilt. The old, disconnected, entrance to the subway is on the left.

116. Ex-LCC 'Type H/R2' car No. 126(II) at Nag's Head, Holloway on route 35. 29 August 1949.

117. Ex-LCC 'Type E/3' car No. 1964 on the Sunday extension of route 31 from Hackney to Leyton.

118. Ex-LCC 'Type E/3' car No. 1939 at the Effra Road change pit in Brixton, south London on route 33.

119. Ex-LCC 'Type H/R2' car No. 104(II) at the Stansted Road junction with Brockley Rise in Forest Hill, south London, on route 35 (17 September 1949).

120. Leyton Corporation 'Type E/3' car 202 on the reserved track at the side of Whipps Cross Road alongside Epping Forest (not on the north Middlesex section). Some of these cars were later transferred to Holloway depot for service on the Kingsway Subway routes.

Route 11 from Moorgate to Highgate Village

121. Ex-LCC 'Type H/R2' car No. 154(II) at the bottom of Highgate Hill, Archway.

122. Ex-LCC 'Type H/R2' car No. 155(II) at Pemberton Gardens, near Holloway depot.

Feltham cars in south London

123. Feltham car No. 2125 at the Tooting Broadway terminus of route 10 in Garratt Lane on a short working to St. George's Church, Southwark (1950).

124. Feltham car outside the ex-LCC Brixton Hill depot. Note the overhead wiring used as the power supply within the former cable tram trailer depot and the 'plough' being inserted under the car to collect power from the conduit system used on the route outside.

Chapter
Six

Tramway Depots
in North Middlesex
and North London

The North London Suburban Tramway operated its single route between Stamford Hill and Ponders End with horse power from a depot at Tramway Avenue in Edmonton. The Company offices were situated on the corner of Tramway Avenue with Hertford Road.

The North London Tramways used the same depot and offices at Tramway Avenue and modified the facilities to maintain steam traction. Following the extension of the original route to Finsbury Park, and with the prospect of commencing a service between Wood Green and Finsbury Park, they built a second depot off Seven Sisters Road in Tottenham to avoid running dead mileage back to Edmonton.

While still a separate company, the North Metropolitan Tramways operated horse trams from three depots in the area: Finsbury Park, Green Lanes and Stamford Hill. Upon taking over the operations of the North London Tramways, it returned the newly acquired lines to horse power and reconverted the facilities at the Edmonton depot accordingly. As the cramped location at the Seven Sisters Road depot was not suitable for stabling horses it is assumed it was closed since the Wood Green service was reallocated to the North Met's own depot at Finsbury Park. Subsequently, the North Met developed additional depot sites at Wood Green and Manor House. The Manor House site also had offices for administering the combined system.

The Metropolitan Electric Tramways converted the Edmonton and Wood Green depots for electric traction, built a new depot at Finchley and used the Manor House site both as a permanent way yard and as its head office for managing its wider operations in north London and Middlesex.

The depots at Green Lanes and Stamford Hill passed directly from the North Met to the LCC and, together with the North Met's share of the joint depot at Finsbury Park, were closed when the lines they serviced were electrified.

Today, only Wood Green depot survives as a bus garage.

Edmonton depot

The North London Suburban Tramways Order 1879 authorised the construction and working of a section of tramway, including the provision of a new road off Hertford Road, named Tramway Avenue. This gave access to the horse tramway sheds and stables which were to be erected on land rented from Thomas O'Hagan which fronted the access to Cuckoo Hall Farm, now known as Turin Road, and was formerly part of Cuckoo Hall Farm estate.

The plan shown in Figure 10 on page 159 is taken from the lease between Thomas O'Hagan and the North London Tramways Company dated November 1890. Figure 11 shows the plan attached to the indenture dated 13 November 1890 between Thomas O'Hagan and a benefit society.

Section 4 of the North London Tramways Act 1882 provided for the North London Suburban Tramway Company to be dissolved and vested in the North London Tramway Company. Thus the benefit of the tenancy of land for a depot at the end of Tramway Avenue passed to the latter company.

The original depot, built in 1880 – 1881, was 250 feet by 185 feet in size. During the next decade it was extended by erecting several car sheds, engine sheds, stables, stores and other buildings to accommodate the growing fleet of horse trams and (between 1885 and 1891) steam tram locomotives and trailers. The Company offices were situated on the corner of Hertford Road and Tramway Avenue.

The investment in the site was such that on 1 November 1890, the freeholder (Thomas O'Hagan) was prevailed upon to grant a lease of the " ... land at the end of Tramway Avenue, together with several car sheds, engine sheds, stables, offices, stores and other buildings ..." for 89 years from 24 June 1890 at an annual rent of £64 1s 3d.

After the purchase of the North London Tramways Company by the North Metropolitan Tramways Company, the new owner reverted to operating only horse trams and had to make hasty arrangements for stabling the horses. It was, therefore, decided in April 1893 to call for tenders to rebuild the depot to incorporate adequate stabling facilities.

Following the take-over of the North Met by the Metropolitan Electric Tramways, the new owners entered into a contract with Messrs Holliday and Greenwood in September 1903 for the reconstruction of the depot, including raising the roof, to accommodate electric trams. The depot was again extended in 1907 so that by July 1908 it comprised car sheds 137 feet wide by 217 feet 6 inches long, covering 10 tracks, each with an inspection pit, and could accommodate a total of 60 cars.

In 1912 the MET made its final extension to the depot buildings by roofing over part of the yard and laying one additional track without an inspection pit – although it later acquired additional land to the north of the depot, up to Causeyware Road, on 16 December 1930.

After the MET was taken over by the London Passenger Transport Board (LPTB) in 1933, further land was purchased on 8 January 1937 to extend the original site southwards. In February 1937 a contract was placed with Ekin and Company for the reconstruction of the premises, across the extended site, as a trolleybus depot. Edmonton depot was converted to trolleybus operation in two stages; tram routes 49A, 59 and 79 were abandoned on 16 October 1938, leaving just route 27 as a tramway operation until 5 November 1938. Route 49A was converted directly from tram to motor bus operation and re-allocated to Enfield bus garage.

On 17 April 1940, the LPTB purchased the freehold reversion in the lease of 1890, thus becoming the freeholder of the entire depot site.

125. Edmonton terminus, Hertford Road at the junction with Tramway Avenue. Former North London Tramway offices in the background.

126. Edmonton depot, May 1931.

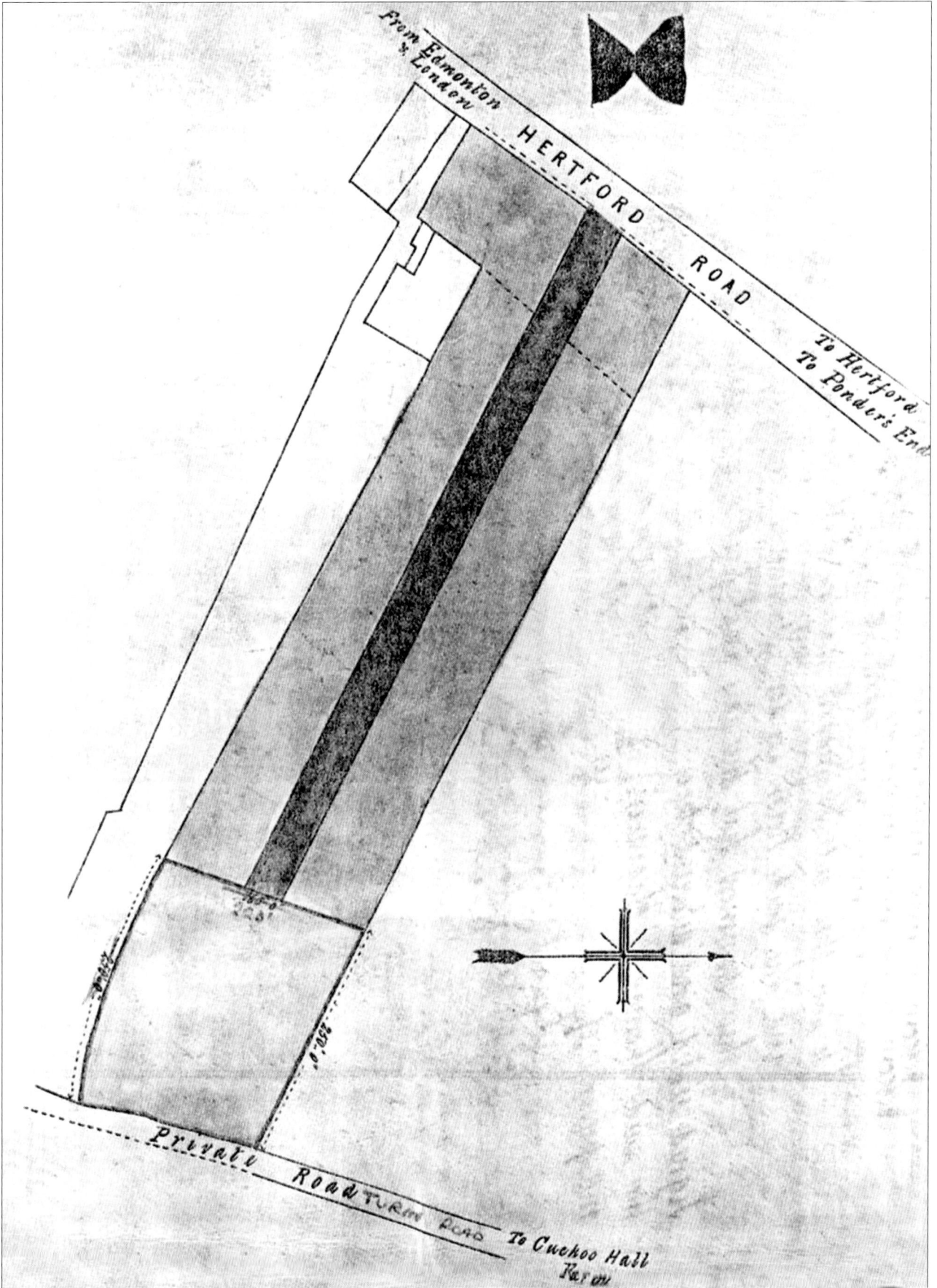

Figure 10. Edmonton horse tram depot: plan attached to lease (1890).

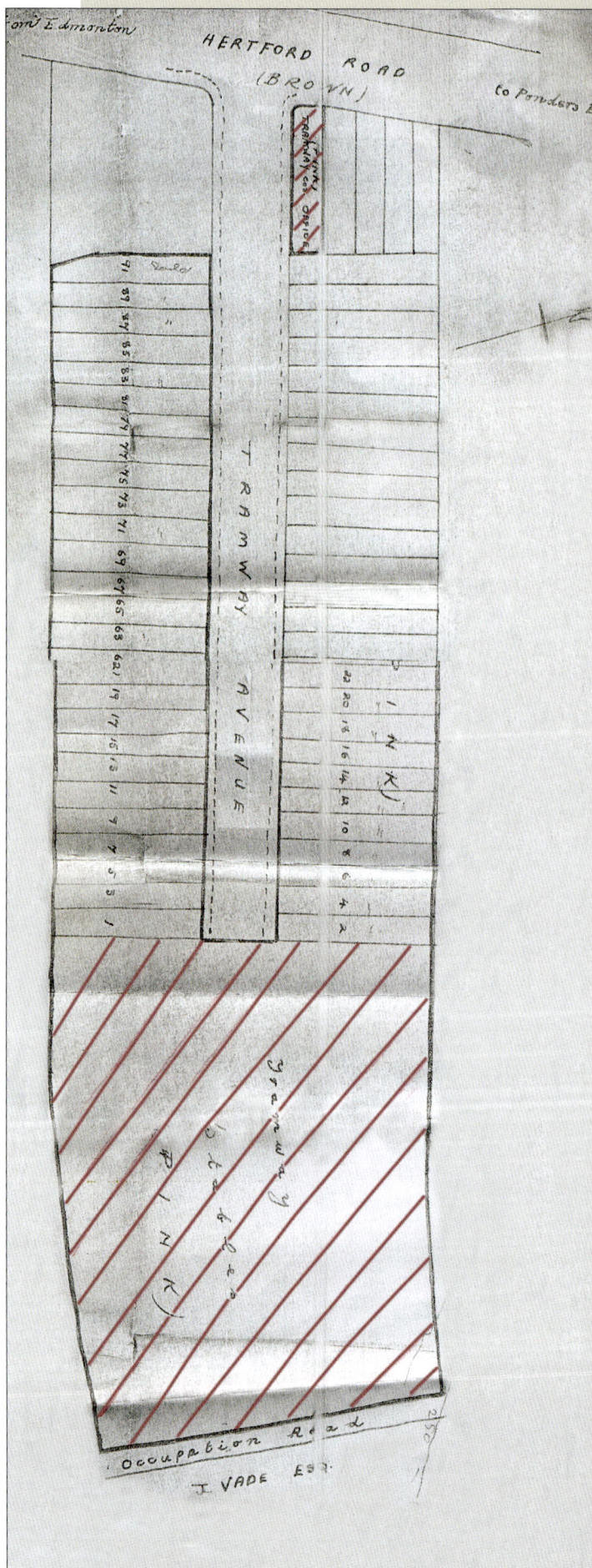

**Figure 11.
Edmonton horse tram depot:
plan attached to indenture
(1890).**

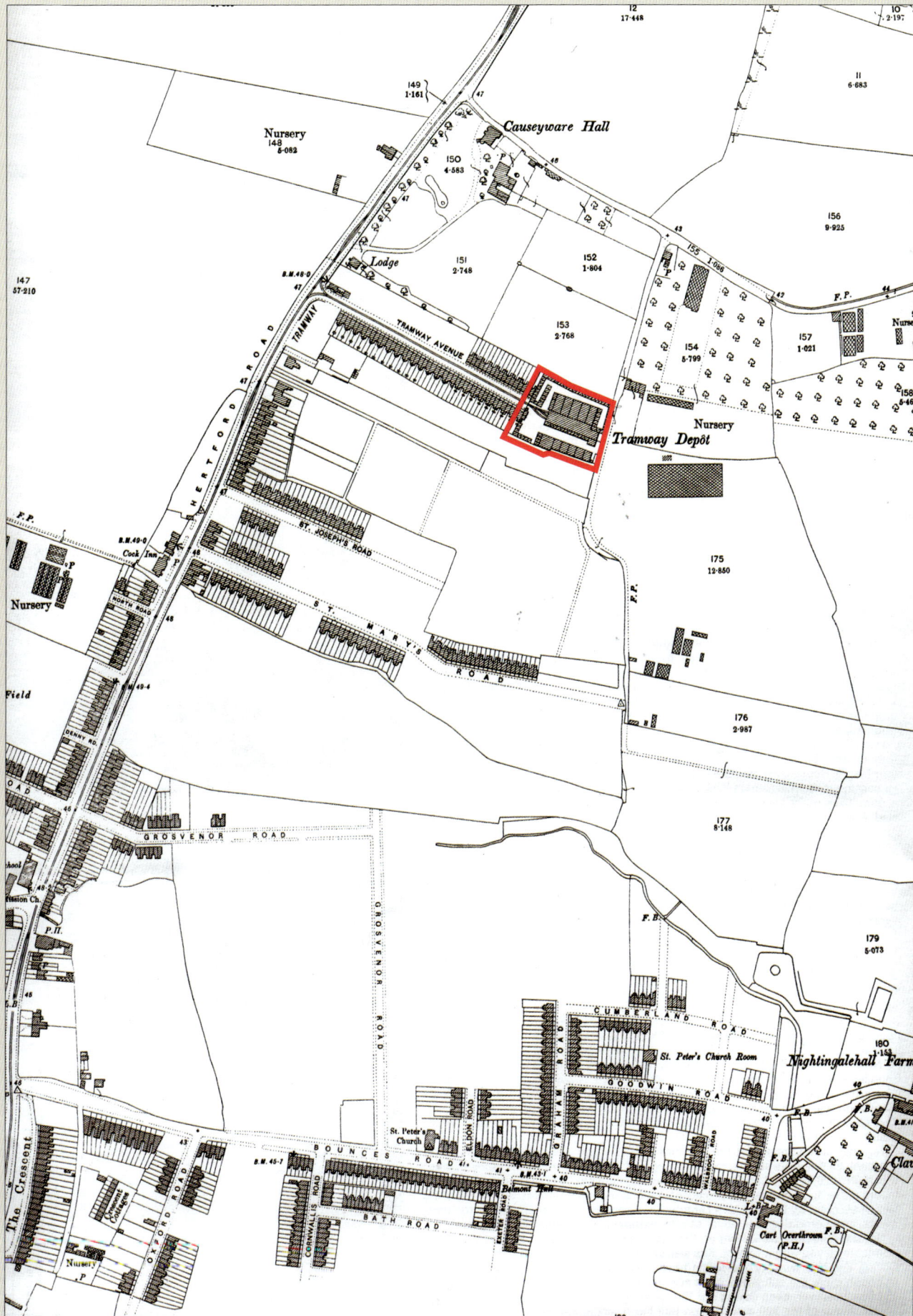

Figure 12. Edmonton tram depot location (1894).

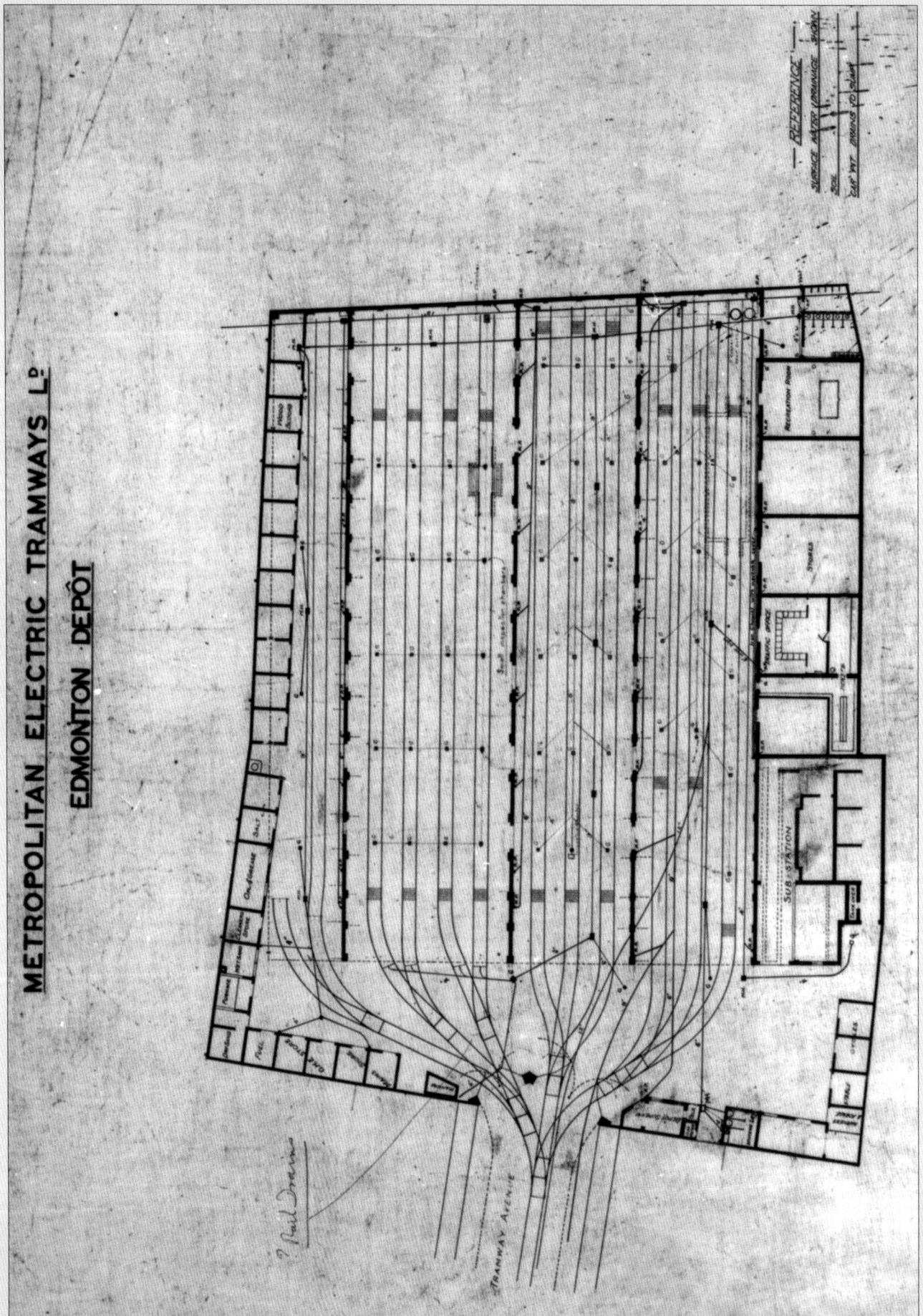

Figure 13. Edmonton electric tram depot layout.

127. Finchley depot, May 1927.

Finchley depot

To provide additional depot capacity for the trams required to operate the MCC's light railway services, the Company purchased a site for a depot and sub-station at Woodberry Grove, Finchley in February 1904. Most of the tram services operated by Finchley depot were in North West Middlesex and, therefore, outside the scope of this book.

As described previously, soon after the purchase the Company realised that it had no access to the site for either the track or the electricity supply cables because the proposed routes were over private roads. Following negotiations with the owners of these roads in June, the Company agreed to the terms providing it were given all the required way-leaves to allow the track and cables to be laid along Woodberry Grove from Ballards Lane to the depot site and other cables from the Great North Road.

In October 1905, the owners of the private roads objected to the tramway poles which had been erected along Woodberry Grove and commenced High Court proceedings against the Company, on the grounds that these poles were not included in the way-leave granted on 1 November 1904 and Company employees had, therefore, trespassed when erecting them.

When the actions were heard in 1907, the first action was dismissed and for the second the owners of the private roads were awarded 20 shilling damages in respect of a technical trespass committed by the Company. The road owners then appealed against the judgements given. Meanwhile, these proceedings had been brought to the attention of Finchley UDC who had inserted a clause in their General Purposes Bill in respect of the adoption of private streets in their area. Royal Assent to this bill was received in 1908, whereupon the Council took steps to declare Woodberry Grove a public highway.

By July 1908 the depot comprised car sheds 173 feet 6¼ inches wide by 148 feet 7½ inches long, covering 15 tracks, each with an inspection pit, and could accommodate a total of 60 cars.

Finchley depot was fully converted to trolleybus operation on 6 March 1938 after the abandonment of tram route 21. The other tram routes operated from Finchley depot, in the north west Middlesex area, had already been abandoned.

128. Comparison of older and new cars at Finchley depot.

129. Horse tram and staff at Finsbury Park depot.

Finsbury Park and Green Lanes depots

Finsbury Park depot was opened on 21 January 1872 by the North Metropolitan Tramways Company to provide tram cars and horses for the route to Moorgate via Holloway and Islington. The entrance was in Seven Sisters Road and the side of the depot adjoined Stroud Green Road. Although the tramway it served was wholly in London, the depot was in Middlesex since Stroud Green Road was the county boundary between the Metropolitan Board of Works, (the forerunner of the London County Council) and Middlesex County Council.

Following the sale and lease back of the North Met lines in the County of London in 1897, the ownership of the depot at Finsbury Park, which was used for services operated by the North Met in both London and Middlesex, was only partly assigned to the LCC.

After the electrification of both the London and Middlesex lines, the depot at Finsbury Park was no longer required and sold. By 1915 the site had become a 'picture theatre', the front entrance of which faced Seven Sisters Road, with a skating rink behind in place of the stables. In the 1930s the whole site was occupied by 'The Rink Cinema'; the former cinema now a wide corridor leading to the new cinema built on the site of the skating rink. This complex closed in 1958 and has since been demolished.

The Green Lanes depot was opened by the North Metropolitan Tramways Company in May 1874 to provide tram cars and horses for its Stoke Newington and Highbury Park line. It adjoined the Highbury Park Tavern in Green Lanes at the junction with Riversdale Road and Highbury Quadrant. Ownership passed to the LCC in 1897 and it was closed at the time of the electrification of the routes it serviced. The LCC had a policy of building large electric tram depots to service several routes across a wide area, in this instance at Holloway.

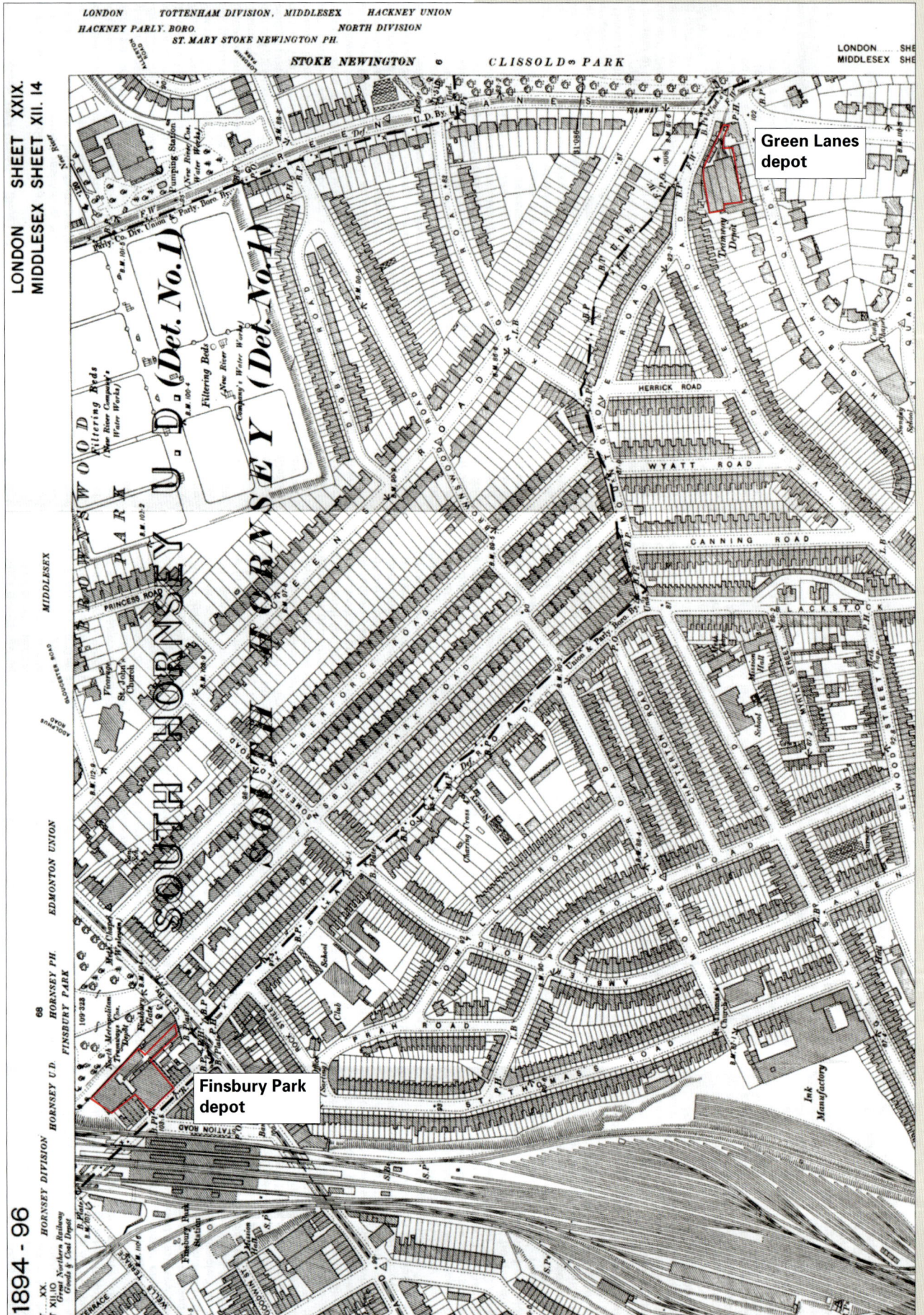

Figure 14. Finsbury Park and Green Lanes horse tram depot locations.

FINSBURY PARK DEPÔT

Freehold part Edged Pink
Leasehold „   „   Blue

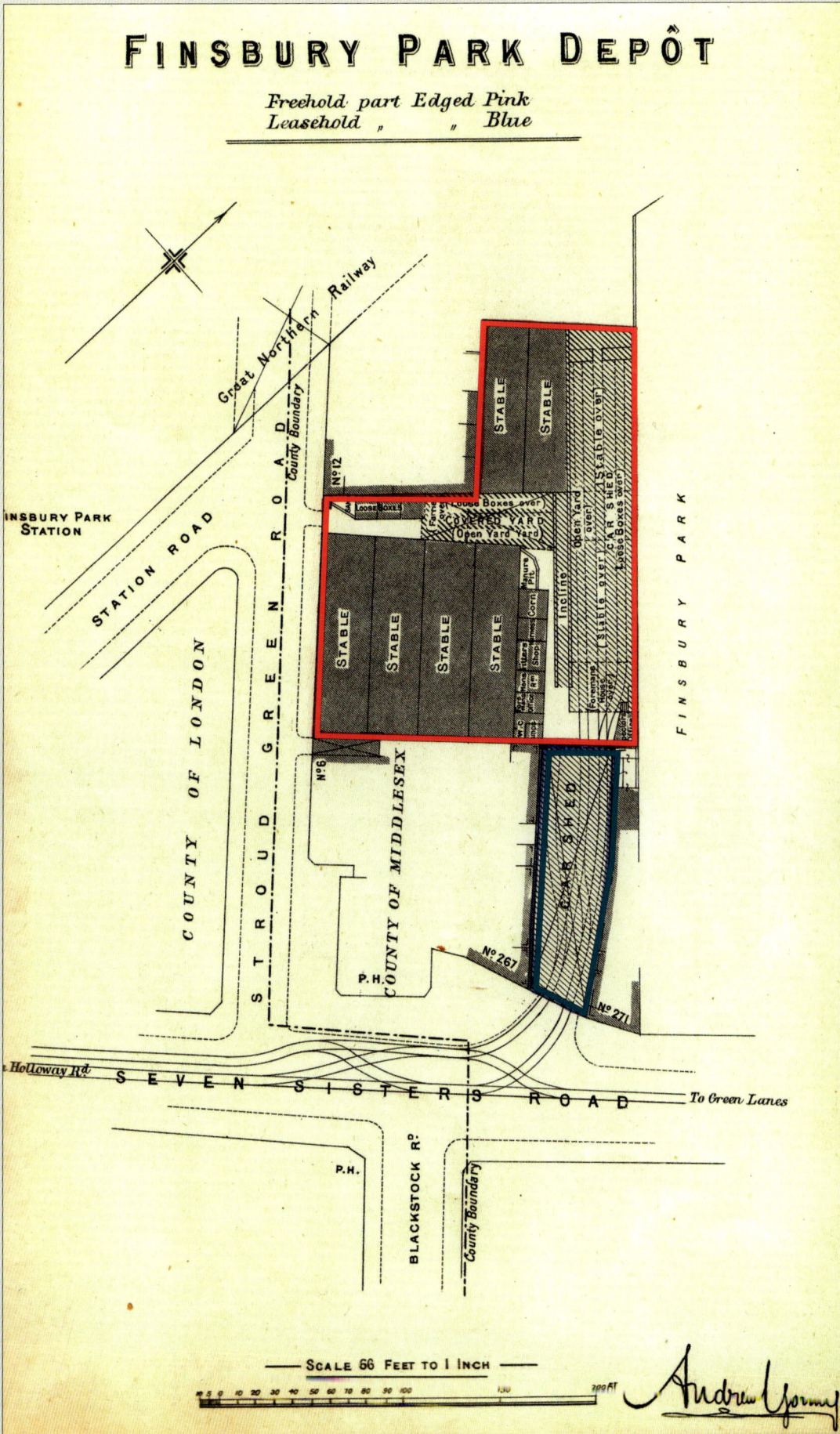

Figure 15. Finsbury Park horse tram depot layout.

GREEN LANES DEPÔT

LEASEHOLD.

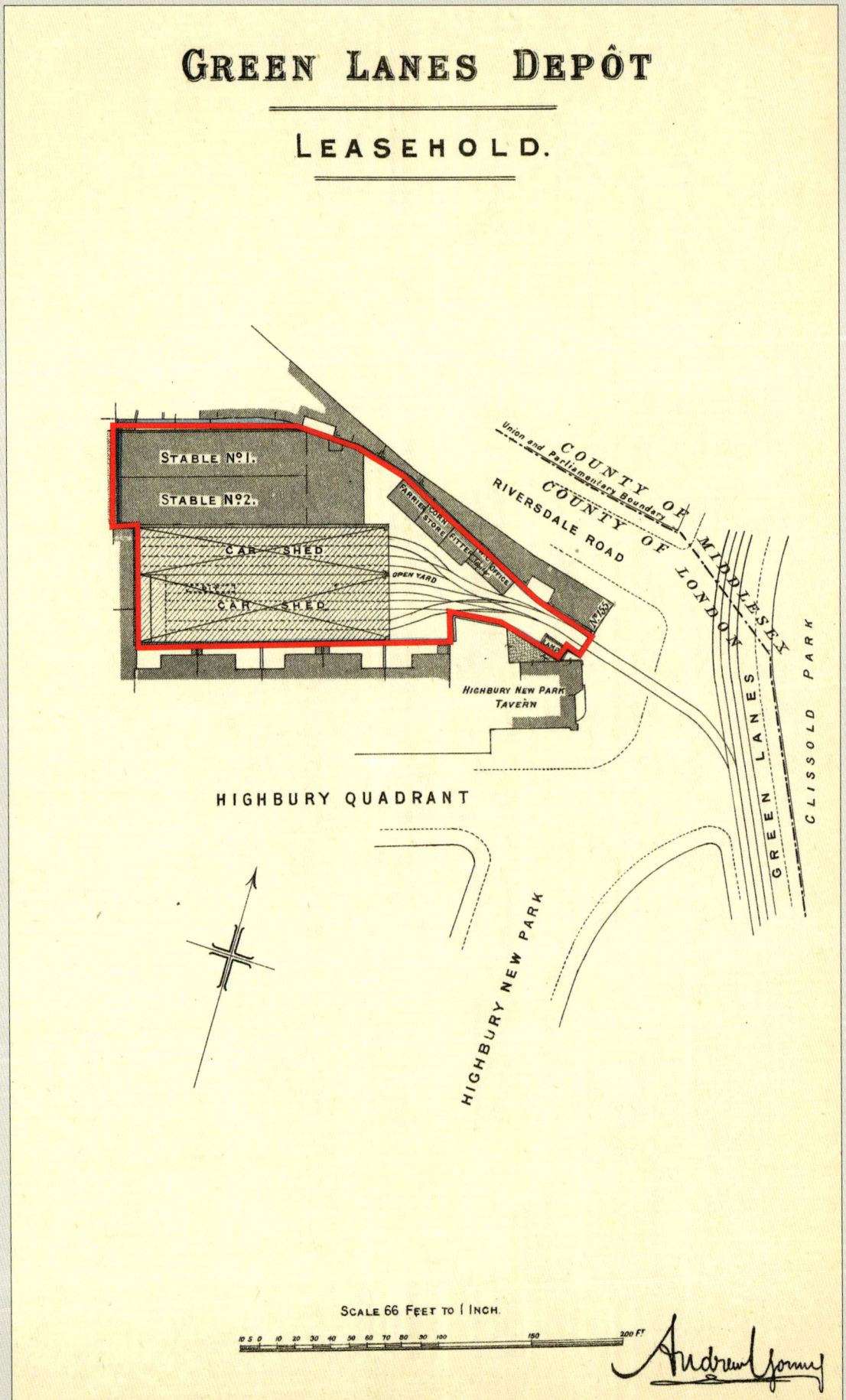

Figure 16. Green Lanes horse tram depot layout.

Manor House depot and offices

The North Metropolitan Tramways Company purchased the site, adjacent to the Manor House public house, in November 1898 and opened a horse tram depot there in 1899. The site was cramped, with the vehicular entrance from Green Lanes alongside the public house and tracks for the cars in a semi-basement under the stables. There was very little room for expansion behind the office block, which faced onto Seven Sisters Road. The depot was only used as such until the Metropolitan Electric Tramways Company opened its first two electric routes from Finsbury Park to Wood Green and Finsbury Park to Seven Sisters Corner on 22 July 1904 since it was not suitable to be converted for double deck electric trams.

In May 1903, the depot was taken over by the permanent way department and instructions were given for minor alterations so that it could be used as a store for overhead equipment and materials. In November 1906, a tender was accepted for more extensive alterations to the property and, at the same time, the engineer was authorised to carry out repairs to and repaint the remainder of the buildings to accommodate the overhead and building maintenance departments as well. At this time the single track leading from Green Lanes to the interior of the depot was re-laid, but could only be used by single deck works cars and 'Type E' passenger cars because of the low entrance. At a later date this track was used by these single deck cars when they became ticket punch cars working between the offices and other depots to distribute ticket stocks and ticketing equipment and collect the cash taken by conductors. The track ran into a paved yard, on one side of which was a wide platform with direct access into the back of the offices.

When football matches were being played at the Arsenal football stadium on Saturday afternoons, double deck cars used on the football specials were parked on the open air section of the single track leading into the rear of these offices for the duration of the match.

The Company authorised additional alterations to be carried out in July 1909 to provide accommodation for the staff and engineers of the North Met EPS Company. Consequently, instructions were given to terminate that company's tenancy of offices in Spencer House, South Place, Finsbury, London on 8 February 1910.

Eventually, the now substantial office block facing onto Seven Sisters Road was used by the traffic and engineering departments of not only the MET but also its sister companies in the London & Suburban Group. For a while, around 1913, it also became the head office of this group of companies.

Following the abandonment of the MET tramways, London Transport also used the property as a medical centre and a recruitment centre. It was sold in the mid-1980s, at the time London Transport was restructured to contract out the operation of its bus services, and radically rebuilt as a housing complex.

130. Manor House tram station, looking towards Amhurst Park, with the entrances to the Underground station shown at this end of each traffic island. The MET offices are on the left.

131. Turnpike Lane tram station on 26 May 1933 with the Wellington public house on the right.

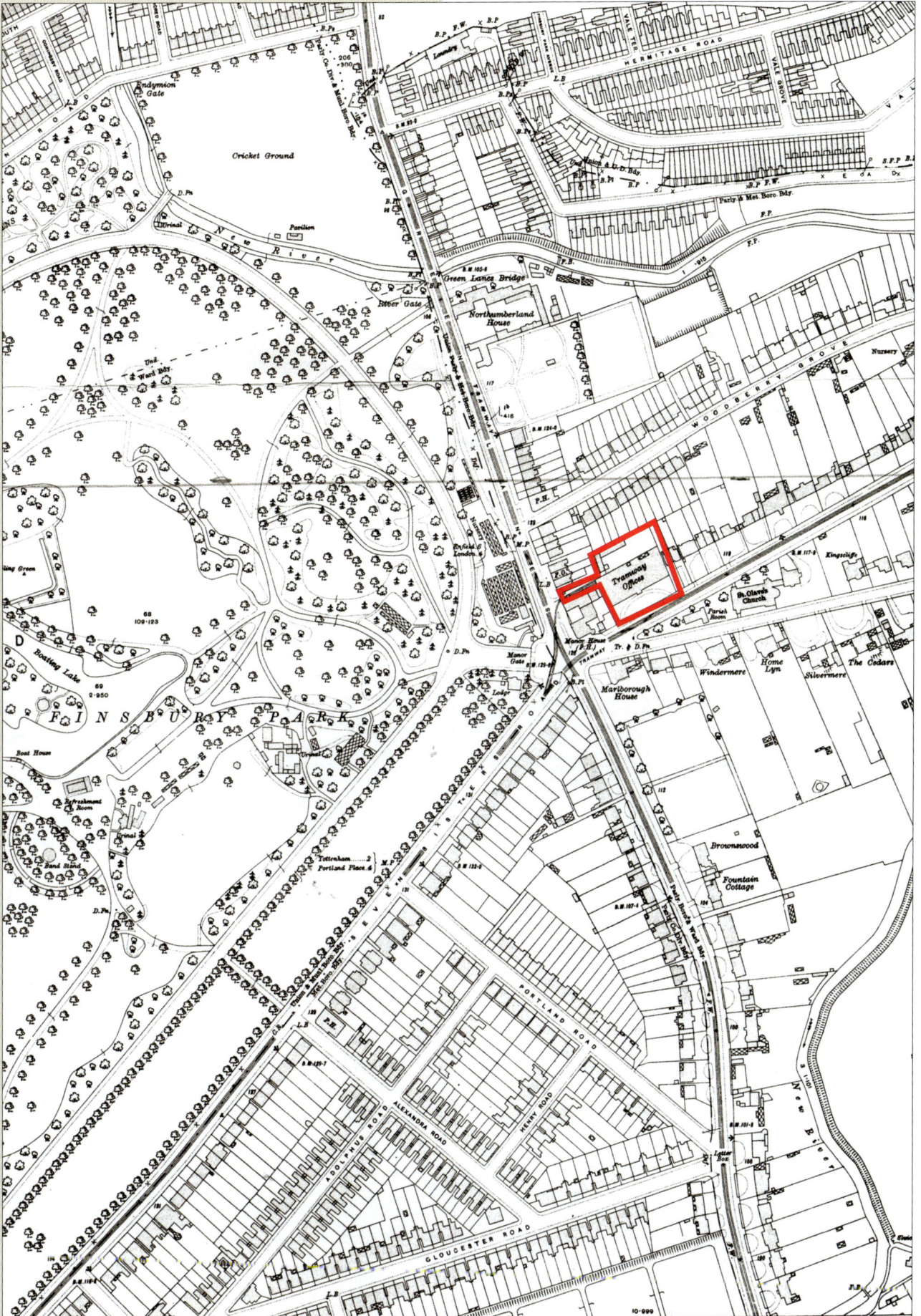

Figure 17. Manor House tramway offices location.

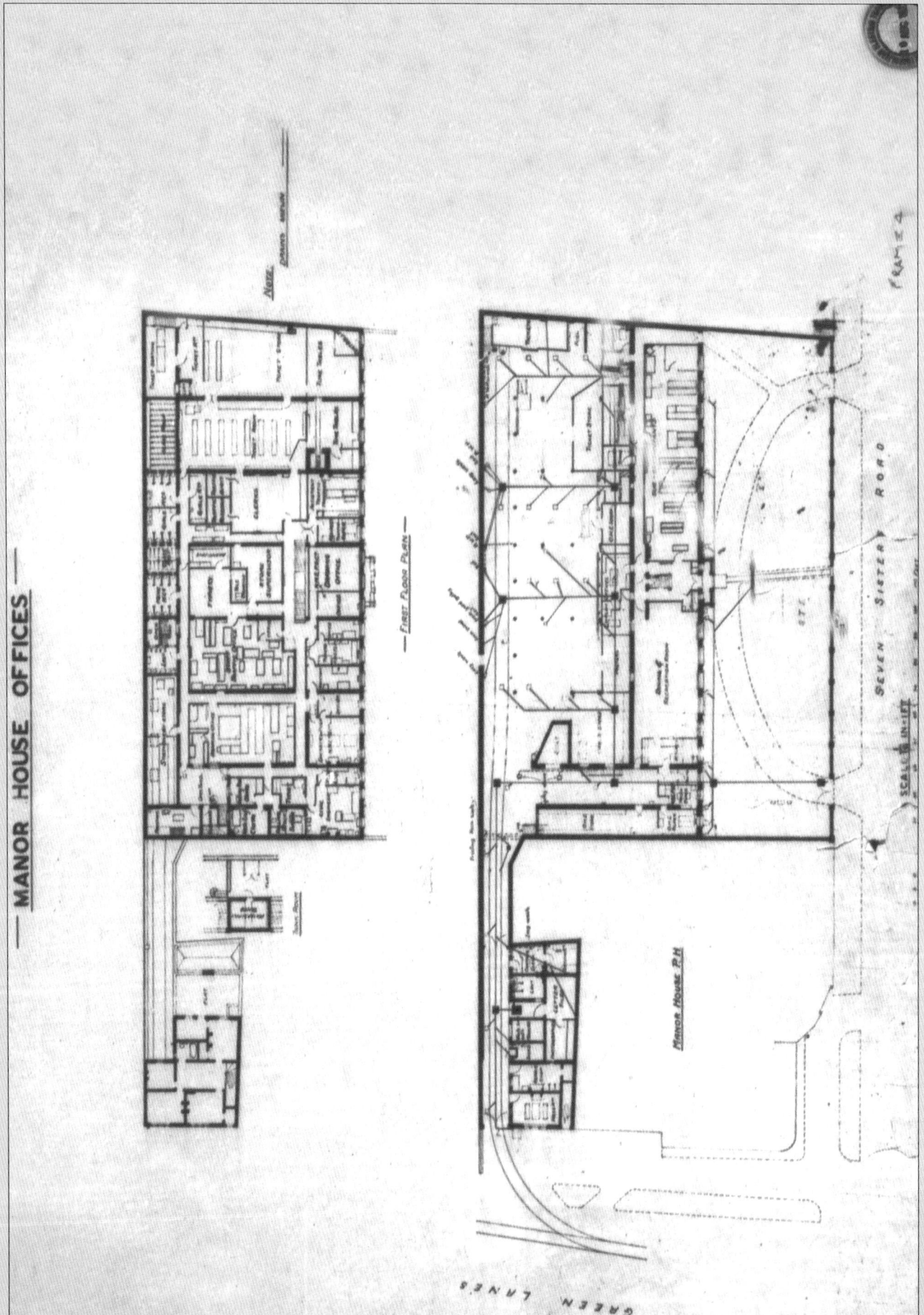

Figure 18. Manor House tramway offices layout.

Seven Sisters Road depot, Tottenham

When the North London Tramways Company extended its steam tramway system from Seven Sisters Corner to Finsbury Park and from Manor House to Wood Green it acquired a site for an additional depot off Seven Sisters Road, Tottenham to avoid running dead mileage back to Tramway Avenue, Edmonton.

The depot was located off Seven Sisters Road by St. Ann's Road, on the right hand side from Seven Sisters Corner. On the north side the site was partly bound by the Midland Railway (Tottenham & Hampstead Joint Line) St. Ann's Road Station (since closed) which was on an embankment.

This small, two-line depot was completed in October 1885 on a triangular site running behind the properties numbered 10 – 20 Kingsford Terrace (both odd and even numbers). A right of way existed along the back of these properties separating them from the depot, which consisted of workshops and a yard. The narrow entrance, which can still be seen, was between a row of shops through the ground floor of the property known as 21 Kingsford Terrace followed by a sharp left hand turn into the depot. It was provided with a weighbridge capable of weighing an engine in full running order and useful to ensure the carts of coke etc were properly laden.

A conveyance for the property was granted to the North London Tramways and is dated 18 January 1884 for a term of 89 years. The unexpired portion of the lease was granted to the North Metropolitan Tramways Company when it took over the North London system upon its liquidation. Under an indenture dated 12 April 1892 between the Liquidator, Receiver and Plaintiff of the North London Tramways Company and the North Metropolitan Tramways Company, powers were given to the latter to use the right of way from Seven Sisters Road to the depot with or without horses, carriages, carts and wagons to and from the private road and under the archway or entrance to it.

There is no record of when the depot was sold, or to whom, but it is assumed that it was closed after the North Met converted the operation of the Wood Green line from steam traction to horse power in August 1891.

Stamford Hill depots

A large depot and stables were built at Portland Avenue in Stamford Hill, about half way along between Darenth Road and Kyverdale Road, in time for the opening of the North Met's line from Moorgate to Stamford Hill on 8 May 1873. Additional tracks were laid in Portland Avenue to Clapton Common by April 1875 so that the depot could also serve the Moorgate to Clapton Pond line and thus allow the unsatisfactory, temporary depot facilities at Hackney to be closed. Ownership passed to the LCC in 1897 and it was closed at the time of the electrification of the routes it serviced.

The LCC had a policy of building large electric tram depots to service several routes across a wide operating area; that for Stamford Hill was constructed nearby at the junction of Egerton Road with Rookwood Road. This was not located directly on any public route and, although just within the LCC area, access to it was via a section of MET-owned track. Consequently, this short section of track north of the Stamford Hill crossroads had to be electrified by both the overhead system for the Company cars in service and the conduit system for the LCC cars working to and from the depot. As well as providing cars for routes operating wholly within the LCC area, after the First World War Stamford Hill depot also operated routes 49 and 53 into the MET area under the joint operating agreements.

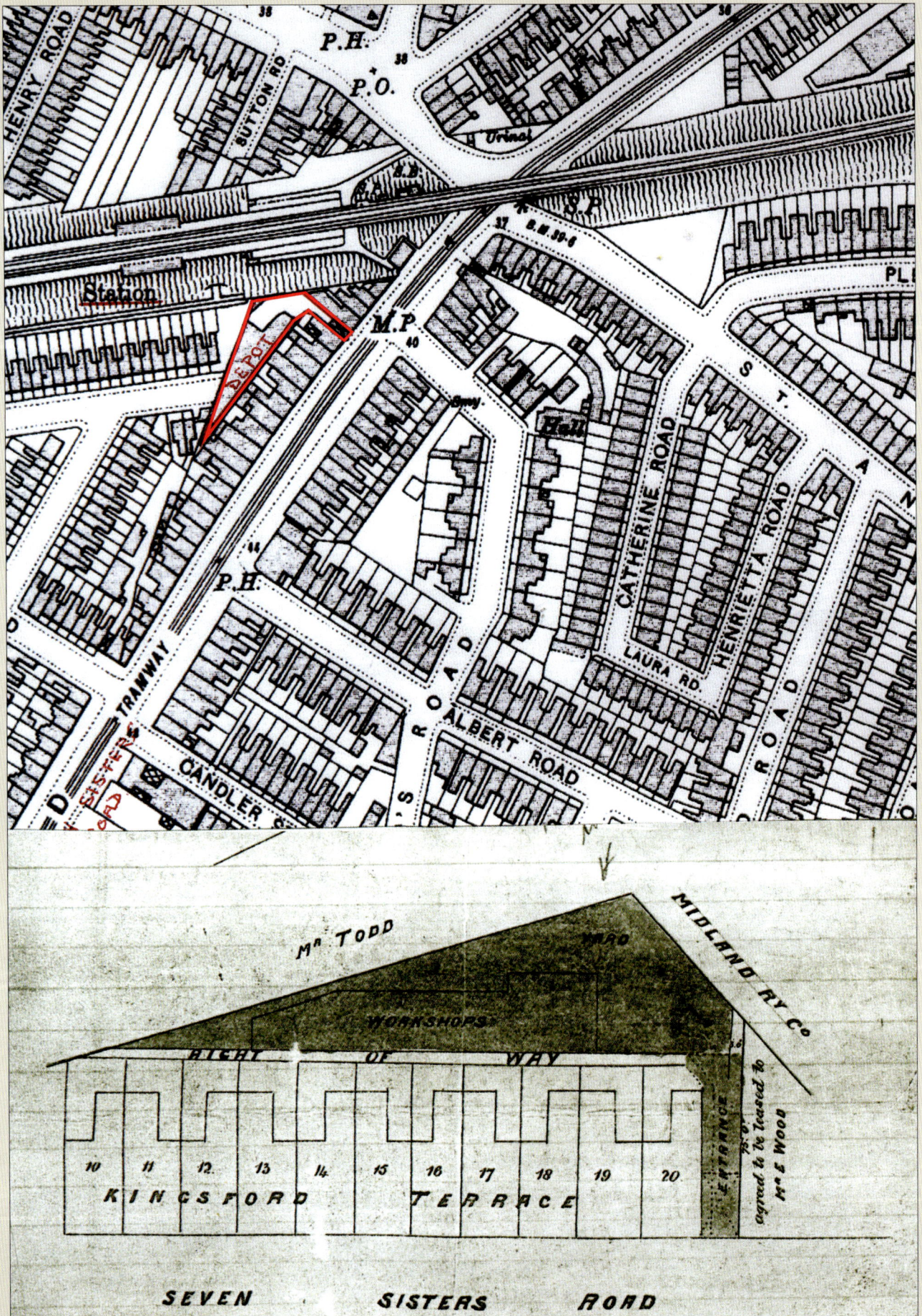

Figure 19. Seven Sisters Road, Tottenham, depot location and layout (1884).

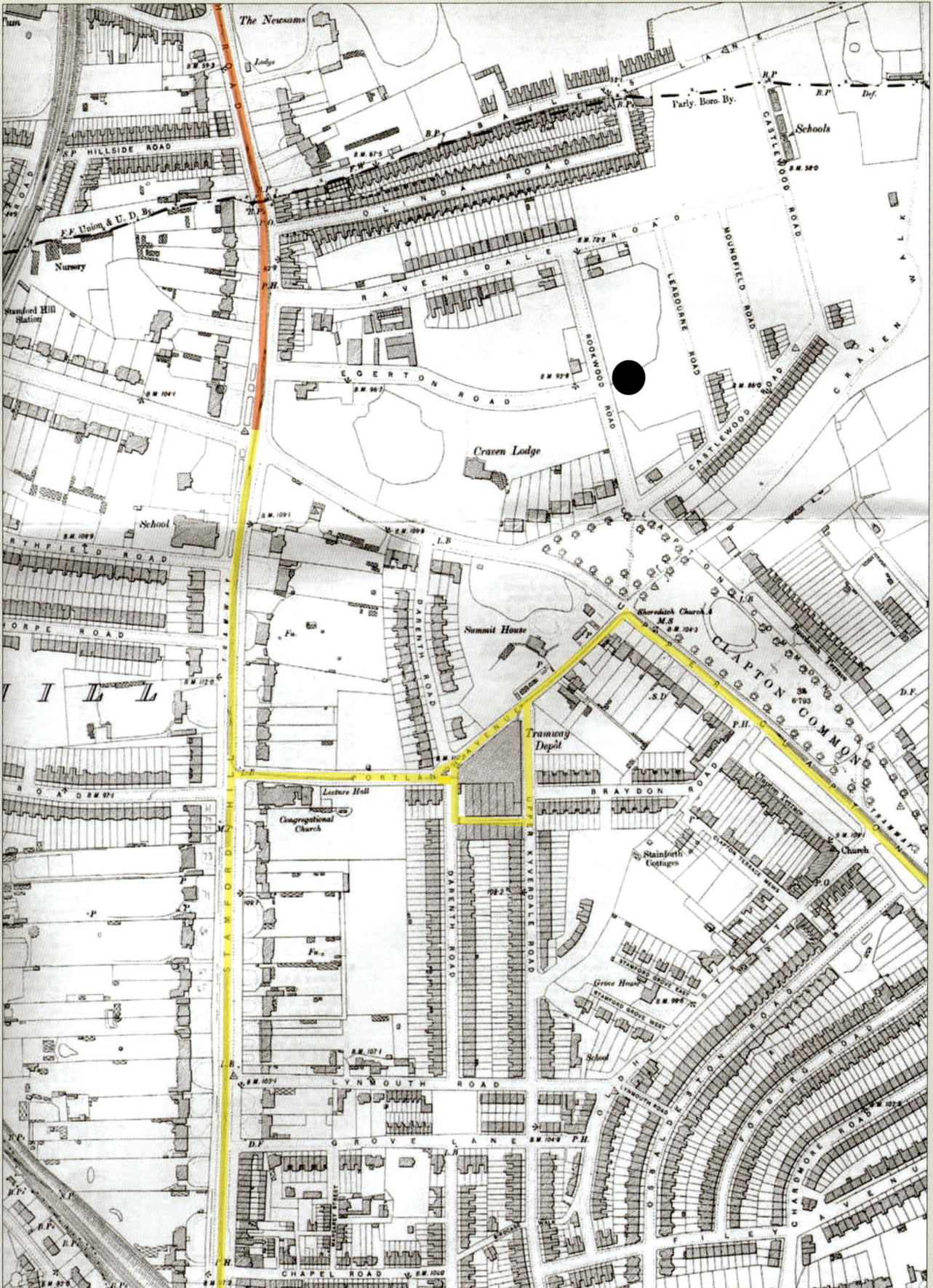

Figure 20. Stamford Hill horse tram depot location.

North Met horse tram routes

North London Suburban horse tram route

Site of subsequent LCC electric tram depot

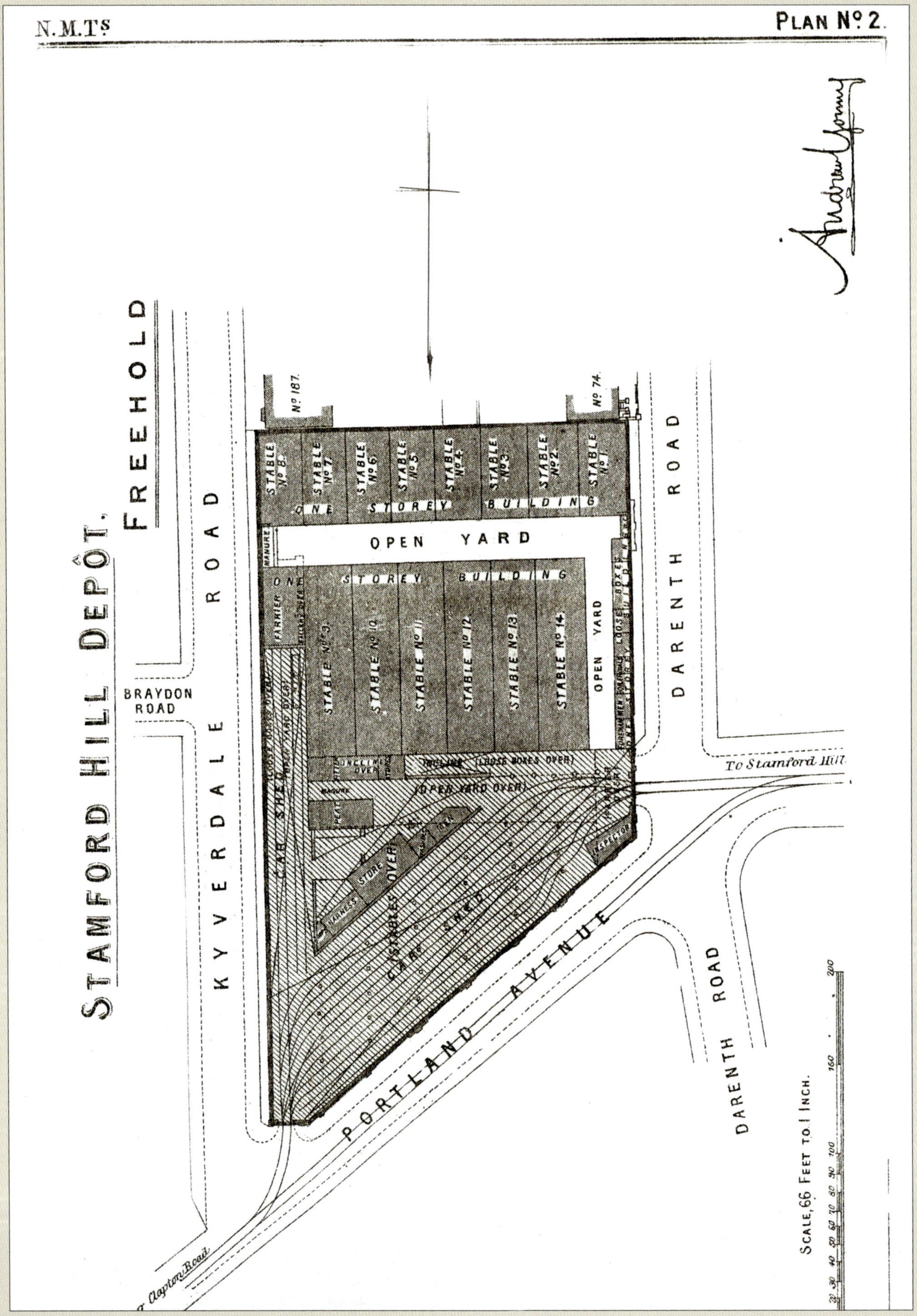

Figure 21. Stamford Hill horse tram depot layout.

132. The entrance to Wood Green depot. The structure over the entrance dated back to horse tram days and was removed in the 1920s.

Wood Green depot

The Wood Green depot at Jolly Butchers' Hill was originally developed by the Metropolitan Tramways and Omnibus Company Limited in 1895 in anticipation of the North Met having to sell its lines and depots in the County of London to the LCC. It was constructed on land adjoining the Three Jolly Butchers public house and comprised horse tram car sheds and stables. The site was bound on the east side by the High Road, on the west and south sides by Hillside Road and on the north side partly by Watson Road and partly by premises forming the property belonging to the Three Jolly Butchers.

In a document dated 30 March 1895, the property is shown leased from the Learoyd trustees (Elizabeth Learoyd, widow and licensee of the Three Jolly Butchers and the brewery company) for a term of 99 years from 24 June 1894 at the yearly rental of £120. Under the terms of this lease the Company was *"required to demolish any existing buildings and, within nine months, to erect and cover in stables, coach-houses, sheds and buildings as a depot for horses, for tramcars and omnibuses in connection with their undertaking"*.

On 2 June 1897 it was sub-leased to the North Metropolitan Tramways Company for 28 years who, in turn, transferred it to the Metropolitan Electric Tramways on 14 November 1902.

The MET purchased additional land to the north west of the depot, comprising the properties numbered 1-8 Watsons Road and the gardens thereof, on 28 January 1903. It then received consent from the lessor of the main part of the site on 31 December *"to alter and adapt the depot with workshops and car housing and storage facilities necessary to work the tramways by mechanical traction except steam"*. Consequently, the rent was increased to £140 per annum. The service of electric cars commenced on 22 July 1904.

Since the building of permanent traffic offices for the depot had been postponed, it was decided in May 1904 to adapt as offices two of the houses in Lordship Lane which had been acquired by MCC in connection with road widenings for the Wood Green to Bruce Grove line. In February 1905, it was decided to screen off part of Wood Green depot as a temporary paint and varnish shop for the cars, pending completion of a permanent paint shop at the new Hendon Depot and Works in North West Middlesex.

133. Wood Green depot, October 1932.

In November 1904 the MET realised the depot was already too small and negotiated with the brewery which owned the Three Jolly Butchers to purchase another piece of land at the rear of the property. The sale was agreed in May 1906. On 16 January 1905, Wood Green Urban District Council agreed with the Company that Watsons Road could be diverted further westward and the property numbered 1 Watsons Road could be demolished to make way for the diverted new road. At the Middlesex Quarter Sessions on 1 July, an Order was made authorising the Company to divert Watsons Road. After the roadworks had been undertaken, the Council leased the site of the former roadway to the Company for £10 per annum. Further land to the north of the depot was acquired on 11 July 1907.

By July 1908 the depot had been enlarged, now comprising car sheds 83 feet 8½ inches wide by 473 feet long, covering seven tracks, of which six had an inspection pit, accommodating a total of 87 cars and including a permanent way yard on the Watson Road side. A further extension was made in 1912, including two additional inspection pits.

On 22 December 1909, the Company sold its

freehold interests in the depot site to Middlesex County Council for £6,295 5s 0d but then leased them back from the Council to operate the Council's light railways. The part of the site already leased from the Learoyd trustees and Wood Green UDC continued to be leased from them.

On 19 April 1932, the Union Surplus Lands Company (an Underground Group subsidiary) purchased further land to the south of the original depot site, fronting River Park Road. Along with the Metropolitan Electric Tramways and the Middlesex County Council Tramways, Wood Green depot was transferred to the London Passenger Transport Board (LPTB) on 1 July 1933. In July 1937 the LPTB acquired the freehold of the strip leased from Wood Green UDC for £10 per annum since 1905 and also received consent to alter the remaining leasehold property for trolleybus operation, the rent being increased to £250 per annum.

The contract for reconstructing the depot for trolleybus operations in 1938 was placed with J. Jarvis and Sons Limited. Wood Green depot was converted to trolleybus operation on 8 May 1938 after the abandonment of tram routes 29, 39A and 41.

134. Feltham car No. 329 at Wood Green depot in MET days.

135. Feltham car No. 2080 at Wood Green depot in LPTB days. Note the reconstruction work being undertaken for the introduction of trolleybuses.

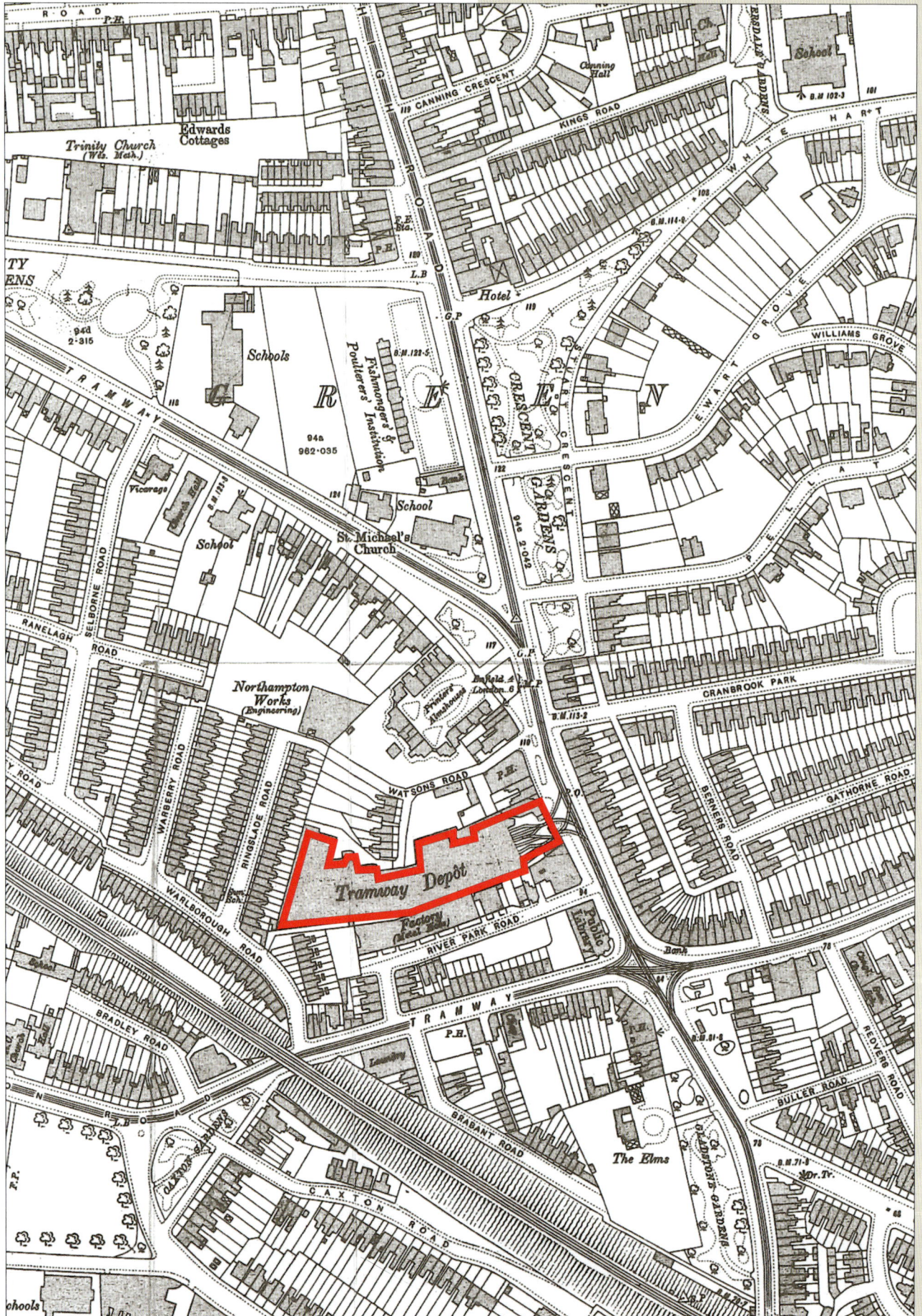

Figure 22. Wood Green tram depot location.

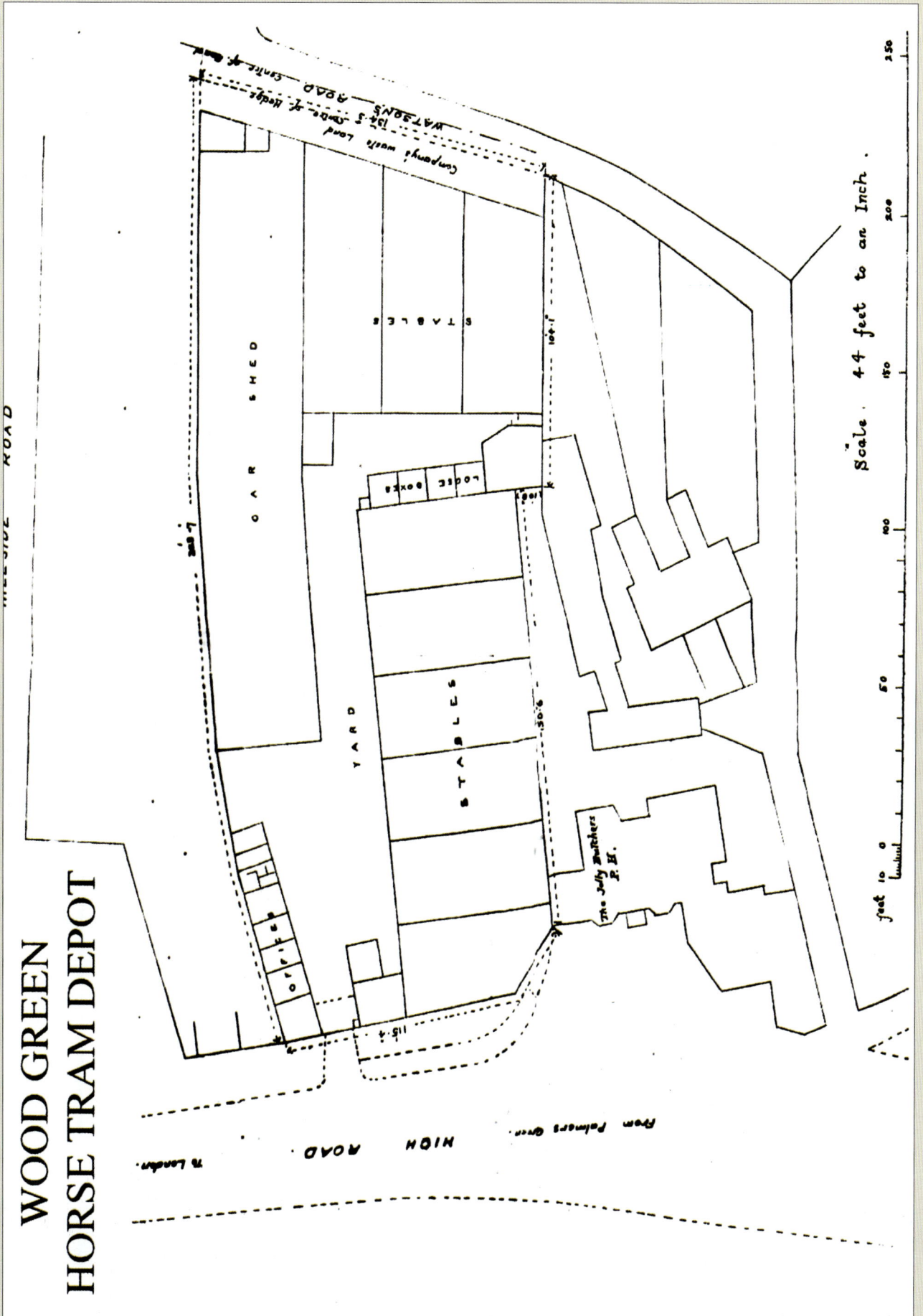

Figure 23. Wood Green horse tram depot layout.

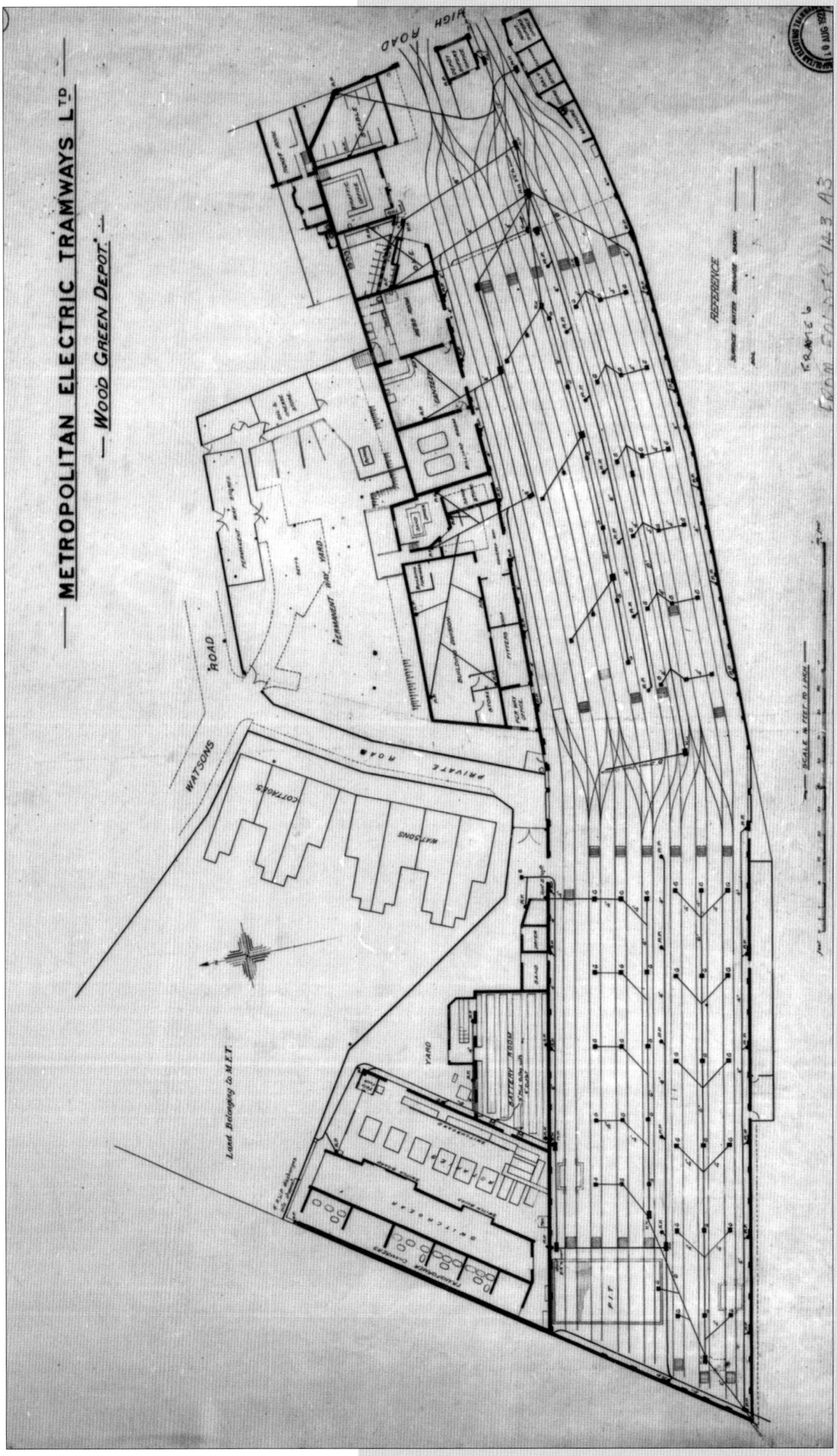

**Figure 24.
Wood Green
electric tram
depot layout.**

LRTA

Since 1937

The Light Rail Transit Association
Advocating modern tramways and light rail systems

LRTA
Since 1937

The LRTA is an international organisation dedicated to campaigning for better fixed-track public transport, in particular tramways and light rail. The Association celebrated its 75th anniversary on 30 June 2012.

Membership of the LRTA is open equally to professional organisations, transport planners and individuals with a particular interest in the subject. Members receive free of charge by post *Tramways & Urban Transit*, the Association's all-colour monthly magazine, as part of their subscription. With tramway and light rail systems being adopted not only in Europe but world-wide, this high-quality journal features topical articles and extensive in-depth news coverage as well as trade news and readers' letters. Details of local meetings in the British Isles are also included.

The LRTA also publishes *Tramway Review* – a quarterly journal devoted to historical material.

Officers of the Association – many with transport industry experience – form part of an extensive network of light rail and tramway information sources, which includes the comprehensive LRTA library.

For more information visit our website: **www.lrta.org**

To become a member of the LRTA go to: **membership@lrta.org**
Postal address: **LRTA Membership, 38 Wolseley Road, SALE, M33 7AU**

For general enquiries contact: **secretary@lrta.org**
Postal address: **LRTA Secretary, 138 Radnor Avenue, WELLING, DA16 2BY**

To order copies of our wide range of books go to: **www.lrta.info/shop**
Orders may be sent by post to:
LRTA Publications, 31 Ashton Road, WOKINGHAM, RG41 1HL

Books recently published by the LRTA include:

Brussels – A Tramway Reborn: 1945-2008	The Belgian Vicinal Tram & Light Rail Fleet 1885-1991
Charleroi's trams since 1940 – Coal, steel and cornfields	Trams through the dunes – The Belgian coastal tramways 1885-2010
Innsbruck's Alpine Tramways	**Coming soon:**
Nottingham's New Trams	Amsterdam trams – From horse car to Combino
PCCs of Western Europe 1950-2010: The tram that Belgium made	Czech & Slovak Tram and Trolleybus Handbook

---

Potential authors of books on subjects relevant to the Association's interests are invited to contact the Chairman of the LRTA Publications Group at 24 Heath Farm Road, FERNDOWN, BH22 8JW